ABOLITIONISM IN THE UNITED STATES AND BRAZIL

A COMPARATIVE PERSPECTIVE

CELIA M. AZEVEDO

GARLAND PUBLISHING, Inc.
NEW YORK & LONDON / 1995

Library of Congress Cataloging-in-Publication Data

Azevedo, Celia Maria Marinho de
    Abolitionism in the United States and Brazil : a comparative
perspective / Celia M. Azevedo.
        p.   cm. — (Studies in African American history and
culture)
    Includes bibliographical references and index.
    ISBN 0-8153-2332-8 (alk. paper)
    1. Antislavery movements—United States. 2. Abolitionists—
United States. 3. Antislavery movements—Brazil.
4. Abolitionists—Brazil. I. Title. II. Series.
E449.A89 1995
973.7'114—dc20
                                                        95-37819

Printed on acid-free, 250-year-life paper
Manufactured in the United States of America

To Professor
Peter Louis Eisenberg,
In memoriam

CONTENTS

PREFACE

When I arrived in New York some years ago, my aim was to understand the construction of the myth of Brazilian racial paradise. My feeling was that if I could understand the history of relations between people of African and European descent in the United States, then I would be better prepared to understand the history of my own country, Brazil, on this particular topic. I had just published a book on the racial views of the nineteenth-century Brazilian elite, and had been surprised by the abolitionists' insistent reference to conflicting race relations in the United States in order to highlight the supposed peaceful relations between white and black people in Brazil.

The writings of Brazilian abolitionists emphasizing the exceptionalism of peaceful relations between white and black people in Brazil allowed me to perceive the myth of racial paradise taking shape. But what I did not know, before researching this book, was that the image of Brazil as a racial paradise had long been circulating among American abolitionists, as part of a vast effort to defeat the Southern American slaveholders and their Northern allies. The reverse example of Brazil—a Catholic monarchy—where the Negro was supposedly well treated both as a slave and a freedman, was used to bring shame to white Americans, and contribute to their repentance for the double sin of slavery and racism.

More than sixty years ago, the French historian Marc Bloch made a vehement call for comparative history. Bloch believed that historians should leave aside the narrow boundaries of their national histories, that is, the mirage of the false local causes, in order to reach a comprehensive vision of history. Comparative history was, in his view, the appropriate method to understand the history of societies as a number of intertwined channels of influence, and also as a vast experience of human diversity.[1]

The words of Marc Bloch gained significance the more I researched and compared the abolitionist ideologies emerging in American and Brazilian societies. Since antislavery movements developed in many countries on both sides of the Atlantic throughout the nineteenth century, comparative history of abolitionism is also the history of overseas connections among abolitionists, either as personal contacts and correspondence, or through reciprocal influences. Thus this book can be read as a historical comparison between abolitionist ideologies in the United States and Brazil, as well as a history of the connections between American and Brazilian abolitionism. The myth of Brazilian racial paradise can be perceived in the making through the history of such connections. After reading this book, the reader might well agree with me that the myth of Brazilian racial paradise is also part of the cultural history of the United States.

The book is divided into an introduction and four chapters. The introduction analyzes seminal studies related to a comparative history of slavery in the United States and Brazil, the evolution of the historiography of abolitionism in each country, and basic problems underlying the comparison between American and Brazilian abolitionism, such as the differences in historical contexts. The first chapter gives a general overview of the basic differences between abolitionism in the United States and Brazil. The second chapter focuses on American and Brazilian abolitionists' views of the slaveholder. The third chapter examines the way abolitionists in the two countries viewed the slave. The fourth chapter compares American and Brazilian abolitionists' reflections on racism, and explores similarities and differences in their proposals with respect to the future of the slave after emancipation.

São Paulo, Brazil
June, 1995

INTRODUCTION

For many years, so-called race relations have been the preferential point of departure of scholars in comparing the histories of the United States and Brazil. What made the two American countries especially attractive for historical comparisons was that, on the one hand slavery shaped their histories in a fundamental way and, on the other hand, both societies seemed impressive for their supposed exceptionalism in race relations.[1] In the eyes of many scholars, the United States stood out as the realm par excellence of racial violence, whereas Brazil stood out as the realm par excellence of racial tolerance, in the past as well as the present.

Much has been done in the last three decades by scholars of both countries to correct the impression that these societies contrasted as hell to paradise. In general, recent studies have discovered more similarities than differences in the experience of slavery in the two countries. And have concluded that what scholars once saw a paradise of racial relations was nothing but a myth.[2]

However comparative history has not yet taken on the challenge of contrasting the paths by which the United States and Brazil achieved abolition of slavery. Slavery came to an end in the United States in 1865 after more than three decades of a continuous abolitionist campaign, and after a four-year civil war left 600,000 people dead and devastated large areas of the South. In contrast Brazil—the last country in the Americas to abolish slavery—experienced just a few years of a fierce abolitionist campaign and commemorated the signing of a Law of Abolition passed by Parliament in 1888 amid massive street marches, public feasts, and house parties throughout the country.[3] Should such contrasting ends to slavery confirm once more that the United States tended inevitably toward racial violence and retaliation, while Brazil tended inevitably toward racial harmony and conciliation? Should we believe that these two distinct paths to abolition derived from distinct racial patterns long inscribed in the history of the two countries?

This book approaches the problem of the differing processes of abolition in the United States and Brazil by analyzing and comparing the ideologies of abolitionism in the two countries. I shall focus on how abolitionists in the two countries raised issues of national identity, citizenship and social justice; how they approached the rationale of race; how the abolitionists' approaches to the above questions in the United States and Brazil were similar and how they were different; and what their approaches can tell us about abolition and its aftermath in the two countries.

Although no one has undertaken to compare the ideological aspects of abolitionism in the United States and Brazil, it is interesting to inquire how the comparative studies of slavery and race relations have approached the problem of the different paths to abolition in the two countries. I will focus on Gilberto Freyre, Frank Tannenbaum, and Carl Degler, because of the enduring influence of their studies over the historiography of slavery and race relations in comparative perspective.

G. FREYRE: THE BRAZILIAN PARADISE

Sixty-two years after Gilberto Freyre first published *Casa Grande & Senzala* (*The Masters and the Slaves*), his argument accounting for supposed racial harmony in Brazil remains influential in comparative studies. The key word in Freyre's thesis is miscegenation. Freyre did not consider Brazilian society to be free from deep economic and cultural antagonisms, with that between slave and master the most serious and profound, permeating the entire structure of colonial Brazil.[4]

But Brazil was exceptional, he argued, in its ability to secure a balance of all those antagonisms by physically as well as culturally mixing different peoples. In contrast to American society, where two inimical parts constantly confronted each other—the white and the black, the ex-slaveholder and the ex-slave—Brazil presented two fraternal parts whose distinct values and experiences had been long interacting in a mutually enriching process that required no sacrifice of one element to the other.[5]

This cultural and physical symbiosis was possible, Freyre believed, because of two peculiar aspects of Portuguese settlement in the New World: the special character of the Portuguese and the ethnic superiority of the Africans taken to Brazil as slaves. As a people, Freyre argues, the Portuguese were undefined. They were neither Europeans nor Africans but both; a synthesis of a long past of cultural and physical interaction that meant the absence of absolute ideals and prejudices.[6]

The tendency toward mixing was transported to the New World and even strengthened when Portuguese men traveling alone met Indian women and shortly after, African women. Freyre suggests that, in contrast to the traffic in slaves to the English colonies, the African trade to Brazil selected slaves of superior ethnic stock in order to attend to the special need of the new settlement in the wilderness: women to make up for the shortage of European women and craftworkers for the mines.[7]

It is interesting to notice here a constant implied reference to relations between Europeans and Africans in the United States. Although Freyre did not explicitly undertake comparative history or try to explain the different paths to abolition, he left the door ajar to the establishment of a nowadays commonplace aspect of the historiographical comparison between the two countries: the effort to interpret slavery and the passage to free labor by constantly referring to the higher or lower level of miscegenation and its social acceptance in each country, as a measure of the social integration or exclusion of the former slave.

As C. Vann Woodward points out, the emphasis upon miscegenation served an important purpose for both Brazilian and American scholars. Freyre, under the influence of his teacher Franz Boas at Columbia University, was able to liberate himself from the shame of being part of a "mongrel" country by stressing that miscegenation was the solution to the race problem and the path to ethnic democracy and social harmony. American scholars were later anxious to expiate the sin of racism by mirroring "faithfully in reverse a Latin American picture of racial felicity and harmony."[8]

F. TANNENBAUM: THE AMERICAN HELL

Just as Freyre promoted the idea that Brazilians are an exceptional people given their harmonious patterns of race relations, so Frank Tannenbaum inaugurated the field of comparative studies between the United States and Latin America in *Slave and Citizen* (1947) by developing the reverse idea, that white Americans are exceptional in their racism against the Negro.

Tannenbaum argued that the adventure of the Negro in the New World had been structured differently in the United States than in any other part of the American continent. Only in the United States had the Negro been socially excluded and denied. Despite his adaptability, willingness, competence, and "complete identification with the *mores* of the United States," "a barrier" had been drawn against him.[9]

Tannenbaum found the roots of such differences in present-day relations between people of European and African descent in the different slave systems, with their distinct legal traditions, social policies and religions. Relying on Freyre's assertions about Brazil, Tannenbaum argued that both the law and the Catholic church protected the slave, recognizing him as a person and a Christian.[10] Since law and religion considered the slave a moral personality, manumission was seen as a right belonging to every slave and his admission to society came naturally. In contrast, the slave system in the American colonies provided no legal protection to the slaves because there were no religious or legal provisions defining them as anything but chattels.[11]

Tannenbaum's approach to the issue of the different paths to abolition follows as a logical consequence of his thesis that different slave systems generate distinct conceptions of the slave. Where the slave was seen as a person and his right to manumission recognized, abolition came peacefully. But where the slave was considered a chattel and the Negro "a slave by nature," abolition could be reached only through a revolution, as in Haiti, or a civil war, as in the United States.[12]

It is significant that for Tannenbaum miscegenation does not stand as a theme of special relevance in comparing slave systems. As he explains, the process of intermingling was not peculiar to

Brazilian slavery, but part of the system of slavery as a whole. For him, "the new race" that Freyre saw emerging peculiarly from Brazil, was being nurtured everywhere for "the dynamics of race contact and interest were stronger than prejudice, theory, law or belief." If there were any difference, it lay in the fact that in Brazil the new race was accepted as a matter of course and had come to be a point of pride.[13]

C. DEGLER: "THE MULATTO ESCAPE HATCH"

The most comprehensive and influential comparative study of recent times used the door left open by Tannenbaum: that the basic difference between present-day race relations in the United States and Brazil arises not from miscegenation itself, but from its acceptance as a matter of course by Brazilian society. But before reworking this thesis and transforming it to refer to a much older cultural difference between the two countries, Carl Degler had to set aside Tannenbaum's fundamental thesis that distinct slave systems engendered different patterns of race relations.

In *Neither Black Nor White* (1971) Degler began by criticizing Tannenbaum's assumptions about the differences between the slave systems. Relying upon a trend of revisionist studies—the so-called School of São Paulo—that from the mid1950's labeled racial democracy in Brazil a myth, Degler showed that legal definitions of the slave, whether as human being or as chattel, were ambiguous in both countries. The ambiguity affected the way the slaves were treated by masters and public officials in the United States as much as in Brazil. As for the Catholic church, Degler argued that its interest in protecting, and power to protect, the slave's humanity were as limited as those of the state. Few plantations had priests and the evidence shows that the church had little official interest in interfering with the institution of slavery.[14]

Degler conceded, however, that an important difference between the two slave systems lay in their approach to manumission. In this regard, Brazil seemed to be more liberal than the United States, given Brazil's considerably higher proportion of free Negroes during the nineteenth century.[15] Yet Degler does not find the reasons for the difference within the Brazilian slave system, as Tannenbaum does, but in the different processes of settlement and economic development in the two countries.

Here one clearly feels the influence of Freyre, mixed with the findings of the revisionist studies, acting upon Degler's thesis. On the one side, people of African descent, whether as slaves or as free men, found a place in Brazil, sparsely populated and with a slave economy concentrating upon staple production. On the other side, economic and demographic patterns worked in the opposite direction in the United States. The economy did not provide a place for those who might be manumitted. A large free white population, increased by an ever growing white immigration from Europe, competed for all forms of labor outside the plantations.[16]

Degler held, in sum, that the difference between social practices in the two countries resulted from accidents of geography, demography, and economy, which in turn produced differing attitudes toward the Negro. In order to understand the "basic origins of the diverging racial patterns" of the two countries, he invited readers to "look behind the practices of slavery," where the "key" to the problem lay hidden.[17]

The key, "the mulatto escape hatch" or the mulatto's social acceptance by Brazilian society, marks the real difference between race relations in the two countries, according to Degler. And if Degler is to be believed, this key explains the whole difference in their histories, because it directed racial and social relations toward increasing violence in the United States and increasing tolerance in Brazil. The mulatto's social acceptance by Brazilian society explains why the argument of black racial inferiority never reached the degree of respectability in Brazil that it enjoyed in United States social thought.[18]

Despite their disagreements on the subject of slavery and race relations in the United States and Brazil, Freyre, Tannenbaum, and Degler converge in paying little attention to abolitionism and its critique of slavery. For all the three authors, the different paths to abolition inevitably derived from racial patterns long established in the histories of the United States and Brazil. For Freyre, extensive miscegenation in Brazilian society provided the key to understanding why Brazil stood out as a racial paradise among other countries with a similar slave past. For Tannenbaum, the key to understanding the evolving distinct racial patterns—racial violence in the United States, racial tolerance in Brazil—lay in the fact that the two slave systems generated distinct conceptions of the slave: the one, as a chattel; the other, as a human being. For Degler, the "mulatto's" social acceptance by Brazilian society explained why Americans had come to think in terms of white or black in matter of race relations, whereas Brazilians took a less rigid view, thinking in terms of neither black nor white. Since each of these authors had a different key to explain the past and present relations between people of European and African descent in the two countries, it is not surprising that the different paths to abolition never became a problem for their comparative analyses.

In dealing with, and comparing, the ideological aspects of abolitionism in the two countries, it is necessary to understand the different historical contexts from which those ideologies emerged.[19] Among the many differences in the histories of the United States and Brazil, four seem especially relevant to understanding the abolitionist ideologies engendered within each country.

First, the different paths the two countries took to political independence reveal a great deal about the differences in the ideas stressed by abolitionists in each of these countries. The experience of Revolution in the United States and peaceful agreement with the Portuguese crown in Brazil—that is to say, the victory of republicanism in the first country and its defeat in the second—made a difference in the abolitionists' ideas about national identity, social and political equality, and citizenship.[20]

Secondly, the extent to which the country as a whole participated in slavery affected the way abolitionists addressed the problems of slavery, free labor, abolition and its aftermath, and relations between people of predominantly European and predominantly African descent. Slavery involved the entire society of nineteenth-century Brazil. A small class of white planters ruled over a majority comprising slaves and a substantial and increasing segment of poor free black people. Slaves and free black people made up a majority of the population at the time the first abolitionist societies emerged during the 1860's.[21] In the United States slavery was unevenly distributed. It was confined to the Southern states after the Revolutionary era and formed a world apart, with its own peculiar culture and society. As to the free black people eventually scattered throughout the country, they formed an insignificant segment of the population in comparison to Brazil.[22]

Thirdly, the experience of European immigration differed in the two countries. The United States may be defined as a country of immigrants for, from its beginning, it played the role of refuge for the poor, oppressed, and ambitious peoples of Europe.[23] In contrast, as a colony of the overseas Portuguese Empire, Brazil received few Portuguese immigrants, and was closed to immigrants from all other coutries during its first three hundred years. Although there were some small-scale rural experiments with European immigrants starting at the beginning of the nineteenth century, mass immigration was not debated until the 1870's and 1880's, and was intimately linked to the debate about slavery and the need for its abolition.[24] As we shall see, these ethnic differences in the composition of the population contributed to abolitionist ideas of race, labor, and social hierarchy.

The fourth point to be stressed is the differences in religions engendered by distinct processes of peopling the two countries. Protestantism in the United States and Catholicism in Brazil, as well as their distinct relations with African religions, imbued with different tones the language of abolitionism in the two countries. Moreover it is necessary to bear in mind the different combinations of religious, humanistic, and scientific theories engendering distinct ethics of human relations among American and Brazilian abolitionists.[25]

In comparing abolitionist ideologies in the United States and Brazil, I tried to keep in mind the importance of these four distinct elements of historical experience—political independence, slavery, European immigration, and religion—for the construction of ideas of national identity, citizenship and social justice. Analysis and comparison of the abolitionist ideologies emerging from the intermingling of these four distinct historical elements should contribute to a better understanding of the different paths to abolition, and of the aftermath of abolition in the two countries.

Broad differences in the timing and geographic extent of abolitionism in the United States and Brazil have also informed my investigation.

Antislavery began to evolve in the mid-eighteenth century. By the eve of the American Revolution, as David Brion Davis points out, a new sensibility towards slavery had emerged on both sides of the Atlantic. There was nothing unprecedented about chattel slavery, but the widespread conviction that New World slavery symbolized all the forces that threatened the true destiny of man marked a turning point in the evolution of man's moral perception.[26]

Davis identified four sources of the antislavery impulse in Western culture, particularly the culture of British protestantism. First, the emergence of a secular social philosophy imposed a redefinition of the place of human bondage in the rational order of being. Second, the popularization of an ethic of benevolence, personified in the "man of feeling," consolidated the idea of man's inner goodness and permitted the rise of a liberal spirit. Third, the evangelical faith in instantaneous conversion and demonstrative sanctification brought a new emphasis on personal responsibility, charity and forbearance. Fourth, primitivism or the idea of the "noble savage" modified Europe's ethnocentrism, making possible a favorable interpretation of the Negro's cultural difference.[27]

All the sources of the antislavery impulse that Davis identified except evangelical faith were present in late colonial Brazil and gained strength, especially after independence. As Davis points out, Catholic Latin America also felt the impact of Enlightenment, the American and French Revolution, and the war of independence.[28]

However, in contrast to the United States, where Quakers and other religious sects founded the first antislavery societies during the mid-eighteenth century, antislavery in Brazil did not go beyond a number of intellectual tracts published from the beginning of the nineteenth century. Antislavery societies were founded in Brazil only after the demise of the African trade in 1850.[29]

Despite the later founding of the antislavery movement in Brazil, the basic content of antislavery thought in the two countries seems to have been similar. In the United States as in Brazil, antislavery meant gradual emancipation over a long period of time.

Davis regards the dominant gradualist frame of mind of the eighteenth century as the logical consequence of prevailing fundamental opinions about progress, natural law, property and individual rights. He insists that one must "abandon the conventional distinction between Enlightenment liberalism and evangelical reaction" in order to understand that, despite sharp differences between evangelicals and rationalists, they generally shared confidence in the slow evolution of a divine or natural plan of historical progress.[30]

Gradualism should also be understood in the context of a world which had just been shaken by violent events accompanying the French and Haitian Revolutions. As Merton L. Dillon reminds us, early abolitionists feared the violent disruption of the entire social order that could result from sudden change in any part of it. They expected that, through rational persuasion, slaveholders would gradually adjust to free labor relation. The desired reform was to come from the slaveholders themselves.[31]

The American antislavery movement, as well as the British one, had reached a crucial turning point by 1830. Davis argues that the emergence of immediatism in Anglo-American antislavery thought can be attributed in part to the truculence and stubborn opposition of the slaveholders themselves, who accused the most moderate critics of radical designs and blocked the path to any reform. In addition, the increasing militancy of people of African descent, both slave and free, accentuated the sense of crisis between 1829 and 1831.[32]

But, as Davis stresses, immediatism was more than a shift in strategy. In his words: "It represented a shift in total outlook from a detached, rationalistic perspective on human history and progress to a personal commitment to make no compromise with sin." In sum, the passage from rationalism to romanticism marked a moment of liberation for the reformer from the ideology of gradualism, that is, from a toleration of evil within the social order.[33]

It is at this moment that the ideological differences between abolitionism in the United States and Brazil become most sharply evident. No such shift occurred in the Brazilian antislavery ideology, although truculent slaveholders and unrest among Negroes also played their role during the 1830's and 1840's. Immediatism emerged in Brazil only during the 1880's, in the context of increasing slave upheavals, a massive flight of slaves from the plantations, and the rise of popular abolitionism in the cities and towns. But, as I will argue throughout this book Brazilian immediatism was founded on reasons of expediency and had none of the religious inspiration that permeated immediatism in the United States.

As important to my investigation as the difference of timing between abolitionism in the United States and Brazil is the difference in their geographic extent. Antislavery thought in Brazil developed as a national debate about the means to end slavery, and especially, about what to do with the freedmen. Books and pamphlets were written by reformers from different parts of the country, especially after the demise of the African trade in 1850. The same pattern occurred when it came to the formation of antislavery societies, which were located in different Brazilian states, north and south, beginning during the 1860's and increasing during the 1880's. Scholars have emphasized that abolitionism in Brazil was an urban movement and national in scope. Also deserving emphasis is the fact that abolitionism became during the 1880's the first national mass movement that raised the issues of freedom and social justice, and with lesser emphasis—as we shall see—the issues of citizenship and racism.

The pattern in the United States was much different. From its beginning, antislavery was sectional in scope. It is true that, on the eve of the American Revolution and after, several Southern slaveholders and politicians—among them Thomas Jefferson and Patrick Henry—expressed their repugnance toward slavery. By the same token, several antislavery societies were founded in Southern states.[34] But there was never a strong antislavery movement in the South. Among the few antislavery societies that developed there, those that were able to gather the most followers supported programs for gradual abolition, accompanied by the immediate removal of the liberated Negro from the South.[35]

Thus, it was the Northern section of the country that gave rise to antislavery as a movement devoted to gradual emancipation in its first phase. During its second phase in the 1830's, Northern antislavery evolved into a larger movement, launching a debate

about freedom and social justice with a strong emphasis on issues
of citizenship and racism.

It is appropriate now to make some remarks about the
historiography of abolitionism in the United States and Brazil. In
comparison to the historiography of abolitionism in Brazil, which is
still in its infancy, the historiography of abolitionism in the United
States is remarkable for its extension and dynamism particularly
from the 1960's to the present time.

Dillon identifies four basic approaches to abolitionism in the
United States. The first belongs to the "nationalist historians" who
wrote after the Civil War. Generally agreeing with the antebellum
assessment of abolitionism, these first historians of abolitionism
were inclined to see abolitionists as moral heroes who played a key
role in bringing about the Civil War and in purging the nation of
slavery. The second approach, introduced by Frederick Jackson
Turner and Charles and Mary Beard, diminished the abolitionists'
role by emphasizing economic and other personal aspects of history.
Abolitionists returned to prominence, but incurred condemnation,
with the third approach, concerned with explaining the causes of
the Civil War. Revisionist writers of the 1930's and 1940's condemned
the abolitionists as fanatics whose agitation had brought about a
needless war. The fourth approach, emerging during the 1960's,
redeemed the abolitionists by emphasizing their concern with race,
prejudice and social justice. Dillon suggests that the modern civil
rights movement gave the abolitionists and their program, tactics,
and frame of mind a contemporaneousness not often enjoyed by
figures of the past.[36]

However, as Dillon and Woodward show, not all abolitionists
gained veneration. The perception that abolitionists were divided
into distinctive ideological tendencies such as the moral reformers
(the Garrisonians) and the antislavery politicians (like the Radical
Republicans) led historians to take sides. Some considered the
Garrisonians fanatics and anarchists, incapable of defining a political
struggle against slavery. Others considered the antislavery
politicians to be less interested in the Negro's rights than in
guaranteeing the availability of free land in the West for white
workers. Finally, some historians chose not to take sides and

rehearse the abolitionists' own arguments. They deemed it of paramount importance to understand the abolitionists in their own historical context, carefully distinguishing between the historians' present time and that of their subjects.[37]

More recently, a new line has emerged in the historiography of American abolitionism. Ronald G. Walters suggests that the boundaries between supposedly distinct ideological factions of abolitionists "need to be surveyed, challenged, moved around, and, for some purposes, abolished."[38] It is time now, he argues, to begin treating antislavery as a whole. To do otherwise is to miss the reasons why a new form of abolitionism, immediatism, emerged during the 1830's.[39]

Although the historiography of abolitionism in Brazil has not undergone so many ups and downs, it is possible to discern distinct phases in the way historians treat abolitionism.

Historians writing during the first two decades of the twentieth century emphasized the revolutionary role of abolitionists, their struggle against slavery and racism, as well as the slaves' revolutionary role in abandoning the plantations in a huge mass movement.[40] But the emergence of the myth of a racial paradise during the 1930's deflected attention from the more radical aspects of abolitionism. Gilberto Freyre overemphasized the role of conservative politicians and a sympathetic monarchy, in order to highlight the unfolding of a peaceful parliamentary transition from slavery to free labor.[41]

During the mid-1950's and 1960's, revisionist scholars shifted the image from a benign slavery to a harsh slavery, once more highlighting abolitionism as a violent social struggle. But the economism permeating many of these revisionist analyses set definite limits to the evaluation of abolitionism as a revolutionary social movement. Revisionists argued that the rise of the industrial revolution at an international level, the evolution of an agrarian pre-capitalist economy toward capitalism, the increasing urbanization and the beginnings of industrialization in some parts of Brazil, and especially the emergence of a segment of progressive planters in São Paulo opened the way to the abolitionist movement during the 1880's. In consequence, they saw abolitionism more as a reflex of inevitable structural changes than as a movement capable of creating new possibilities in history. As for the slaves, they simply followed the abolitionist leaders' plans and devices, according to revisionist scholars. They played no independent role, owing to their alienation and inability to articulate their aspirations politically.[42]

A new revisionism has recently emerged in the historiography of slavery and abolition. Recent scholars have highlighted the actions of slaves themselves during the last decades of slavery in Brazil in order to show that their autonomous upheavals, their alliances with popular abolitionists, as well as their pressures on institutional channels, all played decisive roles in the construction of the abolitionist movement and its ideology. The challenge now for the new historians of Brazilian abolition is to present a more balanced view of the intertwining of slaves' actions with those of abolitionists, without losing sight of the Marxian lesson that people make their own history, but under circumstances directly received from the past.[43]

Finally, I must clarify my use of the terms "abolitionism" and "antislavery". By "abolitionism," I mean that system of thought which had as its central focus the critique of slavery and which stressed the need to end slavery, whether gradually or immediately. By "antislavery," I mean a more generalized posture of opposition to slavery that did not necessarily look toward and fight for abolition.

This study will focus on abolitionist ideologies. For Brazil, I will deal mainly with those who proposed the abolition of slavery, either gradual or immediate. But I will refer briefly to those antislavery reformers whose main concern was to promote the immigration of Europeans (or white Americans) to Brazil in order to replace slaves. By the same token, for the United States I will deal mainly with those who called for the abolition of slavery, especially the immediatists, since they wrote extensively for more than three decades. But I will mention, when necessary, those antislavery politicians whose main concern was to prevent the expansion of slavery to the new territories, rather than to abolish it throughout the country.

ACKNOWLEDGMENTS

Many people in the United States and Brazil made this book possible. I will begin by thanking Professors Barbara Jeanne Fields, Elizabeth Blackmar, Eric Foner, Jean Franco, and Nancy Priscilla S. Naro for reading my work and improving it with their suggestions. Professor Barbara J. Fields helped me in many ways throughout my academic life at Columbia University and my residence in New York. Her critiques, suggestions, and editorial remarks were essential for the outcome of this study although the ultimate responsibility for it remains mine. Other people helped me along the way: Professors Deborah Levenson-Estrada, Richard L. Bushman, David Cannadine and Herbert S. Klein. Many friends and colleagues gave me warm encouragement and helped me in a variety of ways, including: Edna Coleman, Alice Nash, Paul M. Pitman, Nancy Cohen-Lack, Cintia Pamplona, Ana Edite Montoia, Marcia C. Naxara, and Professors Leila M. Algranti, Robert W. Slenes, Marco Antonio Pamplona, Vavy P. Borges and Alcir Lenharo. My sister Silvia A. de Oliveira and my father Roberto M. de Azevedo were always there to help me along the way with any long-distance difficulties.

This book counted on the support of various institutions and people: the Fulbright Commission; the Latin American Scholarship Program of American Universities—LASPAU; Columbia University's Presidents Fellowship; the Institute of Philosophy and Human Sciences at Universidade Estadual de Campinas (UNICAMP), Brazil; the Fundo de Apoio ao Ensino e Pesquisa (FAEP) also of the State University of Campinas; the Fundação de Amparo à Pesquisa do Estado de São Paulo (FAPESP). Ms. Sonia Wallenberg, my adviser at LASPAU, was always availabe to solve any problem related to my stay in the United States. My colleagues of the Department of History at UNICAMP allowed me a four-year leave of absence partially with pay.

I would like to thank the many librarians who helped me in different institutions: Butler Library at Columbia University, especially the Rare Books Division; Barnard Library and Lehman Library, also at Columbia University; the New York Public Library, especially the Schomburg Collection; the New York University Library; Biblioteca Nacional in the city of Rio de Janeiro; Arquivo do Estado de São Paulo, Biblioteca Municipal Mário de Andrade, Biblioteca Central da Faculdade de Direito, all of them in the city of São Paulo; Biblioteca do Instituto de Filosofia e Ciências Humanas and Biblioteca do Instituto de Estudos Lingüísticos, both libraries of the State University of Campinas, in the city of Campinas. I am also grateful to the Department of Inter-library Loans which made it possible for me to read material from distant libraries in the United States.

I am grateful to Professor Graham Hodges for including this book in Garland's series Studies in African American History and Culture. I also owe thanks to Mr. Robert McKenzie, Assistant Editor of Garland Publishing Inc., Ms. Elspeth Hart, Senior Editor of Garland, Mr. Norberto de Paula Lima, and Ms. Ann Mische. Their dedicated and careful work made possible the final edition of the book.

Last but not least, I thank my husband, Josué Pereira da Silva, who read many drafts and was able to suggest the best solution for every problem. Most importantly, he was always by my side.

To my sorrow it is no longer possible to thank Professor Peter Louis Eisenberg. He enthusiastically supported from the beginning my aim of studying the History of the United States and writing a study in comparative history. I dedicate this book to his memory.

Abolitionism in the
United States and Brazil

I
Abolitionism in the Two Countries: An Overview

The movement against slavery demands attention for its insistent defining of international goals and forging of enduring overseas connections in a period increasingly characterized by nationalist movements. As the Irish M. P. Daniel O'Connell stressed during a public meeting of antislavery delegates in London, in 1837, the "community of sentiment," which had been borne on "the wings of the press," had already spread all over the world, strong enough to cross oceans and bring down "the lash of human indignation" upon those horrible criminals, the slaveholders.[1]

Besides flying with the wings of the press, the British abolitionists decided to work with the tools of international organization. Having achieved considerable experience in dealing with different countries in their struggle against the slave trade, and having got rid of slavery within the boundaries of the British empire, the British abolitionists founded a new organization, the British and Foreign Anti-Slavery Society, in 1839. Its goals, to correspond with the abolitionists in America, France and elsewhere, and to encourage them in their struggle against slavery, made clear the need to consolidate and expand the community of abolitionist sentiment all over the world.[2]

By mid-nineteenth century, two major countries on the American continent stood in open challenge to this transatlantic convergence of antislavery feelings. Both the United States and Brazil aroused special indignation for being major holders of enslaved people and for presenting the spectacle of slaveholding classes with solid roots in their countries, which meant expanding

3

economic interests, strong political power, and a deep conviction that slavery was the best labor regime in terms of both profitability and social stability.[3]

However, while the United States had a well-structured abolitionist movement with hundreds of abolitionist newspapers and societies scattered throughout the Northern states, Brazil lagged far behind. But for a few isolated antislavery writers, there was nothing that could evoke the image of a community of abolitionist sentiment in Brazil at least until the mid-1860's. Moreover, despite the existence of a law forbidding the slave trade from Africa, which was decreed in 1831 under pressure from Great Britain, the trade continued untouchable for twenty more years.[4]

One might see as only natural that the transatlantic connections between abolitionists should develop in the first place between American and British abolitionists. As Betty Fladeland shows, relations between these two abolitionisms predated the American Revolution, having been nourished by transatlantic links between Quakers and Methodists.[5] After the separation of their countries, British and American abolitionists continued their cooperation by struggling against the slave trade, experimenting with neighbouring colonization projects in Africa, acknowledging the failure of gradual abolition, and declaring for immediatism in the 1830's.[6]

But despite their common cultural heritage, another reason accounts for this intense cooperation between British and American abolitionists. From the first decades of the nineteenth century, British and American abolitionists began to suggest that American slavery was the worst in the world, and in the entire span of human history. Although both the British West Indies and the American South were actually exposed for the violence of the slaveholders against the slaves in numerous books and accounts by British travelers, slavery in the United States seemed to attract special condemnation. For as O' Connell insisted during an antislavery meeting in 1829, slavery should be incompatible with this "boasted land of freedom." In an imaginary address to Americans, O' Connell asked:

> . . . you threw off the allegiance you owed us, because you
> thought we were oppressing you with the Stamp Act, you boasted of
> your deliverance from slavery. On what principle, then, do you
> continue your fellowmen in bondage . . . ? I will say unto you, freemen
> of America, . . . that you are hypocrites, tyrants, and unjust men; that
> you are degraded and dishonored; and I say unto you, dare not to
> stand up boasting of your freedom or your privileges, while you
> continue to treat men, redeemed by the same blood, as the mere
> creatures of your will . . . . [7]

The assertion proclaimed in the Declaration of
Independence—that all men are born with inalienable rights to life,
liberty and the pursuit of happiness—chased Americans as a ghost
inherited from a golden age when the promise of freedom for all
seemed to point to the exclusion of slavery forever. Therefore,
Americans deserved special censure, not only for being cruel and
harsh toward their slaves, but also for lacking principles and acting
hypocritically toward the rest of the world.

The reverse side of this special focus upon American slavery
was the beginning of the formulation of an antislavery propaganda
that relied on numerous comparisons between American slavery
and slavery in other parts of the world. As we shall see in the next
chapter, the image of Brazil as a country of less cruel slaveholders
began to take shape from this comparative Anglo-American propaganda. But the point to retain here is that by comparing slavery in
the United States unfavorably to slavery elsewhere, abolitionists
revealed their belief that the international movement for abolition
depended on the results of this movement within the United States.

At this point it is necessary to say that I will be dealing with
two levels of comparison. First there is the comparison undertaken
with the benefit of more than a century of hindsight. Systematically
carried out, comparison of abolitionist ideologies in the two countries
will throw light on noteworthy historical features that otherwise
might be taken for granted. Such, for example, is the case of the
"belated and derivative development" of antislavery activity in
Brazil, an intriguing question which historians have not paid enough
attention to, according to David Brion Davis.[8] Another intriguing
circumstance is the enduring Anglo-American antislavery
cooperation, despite the major events of a Revolution and two

subsequent wars setting the two countries apart, and this during a historical period of mounting nationalism throughout the world.

The second level of comparison takes its cue from the reflections of people who actually lived and made our past. From their voices, from the abolitionists' self-interpretation of the present they experienced in the United States and Brazil, one learns that the history of abolitionism in each country is inseparable from the history of the transnational connections between abolitionists. Either by constantly interacting or by mentally comparing their historical situation with that of counterparts in different countries, abolitionists forged interpretations that were essential for their daily antislavery practice.

It is at this second level that one may best savor the mixture of the two dimensions of abolitionism: the international and the national. The international dimension of abolitionism permitted the construction of a discourse on freedom and humanity whose terms would later reach the status of universal truth throughout the world. As Davis suggests, the emergence of an international antislavery opinion represented a remarkable change in moral consciousness and a turning point in man's image of himself.[9] But the national dimension of abolitionism that can be perceived in the American and Brazilian primary sources reminds us that the local, the daily, experience has a special way of shaping reflections about what seems to be universal.

The impulse toward humanitarian reform responded to profound changes that both countries were undergoing. Economic and social changes that had been gradually developing during the eighteenth century gained strength in the United States from the end of the Revolutionary War. Controversies over the distribution of land and the subsequent splitting of towns in New England, the growth of the population by successive waves of immigrants, indentured servants and slaves, the expanding of new commercial and industrial activities in the North and of cotton plantations operated by slaves in the South, the search for land in the West and the increasing speculation over it, were all developments that left exposed the problem of a mounting concentration of wealth and power in the hands of a few. The sense of crisis and the fear that despotism was not limited to the Old World had spread among the population by the turn of the century.[10]

Brazil also experienced huge demographic changes by the mid-nineteenth century. Successive waves of African slaves brought to the Brazilian shores until the closing of the external trade by the Eusébio de Queirós Law in 1850, the natural fertility of the population, and the arrival of the first groups of immigrants brought by private and state enterprises, accounted for a rapid increase of the population. The expanding of large coffee plantations in the Southeast which attracted a huge internal slave trade from the Northeast, foreign investments in railroads and urban facilities, the rise of the first industries in the cities, and the development of an internal market in the cities and their surroundings, imposed a new distribution of the population. By the 1860's and 1870's, while slaves were being transferred in great numbers from the decaying sugar-cane plantations in the Northeastern areas to the coffee plantations in the Southeast, the free white and black people had begun to concentrate in the cities or their surroundings, where new activities offered them new ways of making ends meet. These social and economic transformations engendered new conflicts between the slaveholding classes and gave rise to new urban groups whose economic interests gradually allowed them to draw a critique of the traditional distribution of land, wealth and power.[11]

In both countries abolitionism emerged as one among many reformist movements. If one examines the lives of abolitionist leaders prior to their commitment to the movement for immediate abolition, one will find them involved in other projects of reform. During the 1810's and the 1820's—the age of the Second Great Awakening—the abolitionists-to-be in the United States founded or became members of temperance societies, tried to rescue women from prostitution, distributed bibles to the lower classes, struggled to moralize and educate the working classes, and hoped to solve what they considered "the Negro problem" by sending free black people to Africa as part of colonization nuclei.[12]

During the 1860's and 1870's the abolitionists-to-be in Brazil created literary societies and newspapers as a mean to express their dissatisfaction with the general state of society and politics, joined emerging professional groups, founded educational and cultural societies, debated the relative merits of a republic and a constitutional monarchy, campaigned for electoral reform, the separation of church and state, public education, and supported state or private plans for immigration from Europe aimed at progress combined with a general whitening of the population.[13]

As seems evident from the types of reformist movements in which the future abolitionists first expressed their restlessness and discontent with the general affairs of their societies, the ideological sources from which they drank were miles apart. Indeed, one of the most striking differences between   American and Brazilian abolitionists can be perceived in the tone of their language. The following quotations from abolitionists in each country may afford a first approach to this differing tone:

> We believe slavery to be a sin—always, everywhere, and only, sin—sin in itself . . . sin, in the nature of the act which creates it . . . sin, because it converts persons into things, makes men property, God's image merchandize . . . In other words, because slavery holds and uses men, as mere means for the accomplishment of ends, of which ends their own interests are not a part—thus annihilating the sacred and eternal distinction between a person and a thing—a distinction proclaimed an axiom by all human consciousness—a distinction created by God . . .[14]

> To own slaves nowadays is not a title of honor anymore ... Protected by the government and supported by the House of Representatives . . . , slavery has nonetheless been publicly acknowledged as the reduction of free people to captivity; that is because the present slaves happen to be the children of the imported [Africans], or the very Africans whom the law has declared free for the last forty-nine years.
> By investigating our production one understands that slave labor is the sole cause of the country's industrial and economic backwardness . . .[15]

The differences between these abolitionist statements are obvious. The first, the Declaration of Sentiments from a meeting of abolitionists to organize a state Anti-Slavery Society in Ohio in 1835, is essentially religious and draws its arguments from immutable principles. The second, the editorial of the first number of the organ of the Brazilian Anti-Slavery Society—founded in Rio de Janeiro in 1880—is essentially secular and draws its arguments from reasons of expediency.

Despite the many internal conflicts that divided abolitionists into different groups in the United States, and to a lesser degree in Brazil, it is possible to suggest that when compared to each other American and Brazilian abolitionism exhibit sharp general distinctions.[16] American abolitionism spoke the language of religion in which the image of God imposing a higher law over society is central, while Brazilian abolitionists adopted a lay language in which the central figure is progress and the corresponding human laws.

This characteristic tone of the language of abolitionism in each country points to distinct modes of formulating ideas and proposals of action. On one side, American abolitionism acts according to the idea of an immutable truth governing humanity throughout the ages. The one capable of capturing this truth in his heart must assume as his supreme mission in life the spread of this knowledge, that is, the conversion of other human beings to the divine laws. On the other side, Brazilian abolitionism acts according to the idea of different truths or stages of evolution governing societies in each age. The one capable of perceiving changes in societies and the corresponding truth must struggle to bring others to reason by means of rational persuasion.

In sum, to abolitionists in the United States, the idea of truth was absolute, while to those in Brazil, truth was relative. It is necessary now to elaborate these differences by examining the ideological roots of abolitionism in each country.

Although the idea of natural rights was inherent in abolitionism in general, enlightenment concepts were entrenched in purer form in Brazilian abolitionist discourse. The ideal of social equilibrium and belief in the interrelationship and slow evolution of institutions, which according to Davis formed the eighteenth-century climate of opinion, were characteristic of Brazilian abolitionism from the first antislavery writers to the abolitionists of the 1870's and 1880's.[17] The imbalance of society, caused by heterogeneous classes of masters and slaves, was indeed the first preoccupation which, together with British pressure against the African slave trade during the first half of the nineteenth century, moved the early antislavery reformers in Brazil.

The epigraphs chosen by two of the first Brazilian antislavery authors, João Severiano Maciel da Costa and Frederico Leopoldo Cezar Burlamaque, point to the original enlightenment sources, as well as the reasons why these sources appealed so much to the intellectual spokesmen of a diminutive white elite. In Maciel da Costa, one reads the following quotation from the *Esprit des Lois* by Montesquieu:

> . . . Nothing approximates people more to the condition of beasts than always seeing free men and not being one of them. These people are the natural enemies of society, and their numbers will be dangerous.

In Burlamaque's epigraph, reflection on the dangers of the inequality between free men and slaves becomes more concrete, reminding the reader that modern slavery means the perennial renewal of the inequality between white and black people, and its subsequent risks. The second quotation comes from a speech by De Pradt:

> The phrase trade of blacks means only this: whom will America belong to? to Africa or to America?
> Every cargo of blacks transported to America is . . . a cargo of black animals ready to devour it.[18]

The perception of a perennial war between classes—classes here seen as groups of people of distinct social conditions, morals, and racial origins—allowed enlightenment-inspired Brazilian reformers to acknowledge the impossibility of reaching social equilibrium, which was necessary for the progressive advance of the country and its institutions, while the system of slave trade and slave labor persisted.[19] This perception might have become especially keen after successive waves of slave and free black people's insurgencies revolutionized Bahia during the 1830's.[20] Enlightenment reasoning emphasized the danger of denying the existence of a natural law conferring a birthright of freedom for all human beings regardless of their social condition or skin color.

Although the concept of Providence recurred in these first abolitionist tracts, warning readers that slavery was an abominable practice according to the divine dictum, one senses that God played a mainly decorative role, which   intellectuals with a Catholic background felt obliged to assign. The central concern was not to fulfill whatever God expected from people, but to install a reformed social order where the "public interest"—that is, the ensemble of men of wealth and power—could live in peace, without fearing the actions of those below.

The first Brazilian antislavery reformers seem to have assimilated very solidly the compromise found by Montesquieu between the higher law and the human law. As Davis suggests, Montesquieu acknowledged the existence of a higher law which he defined as an eternal, uniform, and rational system of law limiting even the will of God. However, far from being abstract, this higher law could be grasped only in concrete situations, that is, only by rational inquiry into the different institutions of a country.[21] Within this kind of reasoning, where God could be depicted as responding to different historical situations, human law acquired precedence over divine maxims as well as enough legitimacy to be immune to criticism and transformation other than through the gradual devices of reason.

Moreover, early Brazilian antislavery writers showed a great ability to integrate this rational and balanced view of divine law and human law with the utilitarianism that other philosophers of the Enlightenment, such as David Hume, John Millar, and Adam Smith, began to develop during the second half of the eighteenth century.[22]

The theme of the unprofitability of slavery and its harmfulness to the interests of the elite in the long run was clearly developed by José Bonifácio de Andrada e Silva, later to become known as the Patriarch of Independence and to become the early abolitionist most eulogized by his successors. In *Representation to the Constitutional Convention* of 1823 he presented four theses in defense of gradual emancipation: l. slavery prevents the increase of the population because of the high death rate of slaves; 2. slavery prevents industry;

3. plantations do not generate significant profits because the crops remain under the care of unskilled, indolent slaves who cause great expenses and often run away; 4. slavery causes the devastation of nature.[23]

Although later abolitionists were to raise new issues in their critique of slavery, it is important to remember that these two themes—the social and racial imbalance of a slave-based society and the unprofitability and irrationality of slavery—molded further thinking on the issue of slavery and formed the underpinning of Brazilian abolitionism.[24]

As for the sources of early American antislavery, although Enlightenment thinking was always present, with its emphasis on the natural rights with which all human beings were endowed, religious thinking seems to have prevailed. From the first Quakers of Pennsylvania to the Evangelical sects that had mushroomed throughout the Anglo-American world by the mid-eighteenth century, antislavery tracts were imbued with the ideal of the millenium and the belief that it was the responsibility of each individual to secure the good order of society required by divine law.

Davis argues that the transformation of the idea of sin is the key to the religious origins of antislavery thought. The traditional belief was that, after the fall of Adam, man's natural and legal condition was total subordination to God and a corresponding natural inability to will what was just and lawful. As long as sin was traditionally thought of as a kind of slavery, and external bondage could be justified as a product of sin, one could not fully perceive the moral contradictions of slavery.

However, the latent egalitarianism that Christianity embodied continued to nurture in sectarians' dreams of liberation from necessities arising from sin. The critique of the doctrine of original sin opened the way to a picture of God as a transforming force rather than a fixed point to which man aspires. This shift in the image of God undermined the idea that the existing social order was a necessary compromise with sin. Another related shift in the meaning of history, promoted by millenial sects, substituted the idea of history as a creative process leading to perfection for the idea of nature as a fixed and complete chain of being. Thus, a latent Christian egalitarianism, with its ideals of absolute liberty, equality, and brotherhood, acquired a powerful new meaning when a changed perception of time allowed people to actually struggle for the Kingdom of God in the immediate future rather than continue to dream of a Golden Age forever lost in the past.[25]

As Davis emphasizes, the religious transformation of the ideas of God and sin was undertaken by sectarians far removed in time and space from contact with the institution of slavery. Nevertheless if one wishes to understand the frame of mind of abolitionists like Benjamin Lay, Anthony Benezet, and the first Quakers who began to equate slavery with sin, one has to acknowledge the sources from which they drew religious inspiration, as well as the centrality for them of the idea of sin.[26]

By the same token it is necessary to acknowledge the individualistic tendency imbuing American abolitionism from the beginning. Davis argues that the growth of antislavery thought depended upon the emergence of a new ethic of benevolence whose ideal of individual responsibility replaced the old, disintegrating medieval patterns of charity and social responsibility.[27]

The philosophy of benevolence that emerged in Britain during the seventeenth century responded to the sentiments of those Anglicans who became known as Latitudinarians. Their distaste for theological dogma and the doctrine of original sin, their appreciation of human feeling and sentiment, and their confidence in man's capacity for moral improvement opened the way to a perception of religion as a way of life and a new relationship with the world, rather than as a set of beliefs or prescribed ceremonies.[28] This reaction against Calvinism and its doctrines of predestination and total human depravity nurtured new trends of humanistic thought such as primitivism—the search for models of natural virtue among primitive societies—and romanticism—a sense of internal freedom and virtue.[29]

Up to now we have examined some of the early ideological influences upon the frame of mind of abolitionists in Brazil and the United States. At the root of American abolitionism one finds a growing belief that the kingdom of God will become a reality in the near future as long as responsible individuals substitute virtue for sin, virtue being the right to independence and freedom for all. At the root of Brazilian abolitionism one perceives an increasing desire for social balance, which will be possible as long as the upper class devises appropriate rational policies for incorporating the lower classes into a hierarchical society, where each one recognizes his place and feels himself part of a whole. In sum, on the one side one finds religion central to the framing of later American abolitionist thought. On the other side, one perceives an enlightened secular mode of reasoning as central to the framing of later Brazilian abolitionism.

It is necessary now to examine the social circumstances that contributed to the frame of mind of abolitionists in each country. And here the tone of their discourse points to another striking difference between American and Brazilian abolitionism. The tone of the language of American abolitionism is of one who speaks from outside about a distant and disgusting reality. There lay the South, where slaves carried an unbearable cross imposed upon them by cruel slaveholders, the greatest of all sinners. The poor slaves, the victims, were the brothers to be redeemed.

> Who are the real working bees of the South, who are the authors of all the good we thence derive? . . .— The blacks — the blacks—the blacks . . . .By setting them free, we should injure their masters to the exact amount of their market value, considering them, as these last do, as mere merchantable cattle. . . . Why should we be less fearful of offending them than their masters? . . . If justice, humanity, and the dictates of common interest are of any consequence to a clear view of this question, the blacks are most emphatically our brethren.[30]

Brazilian abolitionism exhibits a quite different tone. It is a voice from within; it is like listening to one who speaks about an enveloping and distressing reality. Here one not only sees but feels the daily spectacle of slavery, slaves being victimized by slaveholders who, by their lack of providence, become in the end the greatest of the victims. The poor slaves, the victims, have also the power to overrun and disrupt the entire society. The tone is a mixture of compassion and fear; the word "brother" does not come out so easily when one speaks from inside slavery.

> The servant issue has reached this point: to save everything, or to lose everything. To save everything means to colonize the freedman, that is, to gradually extract the free worker from the enslaved one by means of discipline and wages; to lose everything means to let the slave learn the path to freedom by means of the irresistible effects of propaganda.[31]

A brief comparison between some aspects of the lives of two of the most influential leaders of abolitionism in each country may throw some light on the reasons for this distinction of tone. Born in 1805 in Newburyport, Massachusetts, William Lloyd Garrison endured a life of hardships and poverty from early childhood. He was the son of a sailing-master who traded corn and flour in Virginia and rum in the West Indies but was suddenly reduced to despairing immobility by President Thomas Jefferson's Embargo Act in 1807. Despite the resistance of his prohibitionist and churchgoing wife, it seems he took refuge in alcohol for his sorrows. After harsh familial conflicts, he abandoned her with three small children to support.

As a small boy, Garrison was apprenticed to different people in different places, including a Quaker shoemaker in Lynn and a cabinetmaker in Haverhill, besides taking many odd jobs in Lynn and Baltimore. He finally began to find his vocation at the age of thirteen, when he was apprenticed to the editor and owner of the Newburyport *Herald*, having rapidly learned the printing trade which opened his way to journalism. As a white boy in New England, Garrison probably had little contact with black people, at that time increasingly segregated.

As for slaves, he probably saw them in the streets at the age of ten during a brief period when he lived with his mother in Baltimore. But slaves reached his mind only through long-distance references, such as the one found in a letter that his mother sent him shortly before her death. She told him about a "Coloured woman" who had been waiting on her with so much kindness that there were not words enough to describe it. Nevertheless this woman was "a Slave, to Man—yet a free Born soul by the grace of God. . . ". She concluded by asking her son not to forget the kind slave, "for your poor mothers Sake . . . ," in case he ever visited Baltimore.[32]

A few years later, already an editor of the Bennington *Journal of the Times*, Garrison followed his mother's advice, aligning the issue of the injustice of slavery with other moral and political campaigns, such as the ones for temperance and for the re-election of John Quincy Adams.[33] After defending abolition in the District of Columbia as a first step toward ending slavery throughout the country, he added that Americans had to be taught to become as excited over the injustices to the slaves in the capital of the nation as they had been over the impressment of ten white citizens by a foreign country during the War of 1812.[34]

The point stressed by Garrison was the need to create a widespread empathy for the Negro slave whose routine of life—people should know—was a permanent imprisonment, and not merely the occasional violence striking free white men in time of war. But if it was difficult enough to arouse this sympathetic sentiment among Northern citizens toward people who lived out of their sight, and miles away, Garrison also experienced the difficulty of convincing someone who lived right in the middle of slavery to awaken to its injustice.

After becoming editor of the Baltimore *Genius of Universal Emancipation*, Garrison finally had the chance to talk face-to-face with a slaveholder. Having published a virulent article denouncing a ship owner from Newburyport who traded in slaves, Garrison was found guilty of criminal libel and put in jail. There he managed to inquire of a Southerner, who was searching for a fugitive slave, what right had he "to that poor creature." Listening to his straightforward and candid reply—"My father left him to me,"—Garrison tried in vain to convince him that keeping that man enslaved was as unjustified as if he kept stolen money from a bank just because he had inherited it from his father.[35]

Talking to this man, Garrison probably felt himself truly an outsider, incapable of reaching the conscience and the world of the slaveholder. On the contrary, for the future Brazilian abolitionist leader, Joaquim Nabuco, slavery had always been a matter of fact, as natural as the air he breathed. Slavery was not a peculiar institution one occasionally hears about and meets face-to-face only in exceptional circumstances. Slavery was his world and shaped his conscience as profoundly as it did that of the slaveholder Garrison met in the Baltimore jail.

Nabuco was born in 1849 in Recife, the capital of Pernambuco, a Northeastern province historically devoted to sugarcane plantations. His mother was the niece of the powerful Marques do Recife (Marquis of Recife)—the leading figure of one of the oldest and wealthiest slaveholding families of that province, the conservative Paes Barretos. His father, José Tomás Nabuco de Araújo, who was to become the eminent Senator Nabuco of the Empire of Pedro II, began his professional career as a judge in a small provincial town. After his marriage to a member of the Paes Barreto family, he was elected representative of his province in Parliament. But he began to attract special attention after he served as the president of the thirty-member jury that condemned to life imprisonment the main leaders of the defeated Pernambuco revolution of 1848—the Praieira.[36]

The Praieira Revolution was the last in a long series of political threats to the endurance of monarchy in Brazil. Nabuco's father was one of a number of young politicians who managed to lay deep roots in the world of politics by supporting the kingdom of the young monarch during its first troubled years. They were afterwards generously rewarded with power, honor and wealth during more than thirty years of political stability.[37]

Joaquim Nabuco spent his first eight years at the engenho Massangana—a sugar cane plantation near Recife. There he lived with his widowed aunt, while his father, accompanied by his mother, moved to Rio de Janeiro, the capital of the Empire and the site of Parliament. From the beginning, he experienced a close relationship with slaves, not only as the mistress's "little son"—as his aunt affectionately called him—but also as a young master himself. At the age of seven he got his second slave as a gift from his aunt, after successfully pleading with her to buy him. The boy was sitting outside the big house when a slave about eighteen years old unexpectedly threw himself at his feet pleading that Nabuco ask his aunt to buy him. He had escaped from a neighbouring plantation after having endured severe chastisements and now feared for his life.

Nabuco recalled many years later that, although he subsequently read *Uncle Tom's Cabin* "a thousand times," slavery would always come to his mind through that unforgettable remembrance of his childhood; he, a small boy having his feet embraced by a youth in tears, and suddenly discovering his power over other people's lives.[38]

Slavery never ceased to be part of his life until abolition in 1888, when he was about forty years old. He never mentioned actually holding slaves during the years of his youth and young adulthood, which he spent in his parents' three-story mansion in the wealthy neighbourhood of Catete in Rio de Janeiro city, and in student residences while he studied at law school in São Paulo and in Recife. But it is hard to imagine a young man belonging to the highest elite not being served by (and profiting from) slaves.[39] He himself acknowledged this inescapable fact by stating in more abstract terms the intimate relation existing between the white Brazilian elite and slavery at the beginning of the 1870's. In an unpublished book written when he was only twenty-one years old, he explained that slavery was the same age as the country. "We were born with it, we live by it . . . Our wealth, where does it come from? From our slave production." And pessimistically he concluded: "abolish slavery today, you shall have abolished the country altogether."[40]

Garrison and Nabuco exemplified in the contrasting details of their lives the fact that abolitionism could germinate in very different worlds over the course of the nineteenth century. Remember the slave; that is what Garrison was first told by his mother, and what he insistently demanded of his Northern readers. He constantly reminded people that, although the Northern states had, one by one, emancipated their slaves during the years that followed the American Revolution, the Southern states, on the contrary, had expanded it. *They*, the others, the Southerners, still held slaves. People had to awaken to this scandalous reality and recall that this peculiar institution actually coexisted with the free institutions of the North.

But Nabuco did not have to remember the slave existing somewhere far away. A slave himself actually woke him to the awkward side of that institution, which was as close as the sugar cane fields of his own plantation. He might have regarded slavery as an unnatural institution, but certainly not as the peculiar institution of others. Slavery was his country. For *we*, Brazilians, still held slaves in this so-called Age of Reason. People had only to open their eyes, to see what was around everyone and everywhere, and compare Brazil with what was going on in the rest of the civilized world.

At this point the old question comes to mind: why people of various backgrounds in different parts of the American hemisphere and in distinct periods of the nineteenth century began to awaken to the reality of slavery? Why should people like Garrison remember the slave and others like Nabuco open their eyes wide to the injustice of holding slaves? Mother's pious advice or the sight of a miserable being pleading for help are scarcely enough to generate more than a fleeting sympathetic thought, before one turns to other and more pressing worldly affairs.

The perception of slavery as an injustice, grown to the point of involving an increasing number of people in a commitment to struggle for abolition, shall command attention throughout this comparative study. Many historians have agreed with Davis that antislavery would not have become a powerful international force had it not been preceded by a revolutionary shift in attitudes toward sin, human nature, and progress.[41] Indeed, abolitionism in its religious version—as in the United States—as well as in its secular version—as in Brazil—crystallized what that revolutionary shift made possible, that is, a new sensibility about the idea of humanity and a belief that the Negro's enslavement was not like other legitimate restraints of social life. In a way, the image of the Negro in cuffs and chains, representing innocent nature undeservedly enslaved, became a powerful symbol of injustice with enough appeal to bring together many different people who felt aggrieved themselves and were discontented with the general affairs of society.[42]

But the different rhythms of abolitionism—Brazil entering the age of abolitionism only during the 1860's—tells us that the assimilation of this humanitarian sensibility depended on a number of circumstances related to the historical development of these countries, their external relations, and the struggles of the free people of African descent and the slaves themselves.[43] In a word, the emergence of abolitionism can only be understood by keeping in mind the constant intertwining of its international and national dimensions.

The following comparison of views concerning the two main characters who actually made slavery—the slaveholder and the slave—held by American and Brazilian abolitionists, and how the abolitionists constructed those views, will show how distinctive could be the assimilation of this humanitarian sensibility.

II
VIEWS OF THE SLAVEHOLDER

When comparing the ideologies of abolitionism in the United States and Brazil, it is hard to avoid noticing the durability of a double discourse of exceptionalism: on the one side a discourse that constructs the image of the Southern American slaveholder as the most cruel master of the modern world, and even of the entire history of slavery; on the other side, a discourse that constructs the image of the Brazilian slaveholder as the most humane master of the day.

As we shall see, this double discourse was not merely a juxtaposition of discourses about different realities, but a single, interconnected discourse, whose double features one suspects could not stand one without the other. It was a comparative discourse, nurtured by abolitionists anxious to understand the world they lived in in order to change it for the better, and firmly convinced that the antislavery struggle transcended the strict boundaries of the nations.

By the mid-1860's, abolitionism as an international movement was beginning to lay roots among Brazilian intellectuals and politicians. The impact of the American Civil War and the defeat of the slave South was too strong to be ignored in Brazil, where around 1,700,000 people were still held as slaves, most of them operating in the main economic sectors.

More than ten years had passed since the Brazilian government, under British pressures, definitively closed the slave trade from Africa. The memory of the humiliations imposed on the nation by the British navy was fast receding into the past, while the recent bloody victory of the Union in the American Civil War contributed to the rise of the perception of Brazil as a peculiar country, that is, a large blot of slavery among the supposedly free and civilized Western countries.[1]

Grasping the spirit of his time, the Brazilian graduate student Francisco Antônio Brandão Jr. solemnly declared in an influential book published in Brussels in 1865 that civilization repealed slavery. This abstraction had been demonstrated by the American Civil War which had just inflicted a "fatal coup" on slavery.[2] The son of a cotton planter of Northern Maranhão, Brandão Jr. asked straightforwardly: who will allow Brazilians alone to continue owning slaves? To him, as a doctoral student of Natural Sciences at the University of Brussels in Belgium able for the first time to take a detached view of his own country, there was only one possible answer: we will be compelled to abolish slavery by force of war and this "will reduce us to the sad situation of that republic [the United States] which was so blooming in the past!"[3]

Other people were able to grasp these essential lessons of historical events in the world they lived in from inside the country. In 1868 the nineteen-year-old Joaquim Nabuco began to devote part of his time to the translation of articles from the *Anti-Slavery Reporter*—the organ of the British and Foreign Anti-Slavery Society. The articles were valuable sources for the political activities of his father, Senator Nabuco, a formerly conservative politician who had recently adopted liberalism as his new banner, and whom young Nabuco expected to become a "Brazilian Sumner" in the near future.[4]

Indeed, there could be no better source than the *Anti-Slavery Reporter* to transmit to Brazilian men of letters a sense of their isolation and shameful peculiarity in the civilized world. There Brazil figured as one of the main targets of the abolitionists, side by side with Turkey, Egypt, South Africa, Spain and Portugal, as well as other Asian and African countries which were considered uncivilized.[5]

However, in contrast to the harsh attacks that American slaveholders endured for more than thirty years of the Anglo-American abolitionist campaign, Brazilian slaveholders were mildly treated and even praised for their putative desire to substitute free labor for slavery. The speeches about Brazil at the Anti-Slavery Conference held in Paris in August 1867, under the sponsorship of the British and Foreign Anti-Slavery Society, reveal the mild tone reserved for this large slaveholding country. One of the speakers, C. Quentin, informed the delegates that slavery was not an institution, a system, or even a dogma in Brazil. Stressing the exceptionalism of Brazil, where slaveholders maintained slavery although detesting it and aspiring to abolish it, he put them above any blame.

> Brazil is in a most exceptional situation: she has received from Portugal this shameful legacy of Slavery; she has not had, like Spain and Portugal, any benefits from Slavery; and she has to support today all the weight of emancipation. If, then, it is just that nations be chastised for their faults, none the less must it be remarked that Brazil has to suffer today for faults committed by other nations, which alone have drawn any profit from them; for Spain and Portugal, which have no longer any slaves but in their colonies, the shock would not be terrible: for Brazil it will be difficult, long, disastrous.[6]

Quentin seemed especially anxious to counteract the arguments of those radical abolitionists who were inclined to raise Brazil "as the principal object of blame." He presented other reasons favouring soft treatment of the Brazilian slaveholders. Having adopted slavery merely as "a shameful legacy of Portugal," Brazil was not even totally responsible for its continuation in the present. Portuguese and other foreigners, many of them French, owned "a notable part of the slaves" in that country. Foreigners treated their slaves "much more inhumanly" than Brazilian slaveholders, who had never practiced "the cruelties which have rendered the planters of the Antilles and of the United States so mournfully celebrated." Last but not least, in the speech from the throne in May of that same year, Pedro II had already pronounced himself in favor of abolition in the future. Meanwhile, he had demonstrated his good faith by conceding freedom to slaves who were being enlisted as soldiers in the war against Paraguay.[7]

In contrast to the numerous delegates and nondelegates from other colonies and countries, such as Cuba and Spain, Brazilians did not attend this conference, as one would expect from a country where a widespread sympathetic inclination towards abolition was taken for granted.[8] But the French abolitionists, who spoke on Brazil's behalf, did not hesitate to praise its native slaveholders for their humanity as well as their desire to begin a process of peaceful transition from slavery to free labor. Where did they draw these ideas from? Did they simply believe the words of the official catalogue presented by Brazil at the Paris International Exhibition which was taking place simultaneously with the Conference?— "The slaves are treated with humanity and are generally well housed and fed . . . Their labor is now-a-days moderate . . . the evening and nights are passed in repose, in the practice of religion, or in sundry amusements."[9]

One should not forget that American slaveholders had exhausted themselves in affirming similar facts about their system, but no abolitionist ever believed them. How, then, could the Conference so unhesitatingly decide against transforming Brazil into its next main target of attack, despite acknowledging its importance by always mentioning it in the first place? As Quentin stressed, there were abolitionists who were inclined to do so.

In the radical counterresolution proposed by Elisée Reclus, Brazil appeared in first place among nations that called themselves civilized and yet proclaimed slavery to be a legitimate institution.

> In Brazil especially, one fourth, perhaps a third of the inhabitants of the empire are, according to law, merely the chattels, the machines of a few large landowners. Agriculture, manufactures, commerce, almost the whole of the public wealth, are founded upon Slavery; and even in a war, called national, a number of the soldiers are slaves, sold by their masters to be sent to their death. The Conference protests against such crimes.[10]

In contradistinction to Quentin's speech, Reclus's counterresolution saw slavery as an institution. But it was not merely one institution among others. Just as abolitionists in the past had denounced slavery as the main feature of the American South, Reclus and his radical fellows showed their eagerness to develop similar arguments for Brazil. In their view, Brazilian slavery should be energetically attacked precisely because the main sectors of Brazil's economy rested upon exploitation of the slave.[11] The ultimate proof that the slaves were treated as mere chattels and not as human beings was that even their lives were being sacrificed in the Paraguayan War, in order to satisfy the pecuniary interests of their masters.[12]

Reclus's counterresolution was not allowed either to be presented and debated, or to be put to a vote of the participants. Only at his stubborn insistence was it even included in the *Special Report* of the Conference. Alleging lack of time to discuss another resolution, the Conference's President, Edouard Laboulaye, did not hesitate to express his disagreement with the political content of the counterresolution. As he put it:

> [T]he little time at our disposal to hear reports upon America and Cuba, would be expended in discussing whether we should put into our resolutions a disagreeable word, more or less, for Brazil.[13]

The official resolution, which was adopted by acclamation, was indeed diametrically opposed, in political content and tone to Reclus's proposed resolution. Whereas the counterresolution chose to celebrate the Haitian Revolution as well as the martyrs of the struggle against slavery such as Vincent Ogé, JeanBaptiste Chavannes in St. Domingo, Louis Delgrés, Ignatius in Guadeloupe, Nat Turner, John Brown in the United States—implicitly suggesting that such revolutionary examples should be followed thereafter—the official resolution chose to omit any disagreeable reference to any country in particular, directing the efforts of abolitionists, instead, toward the respectful persuasion of the governments of countries where the slave trade and slavery still existed.[14]

Supposed external pressure on the Brazilian government to take measures towards abolition has been emphasized by historians as one important spur to the antislavery struggle in Brazil.[15] That may be so; but it is interesting to notice how much softer and less radical was the international abolitionist pressure against Brazilian slavery than it had been against slavery in the American South. Would the history of antislavery in Brazil have been different if radicals like Elisée Reclus had succeeded in imposing their point of view at the Paris International Conference? What meaning would it have had for those isolated radicals like the Brazilian former slave Luiz Gama who sounded like a voice in the desert during the 1860's whenever he demanded immediate abolition and denounced the compulsory enlisting of numerous slaves for the Paraguayan War?[16]

One thing is certain: the Brazilian elite was becoming increasingly sensitive to the demand for emancipation and to the internationally widespread opinion that slavery contradicted civilization. For Brazilian intellectuals and politicians, many of them slaveholders themselves, it might have been a matter of great relief to hear that Brazilian slaveholders were saved from becoming the next big villains of the civilized world. That role had belonged for more than three decades to the slaveholders of the American South, and by the decision of the Anti-Slavery Conference of 1867, they and they alone would continue to be depicted as villains in the public memory of the antislavery struggle.

Perhaps the conservative abolitionism adopted by the international conference resulted from fear of arousing civil wars in other countries, with even worse consequences than those of the American Civil War. Quentin seemed eager to reject any idea of immediatism when dealing with a country like Brazil, where a majority of the population was black and landless. Abolition should be done there under the sign of "transition". Transition: this should be the political banner of abolitionism in Brazil. If not, if abolition came suddenly and without preparation,

> The country could never support this shock, which would have besides, as its infallible result, the crowding back of the blacks into the deserts of the interior, and to creep along the rivers and in the impenetrable forests, a sort of African savage, whom one would never succeed in civilizing.[17]

The nightmare of the Haitian Revolution seemed still fresh in the mind of the Frenchman Quentin. But he believed that Brazil differed from Haiti in having humane slaveholders, who could be reasoned with and persuaded to reform their labor relations.[18]

Although useful for the effort to address in a "respectful" manner the government of the strongest remaining bastion of slavery on the American continent, the notion of the humane Brazilian slaveholder was by no means a recent invention.[19] It was an old idea, so old that one should refrain from trying to state exactly when and where it was born, lest one commit the historian's sin of obsession with origins, against which Marc Bloch warned.[20] But it is possible to detect this picture of the humane Brazilian slaveholder already present among American abolitionists during the 1820's and 1830's.

We may witness the simultaneous construction of the theme of the humane Brazilian slaveholder and of the cruel Southern American slaveholder by following the arguments presented by three American abolitionists during the first decades of the nineteenth century. George Bourne, David Walker, and David L. Child were not simply writers with an arsenal of rational arguments; they were writers with a mission, determined that their arguments should appeal to the hearts of their readers. Thus, they combined a preoccupation with developing accurate arguments with the aim of converting those who doubted the sinfulness of slavery.

In *Picture of Slavery in the United States of America*, the Reverend George Bourne wrote about the sinfulness of slavery in general, but made it clear that he had taken numerous examples of the sinful effects of slavery upon slaveholders from his own observations of slave relations in Virginia over nearly seven years.[21] There were seven sinful effects of slavery upon the slaveholders: 1."a haughty selfconceit;" 2."a marble-hearted insensibility;" 3.sensuality; 4.irascibility and turbulence; 5. injustice and knavery; 6. violence and cruelty; 7. infidelity and irreligion.

Throughout the demonstration of these effects, one could visualize the molding of a myriad of "domestic tyrants" by slavery in the South. The "primary and most permanent notion" a child in a slaveholder's family acquired was that "the slaveholder is a being of superior nature, character, quality and rank." The constant vision of wealthy white couples subjecting wretched black slaves to perennial toil and violence caused the child to grow up with a feeling of "proud self-complacency", that is, the feeling of belonging to "a more excellent order of beings." Thereafter, this arrogant heart would not be able to nurture "genuine religious, moral, or even merely human sensibility."[22] In consequence, the irreligious, immoral and insensible slaveholder acknowledged no restriction upon his power.

> . . . a slave-holder's plantation is his world, where no law rules but his caprices, and no power interferes with his arbitrary mandates.[23]

The picture of the slaveholder, as depicted by Bourne, was meant to arouse a feeling of horror among his Northern readers. How could one help thinking of the slaveholders as monstrous sinners after reading about a woman who systematically whipped her female slaves every Sunday morning before going to church:

> If I were to whip them on any other day of the week, I might lose their work for a day; but by whipping them on Sunday, their backs get well enough by Monday morning![24]

And what about the sight of an irrepressible promiscuity within the slaveholders' houses, where "young ladies elegantly attired" were "attended by their coloured sisters, children of the same father, yet slaves ?"[25]

Despite strong pressure from his Presbyterian peers against his radical abolitionism, the Reverend Mr.Bourne spent his life proclaiming that:

> Every deceased American slaveholder, since the 4th of July 1776, died a man-thief, and a mist of darkness hovers over his grave which no fire of Christian love, that "hopeth all things," can possibly dissipate.[26]

As for the living slaveholders, they were destined to follow the same wicked path as their ancestors for their consciences had become incapable of repenting.

> . . . all arguments which can be deduced from reason, consistency, justice and religion are nugatory . . .
> Hardened by avarice, and seared by long-practised iniquity, their consciences feel not; . . . [27]

Therefore, unless the people of New England started a campaign for "Immediate, unconditional, and universal emancipation!", by expelling slaveholders from the churches as well as from public office, there would be no possible escaping for the slaveholders "from the gulf of destruction and despair which is yawning to receive them."[28]

At this point one may better grasp the key to understanding this attempt to portray Southern slaveholders in such a wicked and horrible light. For how could abolitionists awaken Northern public opinion to the problem of slavery without depicting in lively colors something that was so far from their eyes and so absent from their minds and hearts? At the same time, abolitionists considered the slaveholders to be so imbued with their own world that they could see nothing beyond it. Therefore, the exhibition of the effects of slavery upon slaveholders, featuring true examples from everyday life in the South, was meant to convert the North to the truth of abolitionism. The North, in turn, would press slaveholders to get rid of their fundamental sin. In contrasting the slave South with the free North, abolitionists who acted under the banner "Our country is the world—our countrymen are mankind" helped to inspire their Northern readers with pride enough to allow the rise of a New England nationalism.[29]

Although involuntarily contributing to nationalist perspectives by stressing the New England mission to abolish Southern sin, nothing in Bourne's book would invite the Northern reader to think of Southern slaveholders as set apart from slaveholders of other countries. For as he assured his readers:

> Slavery originated in avarice, indolence, treachery, evil concupiscence, and barbarity: and its constant fruits have been robbery, disease, faithlessness, profligacy of every species, and murder.[30]

Another step in depicting Southern slaveholders as especially cruel slaveholders was taken by David Walker in his explosive *Appeal*, which was published in 1829 and soon caused scandal throughout the country.[31] The son of a slave and a free woman, Walker migrated from Wilmington, South Carolina, to Boston, Massachusetts, where by 1827 he had entered the clothing business, cultivating his mind during his leisure moments, and engaging in activities within the Northern African American community.[32] Although addressing his book to "all coloured men, women and children, of every nation, language and tongue under heaven," he made clear that he intended to defend two interrelated theses exclusively concerning the condition, past and present, of the black people in the United States and their prospects for their future. Writing as a voice from within the black American community—both slave and free— in contradistinction to the ones defined as white Christians of America, or simply," Americans," Walker stated:

> 1. we Coloured People of these United States, are, the most wretched, degraded and abject set of beings that over [sic] lived since the world began, down to the present day . . .

> 2. " . . . the white Christians of America, who hold us in slavery, (or, more properly speaking, pretenders to Christianity,) treat us more cruel and barbarous than any Heathen nation did any people whom it had subjected, or reduced to the same condition.

In sum, "the Blacks or Coloured People, are treated more cruel by the white Christians of America, than devils themselves ever treated a set of men, women and children on this earth."[33]

The reader was not expected to take such words as an anguished complaint without solid foundation in fact. Like almost every other abolitionist who wrote after him, Walker stressed that accuracy based on the observation of everyday life and a reason inspired by God were the essential underpinnings of his work.

> Having traveled over a considerable portion of these United States, and having, in the course of my travels, taken the most accurate observations of things as they exist—the result of my observations has warranted the full and unshaken conviction, that we, (coloured people of the United States,) are the most degraded, wretched and abject set of beings that ever lived since the world began . . . [34]

Over and over, throughout his book, Walker restated his theses in an effort to convince his readers that this was the truth. But truth, or the ability to grasp the truth, only existed as long as individuals made an effort to understand the world they lived in, in order to reach an understanding of God.

> Is not God a God of Justice to *all* his creatures? Do you say he is? Then if he gives peace and tranquility to tyrants, and permits them to keep our fathers, our mothers, ourselves and our children in eternal ignorance and wretchedness, to support them and their families, would he be to us a God of *justice*?[35]

No, God would not be the God of justice if one accepted the idea of an irremediable destiny for black people as victims under white tyrants. But Walker believed that God only acted in one's favor if one expressed the will to overcome a situation of oppression. In the case of the black people the "day of the redemption" would only come when they showed "a willingness . . . for God to do these things for us, for we may be assured that he will not take us by the hairs of our head against our will and desire, and drag us, from our very mean, low and abject condition."[36]

But how could there be willingness to change one's situation in this world without an accurate knowledge of this situation? How could black people grasp the truth of God if they persisted in ignorance and servility?

Despite its inflammatory language, Walker's *Appeal* should not be taken as a mere call for action against the white oppressors. More than this, Walker meant to bring knowledge to the black community, which in the long run would open the way to the emergence of a collective willingness to resist oppression. Then, God would be allowed to show his justice.

To discover the truth of slavery—one of the main sources of "our wretchedness"—Walker invited his readers to make use of history, both sacred and profane. History would permit them to compare their present situation to the past condition of other slaves in other countries. Thus they would find out about their true condition of oppression in the United States.[37]

Walker develops three diachronic comparisons of slavery in order to prove the exceptional wickedness of white Americans, and more specifically, slaveholders.

First he reflects on the sufferings of Israel under heathen Egyptians. Despite being enslaved by the Egyptians, Joseph and his brothers received the most fertile land in all Egypt from the Pharaoh. Would this ever happen to the people of color in the United States? No, even if a black man bought "a mud hole," some white man would doubtless try to get it from him. Moreover, Egyptians would never say that a slave did not belong to the human family. Pharaoh's daughter took Moses, a child of Israel, for her own son; had Moses wished to, he could have become prince regent to the throne of Egypt. In contrast, what did Americans think of their slaves? As people "descending originally from the tribes of Monkeys or Orang-Outangs," or as Thomas Jefferson put it, as "inferior people to the whites, both in the endowments of their bodies and minds."[38]

Secondly, he insists that the sufferings of the Helots under their Spartan masters were considerably less severe than the hardships endured by black slaves in America. The Helots never suffered brutalities like being chained and handcuffed, while being dragged from their wives and children and driven from one end of the country to the other. Nevertheless, the Spartans were no more than heathens, for they lived long before Christ's appearance.[39]

If the first two comparisons proved that the slaves in antiquity were better treated by their masters, never experiencing those physical cruelties, familial disruptions and racism which were so commonplace among American slaves, the third and last comparison showed that the path to freedom was not completely closed to the slaves of Rome. In contrast, white Americans not only enacted laws to prevent slaves from buying their freedom, but prohibited free black people from holding any public office. In sum, once born in slavery, one would be forever a slave; and if born free, a black person was to remain forever tied to an inferior position in society.[40]

The cruelty of the Southern American slaveholders was even more emphasized with the synchronic comparisons presented by David L. Child, a Massachusetts lawyer and one of the twelve founders of the New England Anti-Slavery Society in December 1831.[41] In a speech delivered at the first anniversary of the abolitionist society, Child began by asking "whether American Slavery is or is not the worst in the known world." From the beginning he declared his belief in the affirmative of the proposition. As he argued, many witnesses to slavery in the Southern states and in the West Indies pointed to far more cruelty in the United States than they had seen elsewhere.[42]

But why would the slaveholders of the American South be so peculiarly cruel to their slaves? What were the reasons that led them to distinguish themselves for their cruelty in comparison to other slaveholders in other countries?

Whereas Walker did not press his comparative analysis of the slaveholders' cruelty to the point of seeking an explanation for this putative American exceptionalism, Child faced the problem by pointing to the Southern slaveholders as the ones who best exemplified the meaning of modern slavery. In contradistinction to ancient slavery in Greece and Rome, which he considered "humane" for having begun as an alternative to the custom of killing prisioners of war, modern slavery originated only in the most unremitting greed.

> Its victims are not the captives of open and allowed war; they are the prey of skulking kidnappers and pirates, enemies of the human race. They are seized in the midst of peace, *merely to make them slaves*, not to save their lives when ready to be sacrificed by the hand of war. Modern slavery is not the consequence, but the *cause* of war; not an amelioration of its horrors, but the fruitful source of fresh wars, each with its attendant train of horrors.[43]

However, the rise of modern slavery had not annulled the humane precepts of ancient slavery, such as the legal protection of the slave, the right of manumission, as the slave's right to hold property and buy his freedom. Instead, the Roman civil law, which had brought together all these precepts under the Christian principle that slavery was contrary to natural rights and could only be justified by the laws of war, had been assimilated together with modern slavery by every slave country with the exception of the United States.

> I believe that it is universally true, that the humane provisions of the civil law were adopted from fifty to three hundred years ago by all the continental governments of Europe, who possess colonies and tolerate slavery in them, although, at this time, not one of them tolerates it *at home;*—and that the harsher features of the civil law have been either mitigated or entirely done away by the same governments.
> This observation applies to the Spanish, French, Portuguese, Danish and Swedish colonies. In all of them, the slaves can have property, and can purchase their freedom, as they could in ancient Rome.[44]

Child pointed to numerous examples in order to prove the more benign character of slavery in countries other than the United States. In Cuba, it was not difficult for a smart and frugal slave to accomplish the means to buy his freedom. As the letters by the Reverend Mr. Abbot, written in Cuba in 1828, revealed, food was furnished to the slaves so abundantly by their masters that the fruits of their own gardens could be converted into money.[45]

A number of ameliorations had recently been introduced in the British slave colonies regulating the slaves' selfpurchase of freedom, limiting the arbitrary punishment of a slave by the master, and prohibiting the separation of slave families.[46] But nowhere was the control of the law over the slaveholders, and in favor of the slaves, so strong and effective as in Brazil.

> In Brazil, at present the most populous slave nation, it is still better. There the master is obliged, under a severe penalty, to give his slave a written license to seek another master whenever the slave demands it; a person willing to purchase being found, the magistrate fixes the price.[47]

The United States, on the contrary, made a poor figure. American slaves did not enjoy any legal protection, while Southern slaveholders were allowed the power of life and death over their human properties.

> I have heard of shooting negroes from trees with as little concern, and apparently with as keen a zest, as a Northern sportsman drops a squirrel or a quail.[48]

But Child made sure that it was not only by hearsay that he defended the thesis of the exceptional cruelty of the Southern slaveholders toward their slaves. Horrible murders of slaves recounted afterwards in books by travelers to the South allowed him to conclude that Southern slaveholders were even worse than the despots of the Old World.[49]

> Those generous tyrants [Charles, Elizabeth, the Louises] appear to have thought that it was sufficient that adventurers in the new world should treat bondmen like beasts for the purpose of gain, but not for taste and amusement. Accordingly, we find neither these nor any other sovereign of Europe, encouraging brutality by law.[50]

The next step in explaining this putative American exceptionalism was to point to the reasons why the United States, among so many countries, had been the only one *not* to incorporate the humane inheritance of the Roman civil law, leaving the way instead totally opened to the horrors of modern slavery. The truth was that the United States was the only country where republicanism and slavery coexisted, and therefore, it was a country born in a fundamental error.

> We consented to cement a union with the strong, by sacrificing the rights of the weak. God is against this whole business. It has already converted part of the nation into madmen, and another part into something more harmless, but not more respectable. To be mad is not much worse than to be
> 'Frightened when a madman stares.'[51]

The image of the madmen and the frightened men, standing respectively for the Southern slaveholders and the people of the free Northern states, pointed to the key to the problem of American exceptionalism. Born in error, the Union had abdicated its democratic virtues—justice, fidelity, fortitude—erecting instead the reign of despotic vices—fear, treachery, the petty politics of office-seekers, avarice, and luxury. It was a Union already sapped in its foundations, soon to be left with no trace of virtue or self-respect.

Child implies that the humane civil law inherited from ancient Rome could still make sense in countries where monarchies acknowledged different stations in life for their subjects, but equality before God. Thus, the monarchs played the role of protectors of the weak against the cupidity of the strong. But in a republic, where political equality stood as a principle, there should be no need for a civil law protecting unequal people. The republic was like a "Pandora's box to the slave," but with no hope at the bottom. The "republican slave" was the slave "chained by the hands of democracy and political equality."[52] The republic slaveholder was, then, exceptionally cruel because he enjoyed the most complete impunity.

Up to now, we have seen how the idea of the Southern slaveholder as the most cruel master of all times began to take shape among American abolitionists during the early 1830's. The radicalism of the proposition rested on two basic arguments—that is, that slavery is a sin, and that the American republic is inconsistent—which formed one interrelated truth.

The belief that slavery was a sin permeated everything American abolitionists did for the next thirty-five years. They made a point of convincing the public that slavery was not only an evil, but a sin. It is interesting to follow an imaginary debate about slavery in the United States published by *The Abolitionist* in 1833. In the midst of this fictitious debate between Philo, an abolitionist, and one Mr. B., who opposed slavery but was not an abolitionist, a third character, a South Sea Islander visiting the land of the white people for the first time, inquired about barbarous customs, such as slavery, existing amid civilization. To his surprise, he found out that slavery was not shocking to white people's eyes, despite their belief in a loving God. As Mr. B. explained to him:

> That [slavery] *may* be an evil, I will admit . . . but I do not see that it is a sin. It was practiced at the time our Saviour was upon earth, and he did not condemn it, but by his Apostles, gave directions to servants to be obedient to their masters![53]

The rather timid reply by Philo, the abolitionist, who could only contribute one rather ambiguous biblical quotation—"remember those in bonds; as bound yourselves"—left the South Sea Islander unsatisfied. One may perceive here an implicit criticism of those abolitionists who were inclined to consider slavery an evil tolerated by the Bible. Abolitionists could effectively oppose slavery only when convinced themselves that slavery and the Bible were truly irreconcilable.

But if slavery was not an evil, but really a sin, it should not be seen as a mere sin among others. It should be seen as the SIN, just as it had been portrayed in the vigorous words of the Reverend Mr.Bourne in 1816, later incorporated by abolitionists like William L. Garrison, the Reverend Theodore Dwight Weld, the brothers Arthur and Lewis Tappan, William Goodell, Frederick Douglass, among many others. Quoting profusely from the Bible and from early British antislavery writings, Bourne had declared:

> Slaveholders plead that they are Christians.
>
> . . .
>
> But the BOOK unequivocally declares, that to enslave a man is the highest kind of theft; to purloin children is the compound of all

robbery, as it steals a Father's joy, a Mother's tenderness, a Brother's delight, and a Sister's affection; to excruciate a female by stripes or by violation, is the height of barbarity; to divest man of his rational characteristics is the most diabolical impiety; ... to profane the sabbath absolutely disavows the authority of God, and salvation by Christ Jesus; and to prolong human existence in agony, the mind bereft of all consolation and the body of needful support is a concatenation of crime indescribable.[54]

The second argument supporting the American abolitionist indictment of slavery pointed to the contradiction of a country which had affirmed its independence by declaring to the world the equality of all human beings before divine and human law, but which maintained millions of inhabitants in slavery. The theme of the inconsistency of the American Revolution seemed directed especially at citizens in the North. If not sinners themselves, as the Southern slaveholders were, the Northern citizens were nonetheless guilty of inconsistency with the Union's principles and, in this way, collaboration in spreading the sin of manstealing.

John Kenrick, like Bourne an abolitionist of the so-called "neglected period" of the antislavery struggle—a period that stretches from the interruption of the African slave trade in 1808 to the rise of radical abolitionism in 1831—denounced the Americans' inconsistency a few years after the closing of the second war between the United States and Great Britain.[55] As he stressed, in defence of the supreme principle that all men are born equally free and independent, or in resistance to violations of their rights, the Americans thought themselves justified in appealing to arms, and exposing their lives and property in two desolating wars. Nevertheless, this same people so "jealous of their *own* rights" did not hesitate in treating "their brethren of a different colour" as property just as if "they were oxen and horses."

Yet such is the inconsistency of the white inhabitants of the
United States—a people too who call themselves CHRISTIANS![56]

Kenrick was especially keen to show that inconsistency was not something to be exclusively associated with Southern slaveholders. He reduced much of the merit of emancipation in the Northern states, which had gradually developed as an aftermath of the Revolution, by publicizing the French traveler Jacques-Pierre Brissot's indictment of the Emancipation Act of Pennsylvania in 1780. The first emancipation law of modern slavery was too moderate and protective of the slaveholders' interests, declared the impatient Brissot one year before the opening of the French Revolution. The law did not extend the hope of freedom to those who were slaves at the time of its passing, for slaves were considered property, and property was sacred. But as Brissot argued,

> . . . what is a property founded on robbery and plunder?
> What is a property which violates laws, human and divine?

Furthermore, the law did not allow a slave to be a witness against a free man. It also included the absurdity of providing that a master be reimbursed, from the public treasury, the price of a slave put to death for crime. To this French critic, that was like compensating the master for his tyranny, for the crimes of slaves were almost universally the fruit of their slavery.[57]

It is interesting to notice here the role of the foreign travelers' views in highlighting the inconsistency of the Revolution and its aftermath. To Child, foreign travelers' accounts of the horrors of slavery in the United States helped to bring the truth to light, for foreigners "did not feel their tongues tied by 'the compact'."[58]

The writer Lydia Maria Child—one of the first American women to succeed in publishing under her own name—invited her large public to set aside their prejudice against foreign travelers' remarks. Conceding that those who came from monarchical countries were often unfit to judge republican institutions, she nevertheless recalled the old adage that "an enemy is the best friend" because he is able to perceive "our faults."

> If they really speak truths, do not let us, like the orientals, be
> angry with every one that refuses to call us 'the celestial
> union'—'brothers of the Sun and Moon,'&cx.[59]

Abolitionists considered foreign travelers especially important in revealing the truth of slavery, for they not only publicized the everyday crimes committed by slaveholders against their slaves, but also revealed the responsibility of the North for reproducing the inferiority of black people both as slaves in the South and as free inhabitants of the North. As an abolitionist argued in the 1833 *Annual Report* of the New England Anti-Slavery Society:

> The guilt of slaveholding is national; the evil is national; 'and a common evil implies a common right to apply a remedy.' We, of New England, deeply participate in the guilt of oppression, having early commenced enslaving the natives of Africa, and up to the last hour of the legality of the traffic, actively prosecuted the foreign slave trade. To the South we are now pledging our physical force, in case of insurrection, and giving our cooperation, without which they could not long retain their victims in servitude.[60]

But it seems that nothing proved more vital in highlighting the inconsistency of the American Republic than breaking the heroic myths surrounding the founding fathers. Once more, American abolitionists highly prized the judgments of outside observers. One example among many was the publication in the opening number of *The Abolitionist* of an old letter sent to George Washington by the Liverpool philanthropist, Edward Rushton. After praising Washington's revolutionary role, Rushton warned him that it was not to the Commander in Chief of the American forces, nor to the President of the United States, that he was writing. His business was with George Washington of Mount Vernon, Virginia, a man who, despite his hatred of oppression and love of liberty, held hundreds of "his fellow beings in a state of abject bondage." History would not excuse the hero, and in the eyes of future generations Washington would be nothing but a sinner.

> . . . Oh! Washington, 'ages to come will read with astonishment' that the man who was foremost to wrench the rights of America from the tyrannical grasp of Britain, was among the last to relinquish his own oppressive hold of poor and unoffending negroes.[61]

The children of the founding fathers were also brought to this exhibition of inconsistent revolutionaries and monstrous sinners. Among the many crimes by slaveholders against slaves described in David Child's book, the one committed by a supposed nephew of Thomas Jefferson could be selected as the very personification of the hero of liberty's child reduced to an abject sinner, the worst slaveholder who ever lived. In December 1811, during a "Sabbath", at the plantation of Liburn Lewis, in the County of Livingston, Kentucky, the owner—"a sister's son of the venerable Jefferson"—called his numerous slaves to witness a spectacle of power. They were collected in a gloomy room by the fire to watch the punishment of George, an ill grown seventeen-year-old boy who had broken an elegant pitcher.

> He [Jefferson's nephew] bound him with cords, and, by the assistance of his young brother, laid him on a broad bench, or meat block. He now proceeded to WHANG off George by the ankles!!! It was with the broad axe!—In vain did the unhappy victim SCREAM AND ROAR! He was completely in his master's power. Not a hand among so many, durst interfere. Casting the feet into the fire, he lectured them at some length. He WHACKED HIM OFF below the knees! George roaring out, and praying his master to BEGIN AT THE OTHER END! . . . And so off the arms, head and trunk, until all was in the fire![62]

It is not my intention to assess the veracity of such accounts. Most important for my purpose is to show how the theme of the Southerner as the worst slaveholder of present and past times emerged from the American abolitionists' writings. This tale of horror involving a descendant of Jefferson exemplifies in nightmarish contours the attempt to wake Americans from their inconsistent lives and build a consciousness of human rights embracing everyone, including people of African descent.

As for the efficacy of such tales in actually waking sinners—the slaveholders—and guilty Northerners, the American abolitionists seemed to expect great results. Despite the violent reaction endured by abolitionists, especially during the 1830's, they were proud to hear that their message had reached some hearts and could make converts even among slaveholders. Seen in hindsight, this perception by abolitionists means almost nothing, but if we exercise our imagination we can understand how those Northern abolitionists might have been excited in hearing that the slaveholder James G. Birney from Kentucky opened his emancipation statement with the following words:

> Believing that slaveholding is inconsistent with natural
> justice, with the precepts and spirit of the Christian religion, and with
> the Declaration of American Independence, and wishing to testify in
> favor of them all, I do hereby emancipate, and forever set free, the
> following named slaves . . . [63]

By the end of the 1830's the idea that the United States was exceptionally furnished with the worst of modern and ancient slaveholders was already firmly rooted in the abolitionist imagination.[64] In 1839, the Reverend Theodore Dwight Weld presented an impressive "encyclopaedia" of horrid crimes happening "not in one of the slave states, but in all of them; not perpetrated by brutal overseers and drivers merely, but by magistrates, by legislators, by professors of religion, by preachers of the gospel, by governors of states, by 'gentlemen of property and standing', and by delicate females moving in the 'highest circles of society'."[65] Weld's book was the touchstone of a trend long in formation among American abolitionists, with the support of their British fellows.

However, as we have seen, reference to the "worst" slaveholder always implied either a synchronic or diachronic comparison. During the 1840's and 1850's, readers of the abolitionist press would find a number of references taking for granted that in every country where slavery still existed, with the exception of the United States, people of African descent, both slaves and free, received good treatment from their masters and neighbours.[66] Whether abolitionists only aimed "to shame our countrymen, by holding up the examples of gentleness and kindness towards colored people, which the Spanish colonies and the South American States afford," as David Child seemed to imply, or if they really believed their own claims, is another story.[67] The fact is that they gave prominence to a theme that became part of the imagination of their time, and endured in the historiography of the twentieth century, especially that part that contrasted race relations in Brazil and the United States. The intertwined ideas of the American racial hell and the Brazilian racial paradise are not of recent invention.[68]

By the time Brazilian abolitionism began to take more radical steps in the 1880's, the idea that Brazil had a mild slavery was already circulating in the international marketplace. As we have seen, it traveled from Europe to the American continent and the other way around in a number of travelers' accounts and in the abolitionist press.

Brazilian abolitionists did not escape exposure to such sympathetic views of their country. Some of them, heirs of planters, politicians or merchants, had the chance to travel to Europe and the United States, there taking notice of how Brazilian slaveholders were being favorably compared to the defeated Southern planters. Others, without ever leaving Brazilian shores, would hear of these opinions from their fellow travelers or by reading the many imported French books which were in great demand at book auctions or in the few bookstores available mainly in Rio de Janeiro.[69]

Despite such international influences, Brazilian abolitionists were not totally impressed. They had their own eyes to see what was going on on the plantations and in urban households throughout the country. Joaquim Nabuco, who was considered the most eminent political representative and intellectual of abolitionism during the 1880's, was emphatic about this point in his main book on abolitionism.

> In general it is said that slavery among us is mild, and that the slaveholders are kind. The truth, however, is that every slavery is the same, and as for the kindness of the slaveholder this is nothing but the resignation of the slaves. Whoever would venture to estimate the crimes by slaves or against slaves; whoever could initiate an inquiry about slavery, listening to the complaints of those who bear it; that one would realize that in Brazil slavery is even now as harsh, barbarous and cruel as it was in any other country of the American continent.[70]

As Nabuco acknowledged, the slaveholder would not need to be cruel as long as the slave behaved passively. But once the slave's docility ceased, then the slaveholder's cruelty emerged.[71] In contradistinction to the American abolitionists who depicted the Southern planters as cruel slaveholders independently of the slaves' reactions—the slaves of Jefferson's sadistic nephew did not lift a finger against him—Nabuco approached slavery and the issue of cruelty by depicting a relationship between master and slave. Slavery in Brazil was as cruel as anywhere else, not because the slaveholder was sadistically barbarous, but because he interacted with the slave within a relation of power. Crimes by slaves or against slaves occurring throughout the country proved, in his view, that cruelty was endemic to slavery, that is, to the everyday relationship between master and slave.

However Nabuco, who knew as an insider the meaning of being a planter and a slaveholder, was also a great traveler. In his travels to the United States and Europe during the 1870's and 1880's he had the opportunity of assimilating much of the comparison that had been made between slavery in the United States and Brazil. This fact explains, in part, why in the same book quoted above, written in London in 1882, Nabuco emphasized from the beginning:

> Slavery, to our happiness, never embittered the soul of the slave against the master, in a collective sense, nor created between the two races the mutual hate which naturally exists between oppressors and oppressed beings. For this reason, the contact between them was always free from harshness outside slavery, and the man of color found every avenue opened before him.[72]

Besides assimilating the comparison already made by Anglo-American abolitionists, Nabuco himself had eyes to compare the increasing racism of the postbellum American scene to the recent political measures taken in Brazil, which, despite the existence of slavery, proved to him the lack of racial prejudice in his country.

> The debates of the last legislature, and the liberal style of the Senate enfranchising the freedmen, that is, agreeing to erase the last vestige of the inequality of the former condition, show that color in Brazil is not, as in the United States, a social prejudice.[73]

Was Nabuco too contradictory in acknowledging, on the one side, the harshness of slavery in Brazil, which as he put it was the same as in every other slave country, and, on the other side, the good feelings existing between master and slave as well as between former master and freedman, which had developed in Brazil alone?

More important than dwelling on the contradiction itself is understanding how it came to be rooted in the Brazilian abolitionist discourse. For Nabuco was not the only one to exhibit it. Generally Brazilian abolitionists oscillated from praising the slaveholders for their generosity toward their slaves to denouncing them for their cruelty and crimes against slaves.

Examples of appraisal of the slaveholders' generosity can be found in successive numbers of the *Gazeta da Tarde*, one of the most influential abolitionist newspapers, edited by José do Patrocínio in the capital of the Empire, Rio de Janeiro. The newspaper opened up a special column—"Chronicle of Goodness"—in order to publicize the "liberty letters" offered by slaveholders. For instance, on May 21, 1887, one slaveholder was praised for emancipating two "enslaved" people provided they worked for him for monthly wages for one more year; on June 21, 1887, another slaveholder deserved to have his name in this golden section for granting freedom to six slaves upon condition of working for two more years; on March 19, 1887, a slaveholder from the neighbouring province of São Paulo was praised for emancipating a twenty-three year old female slave on condition of "serving him for three years"—no mention of wages.[74]

Although the *Gazeta da Tarde* always referred to slaves as "enslaved," making clear its belief in the illegitimacy of slavery according to the natural law, one can perceive in this appraisal of slaveholders an attitude of respect toward the human laws, or the laws of the country. The abolitionist Cincinnatus made clear this distinction by explaining the two dimensions of slave property.

> [Slave property] is illegitimate for being an attack against freedom, reason and justice, and at the same time legal for being born under the shadow of the law and having been protected by law.
> It is yet illegitimate for contradicting every natural and moral law; legal, however, for being authorized by every consolidated power of the country.[75]

Despite the respect for a distinction between legal and legitimate that generally permeated Brazilian abolitionism, some abolitionists were more prone to call attention to the cruelty of the slaveholders toward their slaves than to their occasional acts of generosity. This was evident in the harsh tone assumed by the *Redempção*, an important abolitionist newspaper of São Paulo city, the state capital of one of the most thriving Southern coffee provinces.

In contradistinction to the "Chronicle of Goodness" of the *Gazeta da Tarde*, the São Paulo abolitionists created a special column called "Chronicle of Years," beginning always with "it has been years" that so and so . . . , followed by horrid cases of planters and urban slaveholders, as well as managers, drivers, and slavetraders, whipping and torturing to death their slaves, overworking slaves, and harassing abolitionists.[76]

Despite differences among them, Brazilian abolitionists generally remained determined to combine abolition with respect for the laws, which in a slave country was equivalent to respect for the slaveholders' interests.[77] This conservative aspect was much criticized by Luis Anselmo da Fonseca an abolitionist from Bahia. He called attention to the support abolitionists gave to the increasing number of private manumissions of slaves, who then were obliged to work from two to seven years for their former owners.

> Abolitionists have seldom commented on this fact.
> Many of the most sincerely devoted have promoted emancipations under such conditions, praising them in public and in the newspapers, and even inviting the *masters* who have not yet decided in favor of this solution, to do it.[78]

At this point it is necessary to understand what lay beneath the abolitionists' conciliatory policy. We began by recalling that Nabuco, in a single book, dismissed the thesis of the mild Brazilian slavery and admitted the idea that Brazilian slavery nurtured exceptional good feelings between masters and slaves. We further observed abolitionists assuming the role of public sponsors of private manumissions, under condition of work by the slaves, in an attempt perhaps to promote good feelings between masters and freedmen, and in this way, to forge a very special Brazilian solution to the problem of slavery.

One is tempted here to imagine Brazil as a great South, where abolitionists had to struggle for abolition with great caution. Besides, as we shall see in chapter four, by the 1880's Brazilian abolitionists had had ample opportunity to hear what had become of the once great American South. These are certainly important aspects of abolitionism in Brazil. Because they struggled within the last American bastion of slavery, Brazilian abolitionists absorbed much of the historical experience of abolition and its aftermath in other countries, especially the United States.

Nevertheless, in order to understand the differences between American and Brazilian abolitionists it is necessary to acknowledge marked differences in their modes of reasoning. As we have already seen in chapter one, the ideological sources of abolitionism in each country were quite distinct. In the search for the abolitionists' views concerning the slaveholder, this difference plays its role in explaining the more radical tone of American abolitionism, and the more moderate tone of Brazilian abolitionism.

Two elements present in the thinking of American abolitionists and absent from that of Brazilian abolitionists point to a crucial cultural distinction: the idea that slaveholding is a sin, and the idea that slavery is inconsistent with the origins of the nation.

Denunciations of slavery for contradicting the divine law were also part of the Brazilian abolitionist discourse. However, in contradistinction to the American abolitionist discourse, divine law did not occupy a central position in arguments against slavery. Slavery was attacked for being unproductive, backward, a crime against society, a negation of natural rights, an evil, but hardly an abolitionist would think of defining the slaveholders as sinners.

Brazilian abolitionists appealed mainly to social-economic reason, and seldom to the individual's spiritual existence. Nabuco acknowledged this point by stressing that abolitionism in Brazil was not motivated by religious and philanthropic concerns as in Great Britain. In his view, Brazilian abolitionism was essentially a political movement whose goals were to reconstruct the nation on a basis of free labor and racial integration.[79] But such political goals would only be attained if the slaveholders could be persuaded of the superiority of free labor over slavery.

Cincinnatus's arguments expressed well this secular theme being developed by Brazilian abolitionists, whose main weapons were drawn from economics. He offered two proofs in defending the thesis that the free worker was more productive than the slave. First, by examining a comparative table with estimates of the total of exported products per inhabitants for thirty-three countries, the reader could easily ascertain that Brazil ranked last.[80]

To establish his second proof, he divided Brazil in two, the North with a smaller concentration of slaves and the South with a much larger concentration of slaves. The average rate of export per slave for the previous three years increased where there were fewer slaves and decreased where there were more. Despite the fact that the thriving Southern coffee provinces exported considerably more than the impoverished Northern sugar cane provinces, Cincinnatus's estimate of average exports per slave supposedly proved that the Northern provinces were producing proportionally more than the Southern ones. Having in mind the increasing internal slave trade from the Northern provinces to the Southern ones, Cincinnatus implicitly warned that in the future North and South would switch sides, and the Southern slave provinces would be the decaying ones.[81]

João Clapp, the president of the Abolitionist Confederation, summarized this economic trend, which had long been developed within Brazilian abolitionism, in the opening words of a petition to the Rio de Janeiro city representatives:

> Considering that it has been largely proved that slavery is not an economic factor, nor a financial one, and that it only represents a vice within the national organism, which prevents the regular exercise of its functions . . . [82]

Besides the language of economics, Clapp spoke here the language of evolutionism which, by the 1880's, was increasingly making its way among Brazilian intellectuals. In this case Brazilian abolitionists talked like doctors diagnosing an organism whose disease, slavery, had to be extirpated before it was too late.[83]

This secular bent for arguing against slavery by dwelling more on expedient reasons, and less on principles, was reinforced by the historical memory of the origins of the nation. For, in contradistinction to the American abolitionists, who had a Revolution to remember, Brazilian abolitionists often used irony to describe the way the independence of Brazil had been achieved.

The abolitionist from Bahia, Vindex, possibly another pseudonym for Cincinnatus, considered Brazil's achievement of independence from Portugal a mere compromise between colony and mother country. As he recalled, Brazil had paid two million pounds to King João VI, who, in turn, recognized the sovereignty of the new country. But what made it even worse was the fact that Brazilians and Portuguese made war and sacrificed the lives of many patriots in order to conceal these hypocritical machinations between the king of Portugal and his son, Pedro, who became the first king of Brazil in 1822.[84]

It is interesting to notice that while American abolitionists could relate the struggle for liberty to the Revolution, and therefore stress the inconsistency of slavery with the Constitution, Brazilian abolitionists had to search elsewhere for historical memories of the pursuit of freedom. Freedom was the will of the deceived patriots who fell in a hypocritical war; it was the aim of the defeated Pernambuco Revolution of 1817 which defended a gradual abolition of slavery; it was also the intention of José Bonifácio, "the Patriarch of Independence," whose *Representation* in favor of gradual abolition was never presented to the first Constitutional Congress; before it could be presented, Congress was dissolved by King Pedro I, and the Patriarch expelled from the country.[85]

In sum, for Brazilian abolitionists the continuation of slavery after independence could not be considered inconsistent because the winners' intention had not been to build a nation on a new basis, but to forge a new country on the same old basis. If there was something to be highlighted for inconsistency, it was the very origins of the country.

The problem of slavery for Brazilian abolitionists was not a matter of digging for original principles from a heroic past, but of making Brazil consistent with the development of the contemporary world. For them it was a matter of expediency, and above all, it had to be fast. As the "Friendly Address," from the Paris Antislavery International Conference to the people of Brazil, emphasized in 1867:

> Brazil, at this time, retains in slavery many more human beings than any other Christian nation of the world. May it not have in history the dishonorable distinction of being the last [country] to emancipate them.[86]

In 1880, when this address was published by Nabuco's newspaper, Brazil was just one step from achieving this dishonorable worldly record.[87]

III
Views of the Slave

The picture of the slave as a man in chains, with no will of his own, a bound worker under the sole power of the slaveholder, recurs in both American and Brazilian abolitionism. But any similarity between their views of the slave ceases if one goes beyond the central image of the slave as a victim.

We have already seen in chapter 2 that American and Brazilian abolitionists developed different views of the slaveholder. For American abolitionists, slaveholders were tyrants, cruel monsters, sinners, while for Brazilian abolitionists, slaveholders were backward, ignorant people, who might as a result, be cruel to their slaves. Such distinct views led to distinct conclusions. American slaveholders were expected to repent right away from their basic sin—slavery—and liberate their slaves immediately. Brazilian slaveholders needed to be convinced of their ignorance about slavery—a backward system of labor—and given time to carry out the transition from slave to free labor.

By the same token, American and Brazilian abolitionists developed quite different views about the slave. American abolitionists generally pictured the slave as a brother to his fellowbeing, while Brazilian abolitionists pictured the slave as a domestic enemy to the slaveholder and his kin. The two following extracts may help us to visualize the distinct ways in which abolitionists introduced the figure of the slave to their audiences. From the Declaration of Sentiments of the American Anti-Slavery Society at its first convention in December 1833, in Philadelphia, one learns that:

We have met together for the achievement of an enterprise, without which that of our fathers is incomplete; and which, for its magnitude, solemnity, and probable results upon the destiny of the world, as far transcends theirs as moral truth does physical force.

. . .

Their grievances, great as they were, were trifling in comparison with the wrongs and sufferings of those for whom we plead. Our fathers were never slaves—never bought and sold like cattle . . .

But those, for whose emancipation we are striving—constituting at the present time at least one-sixth part of our countrymen—are recognized by law, and treated by their fellowbeings, as marketable commodities, as goods and chattels, as brute beasts ...

. . .

We further maintain—that no man has a right to enslave or imbrute his brother . . .

The right to enjoy liberty is inalienable. To invade it is to usurp the prerogative of Jehovah. Every man has a right to his own body . . . Surely, the sin is as great to enslave an American as an African.[1]

Now we shall see what a Brazilian living in the 1870's was learning from abolitionism. In an appeal to the mothers, the abolitionist Ruy Barbosa compared the slave to the huge, silent and isolated world of the plants.

Look at the smiling leaves of the orange garden. During the day it is all oxygen, which allows life, as well as harmless scents; during the night, under these balsamic exhalations the carbon dioxide enters, which asphyxiates.

So is man.

Whenever enveloped by the bright waves of liberty, he will fertilize the globe.

Yet abandoned to the darkness of oppression, he will spread death throughout the impoverished atmosphere.

Is there anything more innocent than the lovely lily of the valley?

However, by the twilight fill the alcove with them, and . . . well, it is possible that you wake up no more.[2]

In other words, as the Declaration of the Brazilian Anti-Slavery Society more explicitly stated:

We, Brazilians, do not intend to close our eyes to this monstrous mutilation of man any more, to this systematic suppression of the human nature of one million and half of our countrymen of other race.[3]

Two reasons accounting for the differences of approach toward the slave have already been focused in chapter 1. First there is the difference of inspiration—religious on the one side, secular on the other—permeating the two abolitionisms. The reader of the Declaration of Sentiments of the American Anti-Slavery Society was to be reminded of his duties toward the black slave as both a Christian and a child of the American Revolution. The fathers struggled against British tyranny in fulfillment of the divine law that all men are created equal and endowed with inalienable rights such as life, liberty, and the pursuit of happiness. The children must enlarge the divine task of the fathers by attacking the sin of enslaving one-sixth part of "our countrymen" of African descent. This was a most urgent task. For never had the fathers endured a tyranny as harsh as the one suffered by "our brothers" of a "dark complexion."[4] The implicit feeling was that the sin of slavery was even worse than the sin once committed by the British against the American colonists.

No such religious foundation underlies Brazilian abolitionism. Living in an increasingly secularized intellectual environment, Brazilian abolitionists were inclined to use scientific examples in demonstrating the wrongness of slavery.

In Barbosa's words, liberty to men was like daylight to plants. Plants combined with the sun produced oxygen, which allowed life to spread. Similarly, men combined with liberty produced all the good things on earth that allowed civilization to spread. But denied liberty, as the slaves were, they became incapable of producing anything but death around them, as plants in darkness spread dangerous carbonyl scents to any breathing being. The Declaration of the Brazilian Anti-Slavery Society concluded by recurring to a central idea of the Enlightenment: men without liberty are deprived of their very human nature. More implicitly—and we shall see how recurrent was this idea in Brazilian abolitionism— slaves were like beasts, for the denial of liberty meant the suppression of reason, which the abolitionists considered the fulcrum of human nature.

The prevailing secularism of Brazilian abolitionist discourse did not mean that God was always excluded from the scenery. God had the role of framing secular arguments, that is, of bringing to them a bit of a charitable touch, which people brought up within Catholic precepts would judge apropriate in mentioning those who belonged to an inferior position in the social hierarchy.

The above extract by Ruy Barbosa is one of the rare documents left by Brazilian abolitionists where God has a prominent role side by side with a secular argument. It is possible that Barbosa also appealed to religious arguments because he was addressing women, that is, "mothers of family". Mothers of family was a common Brazilian way of referring to elite women. Barbosa made use of this image probably in order to be more effective in reminding them of the special role to which women were destined in a Catholic society— the role of distributing charity.

> You know well the evangelical narrative of Lazarus and Jesus.
> Because of charity, the common origin, the common destiny, you are like Mary, that is, sisters of those who lie down in life in the tomb of slavery.[5]

This is the religious framework that Barbosa ingeniously constructed in trying to capture the attention of elite women of his native Bahia, one of the most important slave states during the 1870's.[6] Implicitly, he showed his readers that women could act as sisters to the slaves—just as Mary (and Martha) cared for their suffering brother Lazarus— for women resembled slaves in suffering, because both occupied an inferior position in life.

Still, Barbosa did not invite his female readers to conclude that they were committing a most serious sin for enslaving their brothers and sisters, the slaves. In contrast to the American abolitionists, who acknowledged the sin of slavery in light of the divine truth of the equality of all human beings, this Catholic-inspired article by a Brazilian abolitionist recurs to the image of a fraternal relationship between elite women and slaves only to suggest to the first that their inferior position in society should make them more sensitive and charitable toward those who were at " the lowest place in the scale of being," the slaves.

And here we approach the second reason for the difference between American and Brazilian abolitionists' views of the slave. American abolitionism was a voice speaking from outside slavery, while Brazilian abolitionism was a voice speaking from the very heart of the slave hierarchy. "Remember the slave" was a favourite theme of American abolitionism.

> Brothers and sisters! who with joy
> Meet round the social hearth,
> And talk of home and happy days,
> And laugh in careless mirth;
>
> Remember the poor young slave
> Who never felt your joy;
> Who early old, has never known
> The bliss to be a boy.[7]

In the Northern free states, abolitionists never ceased to call attention to the fact that far away, throughout the Southern states, slaves were bound to spend their lives in the service of masters. Counting on the support of the slave laws, slaveholders deprived them of every human right, and inflicted upon them umbearable punishments. Therefore "the enemy of the slave" was the master; for, as the Rev. George Bourne denounced, the master "has made open war against him, and is daily carrying it on by uneremitted efforts."[8]

However, in reminding the Northern citizens of the existence of the slave, abolitionists were also inviting them to take sides. An influential pamphlet by the British abolitionist Quaker Elizabeth Heyrick emphasized that "the true friends of justice," could not delay their support for the struggle for the immediate emancipation of "our African brothers," in the distant West Indian colonies. Slavery was a question in which "we are all implicated; we are all guilty . . . of supporting and perpetuating slavery."[9] By 1837, the year this pamphlet was published by the Philadelphia Anti-Slavery Society, and just a few years after Great Britain decreed abolition in the West Indies, American abolitionists had already made Heyrick's immediatist appeal their own by substituting the image of the brother enslaved in the distant American South for the image of the brother enslaved in the distant West Indies.

In Brazil there was no such distance between abolitionism and slavery. As Joaquim Nabuco emphasized in defining the hard tasks abolitionism would have to endure in Brazil,

> our character, our temperament, our entire physical, intellectual and moral organization, have been terribly affected by the influence of slavery permeating Brazilian society for the last three hundred years.[10]

Historians have stressed the fact that Brazilian abolitionism was essentially an urban movement emerging from the economic transformations of the 1870's and 1880's, transformations that opened the way for new activities and new social groups with interests distinct from, and sometimes in conflict with, those of the planters.[11] However one should not overlook the point that slavery was as much a part of the urban as of the rural environment. Besides, many people who became part of these new social groups—professionals, merchants, small shopkeepers, entrepreneurs—and who were eventually inclined to support abolitionism were the offspring of the plantations, and maintained familial and business links with the planter class.[12]

Brazil was by the mid-1870's—in the words of Vindex, a pseudonym of an abolitionist of Bahia—a huge slave quarter.[13] Slavery did not mean merely the relation between slave and master. For Nabuco it meant a great deal more:

> ... the addition of power, influence, capital, and clientelism of every slaveholder; feudalism established in the country areas; the dependance of marketing, religion, poverty, industry, the Parliament, the Crown, in sum the State, on the aggregate power of the aristocratic minority in whose quarters lived one thousand of human beings, that is, beings embruted and morally mutilated by the force of the very system to which they are submitted; and at last, the spirit, the vital principle which animates the entire institution, ... spirit which has been in every history of slave countries the cause of their backwardness and their decadence.[14]

This lively description of the slave power from the inside allows us to understand that when Brazilian abolitionists addressed the problem of slavery they were addressing people formed by that very evolving slave spirit, as they were themselves. American abolitionists from the 1840's onward warned of a slave power rising from an almost alien society—the South—and trying to expand throughout the country and destroy the free institutions of the North. But while American abolitionists wrote about the slave power, Brazilian abolitionists wrote under the slave power, and were themselves formed by its cultural environment. Understanding the Brazilian abolitionist as someone opposing the slave power from within may help us also to understand why the image of the slave as a brother appears so seldom in Brazilian abolitionism.[15]

Brazilian abolitionists would hardly define the master as the enemy of the slave, as did the Rev. Bourne, and so many other American abolitionists after him. Instead, they tended to stress the reverse idea that the slave was the enemy of the master. If they were to be understood by slaveowners themselves and their offspring, Brazilian abolitionists had to draw a picture that would make sense in the everyday life of a planter or urban slaveholder.

Certainly Barbosa's readers could easily grasp the metaphor of the innocent lilies spreading harmful scents in a dark alcove and endangering the life of anyone sleeping among them. Besides the memories of the slave insurrections that punctuated the life of Bahia from the beginning of the nineteenth century up to 1845, readers of news from São Paulo and Rio de Janeiro would already have been instructed about the slaves' restlessness. Evidence shows that more slaves were rebelling during the 1870's than during the 1860's and even murdering their owners. Some actually killed sleeping owners as when four slaves strangled the mistress of a São Paulo plantation in her bed in 1873.[16]

The image of the slave as a domestic enemy, rather than as a brother, should not be seen as a merely tactical device of abolitionists seeking to convince masters and mistresses that slavery was wrong. The view of the slave as a domestic enemy was imbricated in the very origins of antislavery in Brazil, and can be found in a number of antislavery tracts published from the beginning of the nineteenth century.

The Portuguese priest Manoel Ribeiro Rocha, living in Bahia in the mid-eighteenth century, observed that slaves either ran away or became domestic enemies of their masters because of the harsh punishments and bad treatment to which they were constantly submitted.[17] Besides—and here this pioneer of abolitionism in Brazil talks more like a slaveholder—if Adam, despite his innocent condition as well as his healthy nature, fell miserably in sin, "what can one expect from these idle brutes, living in a lapsing and corrupt state of nature, but that they continuously commit, and be fallen, in the capital vices . . . ?"[18]

Other pioneers of abolitionism in Brazil dwelt on the same theme of the slave as a domestic enemy. José Bonifácio de Andrada e Silva, writing on the problems of the foundation of a new nation in 1823, one year after Brazil became independent from Portugal, warned the delegates to the Constituent Convention about the impossibility of having a liberal and perennial Constitution in a country "continuously inhabited by an immense crowd of brutal and inimical slaves."[19]

The problems of a country inhabited by a majority of hostile slaves, posing a permanent risk to the interests of their owners, were stressed by the editors of Andrada e Silva's book in 1840. Writing during the years of increasing British pressure against the Brazilian slave trade from Africa, the anonymous authors of the Preface made clear that they opposed the "trader of human meat" for introducing barbarism right in the middle of the nation's somewhat tardy civilization.

> The existence of slaves, and which is even more fatal to civilization, their perennial importation from the hinterland of Africa, perpetuates the ignorance, the apathy of a numerous class of cultivators, and makes it impossible to thin out the errors, that have introduced the blind routine of past ages in agriculture. The slave does not have any interest in improvement . . . . But conceding that the slave is capable of some advance, the African doubtless is not, given that his intellectual faculties were blunted by the savage life he spent in his native land, and that his disposition resists to any kind of civilization.[20]

By this statement, and many similar ones that one finds in antislavery tracts, it is clear that the idea, permeating Brazilian abolitionism, of the African slave as a domestic enemy was a direct offspring of the old and conflicting relations between slaveholder and slave. Criticizing slavery, in the case of Brazilian abolitionism, did not mean a complete break with the ideology of slavery. For this criticism was imbued with the view of the slave produced by the slaveholders themselves through centuries of enslaving Africans.

Moreover, the idea of the slave as a domestic enemy combines well with ideas inherited from the Enlightenment. Paradoxically as it may seem, the Enlightenment's emphasis on human nature and reason as requiring liberty, ended by producing the image of the slave as a being deprived of reason, and therefore below human nature, that is, more like a beast. In a personal letter to Joaquim Nabuco, the French writer Victor Hugo—a most beloved author among Brazilian abolitionists—summarized the view inherited from the Enlightenment:

> Slavery is man transformed into a beast within man himself. All that survives of human intelligence in that animal life belongs to the caprice and will of the master. There follow abominable scenes.[21]

It is interesting to notice that the recurrent image of the bestial slave could point either to the passive slave—the one who lived sunk in the resignation of a vegetable—or to the violent slave—the one whom nothing would restrain from committing the most barbarous crimes. Passive or violent slaves may appear alternately in the pages of a single author, as is true of the romantic poet Luís Nicolau Fagundes Varela, one of the first Brazilian poets to write against slavery.

Born in 1841 in Rio de Janeiro, Fagundes Varela spent his childhood on the Santa Rita plantation.[22] As with other Brazilian abolitionists who spent the first years of their lives on plantations until their parents sent them to study in the cities of Brazil and abroad, Fagundes Varela was formed within the environment of slavery. His perceptions of the slave might have been a compound of his memories as a slaveholder's child and his readings as a young student of law in São Paulo and Recife, where he caught the ideal of liberty coming from distinct voices, such as Shelley, Byron, Victor Hugo, Lamennais. From this compound there emerged, in one of his poems, the pathetic slave whose reason had been killed by the violence of slavery. Nothing of a human being seemed to have survived in that reasonless slave who passively allowed his butchers to murder him, like a "sheep at the altar," or a "child in the woman's womb."[23] By the same token, in another poem, nothing of reason seemed to exist in that once docile slave who lived for the sole idea of revenge after his sister died under torture; he ended up killing the master's son with his own hands.[24]

Brazilian abolitionists also pointed to the frailty of reason among slaves who supposedly had been treated well. To young J. Nabuco, the case of Tomás—whom he defended from capital punishment while still a law student in Recife—exemplified the abolitionist presupposition that slavery repealed reason, that is, the ability to behave as a human being. By 1868 Tomás was a docile slave of twenty-five years who had been educated "as a free man", in Olinda, Pernambuco. "No one mentioned captivity. He worked for his mistress and for himself with stimulus and consciousness." One day, however, his mistress died and someone sent him to be whipped at the town's main square under the eyes of its inhabitants. From then one the slave's character went through serious changes. He became a beast. He ran away only to come back for a cruel revenge against the authority he presumed to be the cause of his humiliation. He shot him and was imprisoned. "He was not a man any more, it was a tiger that one held in chains. Even being chained, he was terrible." He killed another man while attempting to escape prison. Nabuco's plea notwithstanding, the prosecutor insisted on the death penalty for "a man already condemned to it!"[25]

Nabuco, as well as a number of Brazilian abolitionists, never ceased to recall those lively memories of slavery which underlay their supposition that a slave was like a beast, that is, less than a human being. Of course, the memories were not only in the past. They were alive, always being reproduced—or threatening to be reproduced—in the present of those who lived in Brazil up to the last day of slavery. Abolitionists as well as slaveholders would agree with Nabuco that if abolitionist propaganda reached the slaves' ears, the most influential and powerful class would be exposed to "the barbarous and savage revenge of a population which has been maintained up to now at the level of the animals, and whose passions, once having broken the brakes of fear, would not acknowledge any limits in the way of obtaining satisfaction".[26]

The awkwardness of an abolitionism continuously engendering the image of the evil slave might well surprise scholars acquainted with American abolitionism, with its emphasis on the slave as brother.[27]

It is necessary to emphasize that stereotypes of the brutish and evil slave had roots in the Brazilian slavery environment as well as in the assimilation of enlightened literature by Brazilian abolitionists. Indeed, the philosophers of the Enlightenment themselves began their humanistic reflection on the problem of slavery by a scrutiny of the increasingly alarmist reports and letters coming from the governors and officials of the West Indies to France from the beginning of the eighteenth century onwards.[28] British and American abolitionists made use sometimes of the image of the evil slave. The British abolitionist William Wilberforce deserved an epigraph in Nabuco's *O Abolicionismo*.

> If the native intelligence and the independence of the Britons cannot survive in the insalubrious and adverse climate of the personal slavery, how could one expect that the poor Africans, with no support of any sentiment of dignity or of civil rights, would not yield to the evil influences to which they have been subjected for so long a time, and would not become depressed even below the level of the human species?[29]

Like Wilberforce, Garrison—one of the main voices of American abolitionism in its purest religious form—pictured the slave as far below the human nature. In attacking the American Colonization Society, Garrison pointed out that the slaves were "the most vicious, degraded and dangerous portion" of the American people, and for this reason could not have any role in civilizing and evangelizing Africa.[30]

However there was indeed a difference of focus between the American and Brazilian abolitionists' views of the slave. As we have already seen in chapter 2, American abolitionists seemed to have elected the slaveholder as the main figure of American slavery to be put on trial; for the slaveholder was the worst of the sinners, the villain who lived by denying the truth of God every single second. As for the slave, the reader of the American abolitionist press will not be able to go far beyond the image of a forgotten and victimized brother. When American abolitionists eventually mention slaves' vices and degradation, they never come down to details, as they usually did in minutely describing slaveholder's crimes and vices. Moreover, during the 1840's and 1850's, the narratives of fugitive slaves emphasized the image of the brother slave by pointing to slaves as moral men and women struggling for justice to the point of risking their lives in dangerous escapes and confrontations.[31]

In contrast, Brazilian abolitionists were more inclined to put the slave on trial; for the slave, because he was a slave—that is a man deprived of reason, and therefore reduced to the condition of a beast—as well as a descendant of a race radically different from his owner's, could not be anything but an enemy to the powerful class. In other words, for American abolitionists, the slaveholder was evil, while for Brazilian abolitionists, the slave was evil.

Up to now I have suggested that differences in inspiration—a more religious abolitionism in the United States and a more secular abolitionism in Brazil—as well as differences in social positions—American abolitionists speaking from outside slavery, Brazilian abolitionists from within—may help us to understand distinct views of the slave. It is time now to introduce a third crucial difference. The relationship between abolitionism and the black community in each country may also explain the reasons why American abolitionists were inclined to picture the slave as a brother, whereas Brazilian abolitionists tended to represent the slave as an enemy.

Historians of American abolitionism have pointed to cooperation as well as conflict underlying the relationship between white and black abolitionists, beginning with formation of the first abolitionist societies in the years that followed the American Revolution.[32] Although some put more stress on cooperation and others, more on conflict, all agree that when white abolitionists met black abolitionists, they were meeting people with feet firmly planted in the African American community, that is, a small but expanding Northern community with its own institutions.

Besides giving free rein to racism, the politics of repression, which increasingly segregated black people from white people throughout the Northern free states from the first decades of the nineteenth century onwards, resulted in a strengthening of the social cohesion of African Americans. As Carol Buchalter Stapp shows with her research on antebellum Boston probate records, the African American community was remarkable for its network of members, its commitment to community organizations, and for its geographic cohesion. In her words, the data "all imply the merging of the personal and public, the private and civic."[33]

However, the fact that African Americans were already living in a segregated community in the North by the time abolitionism arose as a movement committed to immediatism does not imply a lack of communication between black and white abolitionists. On the contrary, "the two abolitionisms"—as they were baptized by Jane H. Pease and William H. Pease in stressing the conflicts—were intimately intermingled by historic and religious heritage.[34]

To begin with, Northern black people were very early, during the seventeenth and eighteenth centuries, incorporated into the emerging European American culture. As Ira Berlin suggests, a small population of slaves living in close proximity to a majority of white people quickly learned English, the Christian religion, "the white man's ways." In learning "the white man's ways," Africans became African Americans without leaving aside their African inheritance, which was reawakened by each newly arrival of African slaves.[35]

Thus, by the time of the American Revolution African Americans had accumulated enough intellectual instruments to struggle in defense of their rights as citizens, and on the terms of European Americans: that is, for the emancipation of America from British tyranny, as well as for the abolition of another tyranny being practiced on American territory—slavery. As Leon F. Litwack emphasizes, African Americans took the new Declaration of Independence at its word when it affirmed the freedom and equality of all men.[36] After emancipation in the Northern states, African Americans continued to fight for abolition throughout the country, as well as against the increasing racism that weighed heavily on the Northern black community.

By 1794 the emergence of the Negro independent church—"the most dynamic social institution in the Negro community,"in the words of Litwack—had improved the African

Americans' ability to solidify their cultural inheritance, to draw their own interpretations from the Bible, and to criticize the inconsistency of the white children of the American Revolution toward their black brethren.[37]

In sum, my point here is that the Northern African American commmunity—small as it was, and increasingly attacked and segregated by the 1820's—was nevertheless able to make itself heard and understood by a small number of religious-oriented European Americans who were equally distressed by the emerging feeling that the American Revolution had failed in its highest humanitarian promises. It is illustrative of the intellectual bridges linking black and white reformers that in 1832 twelve white men—among them William Lloyd Garrison—founded the New-England Anti-Slavery Society in a school-room under Boston's African Baptist Church. That event exemplifies both the physical separation of white and black people, and the intellectual convergence of black and white reformers; the black reformers allowing a white abolitionist meeting in their headquarters, and the white reformers committing themselves to a double goal: the cause of immediate abolition and the improvement of the political and economic position of Northern African Americans.[38]

If we take Brazilian abolitionists at their word, we would conclude that people of African descent were either too ignorant to understand the enlightened goals of abolitionism or too anxious too cooperate with the authorities in maintaining the *status quo*. Slaves and their freeborn enslaved children—that is those who were born after the Free Womb Law of 1871—were incapable of fighting for their rights. In pointing to the role of abolitionists as defenders of the "Negro Race", Nabuco considered that slaves had neither means to rationally defend themselves nor consciousness of their rights as human beings.[39] As for the numerous free black people, be they poor or rich, they did not care for abolition.

In an indignant tone, a writer of the *Redempção*—a São Paulo abolitionist biweekly newspaper—denounced the "slaveocrat mulattoes and blacks," and affirmed that abolitionism was mostly a white man's business. Some people explained the pro-slavery inclination of the majority of the Negroes by recalling their lack of education. But for this writer, the explanation lay in slavery: free negroes believed that "freedom made them white," and that slavery make men black; therefore, they would be ashamed to defend "their race." He concluded that many generations would pass before they could reach those proper sentiments belonging today to those who never had "slave blood" among their ancestors.[40]

However they accounted for the supposed pro-slavery inclination of free black people, one commom aspect may be deduced from the above abolitionist statements: the lack of intellectual communication between white abolitionists and the black inhabitants of Brazil. It is clear, furthermore, that abolitionists did not acknowledge any possibility of intellectual interaction with people from the slave quarters. Setting aside the prejudice permeating these abolitionists' views of the black people of Brazil, one wonders if abolitionists could have thought differently. For although Brazil did not have institutional segregation of free black people at the time of the rise of abolitionism, the white elite and black people—free and slave—lived in two worlds apart.

In considering the social environment from which abolitionism germinated in Brazil, two demographic facts deserve attention. In contrast to the Northern United States, where white people constituted a majority of the population from colonial times, Brazil's majority was of African descent. Despite the scarcity of statistics for the nineteenth century, it is probable that on the eve of Brazilian Independence there were more than 2,500,000 people of African descent—slave and free—compared to a little more than 1,000,000 people of European descent.[41] Fifty years later the demographic balance remained approximately the same. Although the first Census of 1872 did not include the variable color, it is possible to presume that most of the more than 8,200,000 free people were of African descent, in addition to the population of around 1,500,000 slaves.[42] At that time, politicians favoring American and European immigration warned insistently about the risks of having a country mostly inhabited by black people. Five years after the Census one of these politicians, the abolitionist Domingos José Nogueira Jaguaribe Filho, estimated that there were only 3,800,000 people of "white race" in a total population of around 10,000,000.[43]

The second demographic fact helps to explain why the white population remained so small up to the 1880's, when mass immigration from Europe to Brazil began for the first time. In contrast to the United States, whose slave trade from Africa ended in 1808, Brazil continued to import African slaves until 1850. British pressure against the slave trade seemed only to stimulate it. More than 700,000 African slaves entered Brazil from the 1830's, when a treaty between Great Britain and Brazil forbade slave importation, until 1850, when the Brazilian Congress finally voted for the abolition of the slave trade from Africa.[44] Thus, foreign immigration to Brazil began gradually to attract the attention of planters and politicians after the extinction of the African slave trade.

Taking into account these two demographic facts, which point both to the numerical predominance of people of African descent and to the continuous renewal of the African presence in Brazil by the slave ships coming from the other side of the Atlantic, one may visualize better the world the white elite abolitionists lived in. It was a small Europeanized world whose meaning Nabuco synthesized in one sentence: "Our sentiment is Brazilian, our imagination European."[45] As for the rest—if that is the right word to denote the massive surrounding African Brazilian world— it remained foreign, in cultural terms, to the abolitionists.[46]

The strength of the African cultural world in nineteenth-century Brazil may be visualized through the very peculiar Catholicism to which black people gave rise, despite control by the clergy. As Roger Bastide suggests, black Catholicism was the precious shrine that the white Church unwillingly offered to Africans taken to Brazil. In this shrine, Africans and their offspring on Brazilian plantations and in urban households kept the most important values of their native religions. They kept these religious values, not as relics, but as "living realities."[47]

Although Catholicism was able to maintain the unity of its dogma, the heavy influence of African cultures over the dominant class's religion generated another Catholicism with a different cultural perspective. The black religious brotherhoods with their African ethnic distinctions, the black saints and their special feasts, with small black angels opening the holy processions of black followers, and especially the annual ritual of the *Congadas*, with local churches sponsoring the coronation of an elected pair of black sovereigns, all testify to the power of African religions in creating a new type of Catholicism in Brazil.[48]

Bastide calls attention to a further essential point, which may help to explain the differing relations between abolitionists and people of African descent in the two countries, as well as how such different relations contributed to the emergence of distinct views of the slave. In the United States the separation of white Protestantism from black Protestantism was completed with the emergence of a black religious leadership. In Brazil, by contrast, the white church gradually accommodated black Catholicism. By preventing the complete segregation of the two Catholicisms, the white Church maintained control over its black followers. Bastide argues that the incomplete separation between the two Catholicisms prevented black people from achieving race consciousness through the mystic experience.[49] Bastide suggests however, that if white Catholicism was able to keep its control over black Catholicism, the same cannot be said for the vast field of African religions, which survived in secret African divine services—the *candomblés*— and under the control of black chiefs.[50]

Perhaps more important than the absence of a separate black Catholic leadership in Brazil is the fact that reading the Bible does not have the same relevance in Catholicism that it has in Protestantism. In nineteenth-century Brazil, reading of the Bible was confined to the clergy, who, during Sunday sermons occasionally translated from Latin to Portuguese certain texts that interested them, according to their interpretation.[51] In contrast, at the turn of the eighteenth century, the Bible in its English version was already becoming a crucial weapon in the hands of black American priests and their followers in vindicating their rights as human beings.[52] Moreover the American Revolution, with its Christian and Enlightenment-inspired Declaration of Independence, accorded people of African descent a powerful weapon in defending their right to be American citizens.

In sum, in examining the relationship between abolitionists and people of African descent in Brazil one will hardly find any kind of intellectual bridges making communication between them possible. There were no religious or political texts cementing a common ground between them and shaping their views of the slave. Abolitionists on the one side, and the mass of people of African descent on the other, although interacting daily in a thoroughly slave country, lived in two worlds apart in terms of social position as well as of profound cultural differences. As for the few Brazilian abolitionists of African descent who were able to rise to the social world of the white elite, they looked upon the surrounding African Brazilian world with eyes as foreign as those of their white comrades.

Much has been said about the rise of the "mulattoes" in nineteenth century Brazil since Gilberto Freyre published his seminal argument on the issue.[53] According to Freyre, two new and successful forces rose in Brazilian society from the beginnings of the nineteenth century onwards: the "bacharel"[university graduate] and the "mulatto". The "mulatto" himself was often a holder of a bachelor's degree. Both of them were living expressions of the modernizing transformation that began to rupture the traditionally exclusive power of the planters.[54] These were young men in their twenties who usually graduated in Law or Medicine from the few colleges existing in Brazil or from European universities.[55] Many of them were planters'sons, who returned to the plantations only to realize that they could no longer accept the old way of life. As Freyre notes, the Europeanized university graduates looked with profound comtempt and repugnance at the African ambience that the slaves had brought to the plantations.[56] The situation of the young "bacharel" of African descent was especially difficult. His passage into the white, Europeanized world of the intellectual elite by no means meant acceptance of his African ancestry by his white peers, but only a refined effort to forget that ancestry.[57] But the effort of forgetting had limits, and as Freyre shows, it was in the most intimate field of love and marriage that the "bacharel" of African descent risked being suddenly reminded of his origin.[58]

Brazilian abolitionists of African descent lived in the white world of the urban elites, were imbued with European culture, and like their white peers, could hardly feel any cultural empathy with the surrounding African Brazilian world. Thus one should not be surprised at the most repugnant black characters produced by José do Patrocínio for his novel *Motta Coqueiro*. In describing the hideous countenance of the black butcher, Patrocínio reminds his readers that "the whites" had made a beast of him, preventing him from achieving sentiments of family, religion, and citizenship.[59]

The "peculiar sensation," the "double-consciousness" that W. E. B. Du Bois attributed to himself as an American citizen and a Negro "of always looking at one's self through the eyes of others," would not have been unfamiliar to abolitionists of African descent living in Brazil during the 1870's and 1880's.[60] Yet, since they had effectively passed into the white world and therefore, in contrast to American abolitionists of African descent, did not live within a black community, they seem to have believed that their antislavery struggle should not go beyond the narrow goal of abolition of slavery. Their "twoness" was not to become a public issue.[61] The engineer André Rebouças made that clear when he asked the editors of a paper not to mention that he had danced with the Princess Isabel, the daughter of Pedro II, Emperor of Brazil, during a dancing party in 1868. Rebouças dismissed the awkwardness which the fact inspired in the editors, by reminding them that he had already danced with other ladies of society. Although that fact should not be seen as unusual, it should not be made public "because of a thousand reasons of inconvenience.[62]

The intellectual bridges existing between white abolitionists and the black community in the Northern United States are mostly apparent in the abolitionists' effort to prove that the black was a human being with rights equal to those of white American citizens. Through the combined goals of abolishing slavery and abolishing racism, which distinguish American abolitionism, one senses a constant search for empathy with the slave as well as with the free black people living in the North.[63]

The search for empathy with the slave, and the black in general, begins with the search for the past glory of Africa. Black and white abolitionists agreed that Africa in the present had nothing to offer as a contribution to progress and civilization. To Walker ignorance was the word to define the present state of Africa.

> Ignorance, my brethren is a mist, low down into the very dark
> and almost impenetrable abyss in which, our fathers for many centuries
> have been plunged.[64]

Garrison dwelt on the same theme of Africa as a land of
darkness in attacking the colonizationist plan to send emancipated
slaves and free black people to Africa to civilize the African continent.
To him Africa was indeed a "heathenish country," whose salvation
called for well-prepared missionaries, such as the ones who had
been sent to the Sandwich and Society Islands, and portions of
Burma, Hindustan, and other lands.

> A hundred evangelists like these, dispersed along the shores
> and in the interior of Africa, would destroy more idols, make more
> progress in civilizing the natives, suppress more wars, unite in amity
> more hostile tribes, and convert more souls to Christ, in ten years, than
> a colony of twenty thousand ignorant, uncultivated, selfish emigrants
> in a century.[65]

But if abolitionists considered Africa the land of ignorance
and heathenism, they made clear that this distressing present
situation was not to be understood from a racist perspective. To
Walker the "wheel of events" was part of the history of rising and
falling, from which no country in the world could escape.

> Fortune and misfortune, two inseparable companions, lay
> rolled up in the wheel of events, which have from the creation of the
> world, and will continue to take place among men until God shall
> dash worlds together.[66]

In discovering this decaying land all that Christian and
enlightened individuals of Europe, and some of Asia had done was
to plunge the African ancestors "into wretchedness ten thousand
times more intolerable, than if they had left them entirely to the
Lord." But in adding to their miseries Christians tell them "that they
are an *inferior* and *distinct race* of beings . . . "[67]

It was to contradict this rationale of race that Walker dismissed
the presupposition that Africa as a land of darkness had no past,
and took the first steps towards writing the history of Africa from
the point of view of the oppressed Africans. In the past Africa had
been a land of light, for learning, that is, the arts and sciences,

originated among "the sons of Africa or of Ham," and "was carried thence into Greece, where it was improved upon and refined" as well as later among the Romans. What made Walker so sure that the arts and sciences had been initiated by Africans was that Africans were the inhabitants of Egypt, which historians usually claimed as the cradle of world civilization.[68]

During the 1840's the theme of Africa as a land of light in the past received a more detailed treatment from another abolitionist of African descent. In an address to the Female Benevolent Society, the Reverend Henry Highland Garnet invited his audience to forget for a moment the desolation in which black people were immersed, and look upward towards "the bright scenery of the future." In considering the present as "the midway between the Past and the Future," Garnet suggested that the best way to visualize the bright future of "the colored people" was to depict the glorious past of Africa. The biblical narrative offered essential evidence that Africa had been once a land of light. For Ham, one of the three sons of Noah, was the first African; and Egypt was settled by an immediate descendant of Ham called Mesraim. But besides the Bible, "uninspired history" also provided evidence that this "brilliant era" was made by Africans alone.

> We learn from Herodotus, that the ancient Egyptians were black, and had woolly hair. These people astonished the world with their arts and sciences, in which they reveled with unbounded prodigality. They became the masters of the East, and the lords of the Hebrews.[69]

In pointing to the glorious past of Africa, Garnet did not forget to suggest the degraded past of "Anglo Saxons."

> At this time, when these representatives of our race were filling the world with amazement, the ancestors of the now proud and boasting Anglo Saxons were among the most degraded of the human family. They abode in caves under ground, either naked or covered with the skins of wild beasts. Night was made hideous by their wild shouts, and day was darkened by the smoke which arose from bloody altars, upon which they offered human sacrifice.[70]

Two purposes seem to be at the root of Garnet's speech. First, by calling attention to the reverse histories of Africans and "Anglo Saxons" in the past—Africa as a land of light, Europe as a land of darkness—Garnet implied that the future might bring the same historical reversal. For if the present was "the midway between the Past and the Future," the future could recapitulate the past as the closing of a life circle. Secondly, the need to prove that the black was a human being with equal rights to any other human being required that the black be attributed a history of his own—the history of Africa, just as white people could dwell on the history of Europe. Otherwise, Africa would appear as a land eternally destined to degradation because of God's punishment, or, as scientists were increasingly assuming, because of the inferiority of the "African race."

White abolitionists partook of the same purposes by incorporating the theme of the glorious past of Africa side by side with the theme of Africa as a land of darkness in the present. In *The Oasis*, published in 1834, Lydia Maria Child included a special poem on the subject:

> Thebes! what a glory on thy temples sate,
> When monarchs, hardly less than gods were thine
> Though mystery and darkness shroud thy fate,
> The glimpse imagination give us is divine!
> . . .
> The poor despised negro might look up,
> And smile, to hear that Greece, that classic Greece,
> Refused not to partake the enticing cup,
> Which swarthy Egypt tendered with the arts of peace:
>
> That the proud white man sought in ages back,
> The intellectual fire that lights his brow,
> And found it too, among a race as black
> As the poor slave he makes his victim now!
>
> The heir of Africa may not always be
> The "lowest link" in this our being's chain;
> There is a magic power in liberty,
> To make the smother'd flame break out and blaze again.[71]

Besides reminding white Americans that they owed the black Americans not only their physical survival, but also their spiritual life, L. M. Child introduced here another of the favorite themes of American abolitionism: the sublime slave struggle for liberty. In commenting on the danger of slave insurrections, one writer for *The Liberator* made clear that when slaves fought for their liberty, they were only listening to God's will.

> Oppression and insurrection go hand in hand, as cause and effect are allied together ... The last [insurrection] was the memorable one in Southampton, nicknamed, in the contemptuous nomenclature of slavery, Nat Turner. The name does not strike the ear so harmoniously as that of Washington, or Lafayette, or Hancock, or Warren; but the name is nothing. It is not in the power of all the slaveholders upon earth, to render odious the memory of that sable chieftain. Resistance to tyrants is obedience to God, was our revolutionary motto. We acted upon that motto—what more did Nat Turner? ... In claiming this right for themselves, the American people necessarily concede it to all mankind.[72]

The theme of the Americans' hyprocrisy generally appeared intermingled with the theme of the beauty of the slaves' struggle for liberty. For if white and black people were equal children of God, why wouldn't both equally resist to tyranny ? Yet Americans insisted on denying this right to any but the white part of mankind.

> Ye patriotic hypocrites! ye panegyrists of Frenchmen, Greeks, and Poles! ye fustian declaimers for liberty! ye valiant sticklers for equal rights among yourselves! ye haters of aristocracy! ye assailants of monarchies! ye republican nullifiers! ye treasonable disunionists! be dumb! Cast no reproach upon the conduct of the slaves, but let your lips and cheeks wear the blisters of condemnation![73]

To the author of *The Liberator*'s editorial on the Virginia insurrection, shortly after the event, the memory of the American Revolution was irresistible. The slaves did not need incentives from the abolitionists to resist slavery. Besides the incentives coming daily from the slaveholders' violence, they would find others "in every valley, on every hilltop and mountain, in every field wherever you and your fathers have fought for liberty . . . ."[74]

But the call for liberty was not only nurtured by the memories and constant celebration of the American Revolution. The "voices" of liberty were all over "in the air"; the slaves received "sounds from across the ocean, invitations to resistance above, below, around them!"[75]

Sounds of liberty were coming from distant Brazil, where the slaves in Bahia had just rebelled, causing an enormous battle in the streets of the city and the death of 150 to 170 people. After a detailed description of the bloody march of around 1,000 slaves throughout the city, including an assault on the provincial president's palace, *The Liberator*'s editor emphasized that although defeated,

> . . . they displayed the greatest intrepidity and fearlessness, many of them rushing on the bayonets, when they found their project defeated, thus preferring death to continuance of Slavery.[76]

But what made the call for liberty irresistible for the slaves was the memory of a successful slave insurrection, the Haitian Revolution. For the first time in the history of slavery, slaves rebelled, expelled their tyrants, and assumed the political power of a former European colony. Moreover, this had been a Revolution of *black* slaves, a living expression that there was hope for the future of the American slaves. In his concluding remarks to his book on "the tyranny and cruelty of American Republican Slave-Masters," D. L. Child expressed his admiration for Haiti and his best wishes for its future:

> Precious beyond expression to the colored man, is the example of Hayti and the character of her noble deliverer, Toussaint L'Ouverture. The white man's blood ran not in his veins, but the milk of kindness was around his heart.
> . . .
> May she act worthy of her great destiny. In my view, she is now the depository of the greatest trust of God to man. Philosophy and philanthropy strain their eyes towards her. Ethiopia stretches out her hands unto God for her.[77]

Haiti as the American slaves' great hope of deliverance from the present sorrows was one of the common readings of the revolutionary event by American abolitionists. Another reading was that Haiti offered the living proof that people of African descent were not inferior to white people. Therefore Haiti stood also as the black's great hope of deliverance from the sorrows of racism.

Writing about the common charge that black people constituted an "intellectually inferior race", a lecturer to the New-England Anti-Slavery Society recommended those who believed in such theses to read Denhan, Lang, and Clapperton where they would find evidences of "curly haired kings, sable skinned generals and thick-lipped poets."

> But what need to go so far for argument, to refute this calumny, when we have them almost at our doors. Look at Hayti!
>
> . . .
>
> Thirty years ago, her now free inhabitants were slaves, as miserable and degraded as any that disgrace the soil of the continent. What are they now? They are not only free, but more accomplished and better informed, as a people, than many nations of Europe. Hayti broke the bonds of her thralldom alone; alone she contended with success against the utmost efforts of the most powerful empire of the earth; ay, she shared with England the honor of having effectually resisted Napoleon Bonaparte in the zenith of his military and political omnipotence. Now she has her laws, her schools, her orators, her statesmen. I may say with safety that not even our own country has made so great advances, considering the differences of advantages.[78]

Although inclined to praise the slaves' struggle for liberty, abolitionists were not equally prone to welcome violence. To the ones who insisted on depicting the Haitian Revolution as a bloody, and unmerciful scene, abolitionists' common answer was that violence in Haiti was due to Europeans. Like the lecturer just quoted, Heyrick emphasized that the history of emancipation in Haiti as well as of the conduct of the former slaves for thirty years after the event had been one of peace and order. The emancipated slaves became disciplined free workers, and never thought of avenging past injuries.[79] As for the alarming news coming from Haiti during the 1810's, accounting for the bloody conflicts between rival chiefs and their followers, Prince Saunders attributed them to the "abominable" French principles. These principles, which had pervaded France for a long time, and extended to Haiti had "undoubtedly had an extensive influence upon the character, sentiments and feelings of all descriptions of its present inhabitants."[80]

In sum, the Haitian Revolution as a model of a successful struggle by slaves for liberty was a permanent theme permeating American abolitionism. A few years before the Civil War, abolitionists presented the Haitian Revolution as a lesson of history, and a warning for the future of the United States, to those who still closed their eyes to the problem of slavery, or adopted a mere non-extension posture. In a lecture on "the capacity of the Negro Race for self-government and civilized progress, as demonstrated by historical events of the Haytian Revolution, and the subsequent acts of that people since their National Independence," James T. Holley suggested that there was a "close resemblance between the policy of the free colored people, and the whites of this country, with the policy of the same classes in St.Domingo" in the past. At the eve of the Haitian Revolution, the white colonists denied that the free black people of the island should have equal political rights with them. The free black people committed a similar mistake by assuring the white people that they did not intend to interfere with slavery. The well-known destiny of both white and black colonists of Haiti would probably be partaken by white and black Americans.

> If they continue to pursue the partial and selfish policy they have commenced, the task of liberating the nation from the despotism of the slave power will have to devolve on the four millions of despised slaves. If the 'spirit of liberty' is to be found anywhere, in this country, it is to be found among *them*, as their sacrifices to *escape* into freedom already proves. Their love of liberty should put the proud Anglo-Saxon race to the blush, who seem to have lost the capability of contending for any thing but the extension, not the extinction, of human bondage.[81]

The themes of Africa as a land of light in the past, the perennial slaves' struggle for liberty, the glorious Haitian Revolution, were all part of a well-coordinated effort by black and white abolitionists to create empathy with the slave, as well as with blacks in general. Interwoven with those themes was the emerging idea that to be black was a gift of God, and therefore that there was beauty in being black. David Walker was very explicit on this matter:

> They think because they hold us in their infernal chains of slavery, that we wish to be white, or of their color—but they are dreadfully deceived—we wish to be just as it pleased our Creator to

have made us, and no avaricious and unmerciful wretches, have any business to make slaves of, or hold us in slavery.[82]

Garrison seems to have assimilated this idea, briefly stated by Walker, and shaped it into an affirmation of the differences of mankind as a proof of the exuberance of God's creation.

> ... I would as soon deny the existence of my Creator, as quarrel with the workmanship of his hands. I rejoice that he has made one star to differ from another star in glory; that he had not given to the sun the softness and tranquility of the moon, not to the moon the intensity and magnificence of the sun; that he presents to the eye every conceivable shape, and aspect, and color, in the gorgeous and multifarious productions of Nature; and I do not rejoice less, but admire and exalt him more, that, notwithstanding he has made of one blood the whole family of man, he has made the whole family of man to differ in personal appearance, habits and pursuits.[83]

Thus, in arguing against those who acknowledged different races of man and dismissed the idea of a single "family of man," Garrison ingeniously insisted that to be black, as to be white, was part of the well-planned creation of a God to whom beauty existed only as long as there was difference in nature. Therefore the individual differences existing between men were to be at the root of the presupposition permeating the abolitionist central idea of equal rights for all mankind.

As there were no intellectual bridges linking abolitionism to people of African descent in Brazil, one finds hardly any sentiment of empathy towards the slave, and the Negro in general. Themes which, as time went by, shaped a kind of abolitionist common sense in the United States were absent from Brazilian abolitionism. The theme of Africa's brillant past was unknown to Brazilian abolitionists. If Africa ever came to mind, it was because of its misery, ignorance, and ugliness. Africa was irremediably the land of darkness.

The problem to which Brazilian abolitionists constantly referred was that Africa had exported its vices to Brazil, along with thousands of slaves. As Nabuco explained,

When the first Africans were imported to Brazil, its [Brazil's] main inhabitants did not think—it is true that even if they reflected about it, this would not prevent them from doing it, for they were not imbued with Brazilian patriotism—that they were preparing for the future a people compounded in its majority of slaves' descendants . . . The main effect of slavery over our population was thus its africanization, saturating it with black blood . . . .

Called by slavery, the Negro race by the mere fact of living and reproducing, increasingly became the most considerable element of the population . . . . That was the initial revenge of the victims. Each slave womb gave to the master three or four kids which he reduced to money; they went on by multiplying, and therefore the vices of the African blood ended up by making their way into the general circulation of the country.[84]

The "africanization" of Brazil was then an inheritance from the "mother country", that is, Portugal, which had impressed a "spot" on every possible aspect of Brazilian society, including language, social manners, education.[85] Africanization was thus the ensemble of African vices circulating, along with the slaves, in Brazil. But what did Nabuco and other Brazilian abolitionists mean by African vices?

The first vice arose from African superstitions, which had corrupted religion in Brazil. Nabuco believed that Africans were incapable of religion, because they could not understand the metaphysical principles that constituted the superior level of religion. Immersed in their fetishism, Africans saw in their images not the symbol, but the very substance, of the superior being. They did not learn anything from Catholicism but the exteriority of the rites.

Baptism to them is water; marriage, the junction of hands; God is the clay; Jesus is the cross; none of them goes beyond the symbol; none trespasses the form. This makes them completely lost to any religious sentiment, for one can not consider as religion this mere catholic fetishism, for the images of the catholic service are to them variations of the images which their parents adored at Guinea and Kongo. Since no one is concerned about them, they live without any notion of honor, of duties towards morality and religion.[86]

Thus, the lack of a truly religious sentiment prevented slaves from acquiring the basic notions of morality that cemented marriage, family, and social contacts in general.

Another African vice whose effects were visible in the state of backwardness of Brazilian society was laziness. Although acknowledging that slaves had been "docile" and "strong" workers, capable of withstanding heavy field work, Jaguaribe Filho implicitly suggested that Africans worked only under compulsion. For work as the source of goods, improvement and progress was almost absent from African history.

> But when we think that the huge black population that inhabits the African continent, for more than three thousand years, has not taken one step ahead, that man there is a thing with no importance, which is miserably traded, similar to the animals that one domesticates in order to extract from them a gain, that the contact between the peoples has been unable to civilize it [the African population], neither change nor take it from the apathy and misery which seems to be its greatest pride: when one reflects that [the African population] scattered throughout the world does not exhibit as other peoples the love for the homeland, nor the stimulus which guides every man in search of wealth and education, then it seems that one has the right to say nothing more, nor to predict the future of such an unfortunate race.[87]

The theme of Africa as a land of vice was not a creation of Brazilian abolitionists writing during the 1870's and 1880's. Like the view of the slave as a domestic enemy, which imbued Brazilian antislavery from its beginnings, the view of vicious Africa was already present in the writings of the first antislavery reformers. One year before the independence of Brazil, João Severiano Maciel da Costa advised his "Brazilian countryfellows" to cease the importation of evil slaves from Africa. As he argued,

> ... the condition of Africans in their country ... is horrible, for living without a secure asylum, with no morals, no laws, in continuous war, and a war of barbarians, they vegetate almost at the level of irrational beings, they suffer a cruel captivity, and they are victims of the caprices of their Despots whom they pay with life for the lightest faults.[88]

But besides the combined themes of Africa as a land of vices, and the slave as the main source of transmission of such African vices in Brazil, abolitionists were increasingly incorporating the growing scientific rationale of race to their views about the slave by the 1870's and 1880's. Social Darwinism made its entrance simultaneously in American and Brazilian society. But the thought of Herbert Spencer, which systematized the implications of Charles Darwin's evolutionism in fields other than biology itself, became influential in Brazilian society before the abolition of slavery, and not after, as happened in the United States.

In Spencer, Brazilian abolitionists found intellectual weapons to prove the urgent need to get rid of slavery. Brazil, like every other country in the world, was subjected to a general law of evolution, and needed now to leave behind its "militant phase", that is, the phase during which society is organized chiefly for survival and cooperation is compulsory. The next stage in evolution would be the "industrial phase," during which the individual and his right to life, liberty, and property would be respected, and cooperation would be voluntary.[89] In Spencer, Brazilian abolitionists also found the "evolutionary optimism" which underlay their presupposition that the emancipated slaves would have the chance to mentally develop towards the needs of civilized life.[90] As Nabuco argued, many of the unfavorable influences of slavery over the country "could be attributed to the Negro race, to its backward mental development, to its barbarous instincts, and also to its rough superstitions;" but for slavery, contact between white and black people would have brought about the mental elevation of the "Negro race" to the superior level of the "more advanced race," that is, the race of "caucasian blood".[91]

Social Darwinism intermingled with Positivism, another influential theory making its way in Brazilian society beginning during the 1860's. In assimilating the thought of August Comte, abolitionists also found reasons for being optimistic about future relations between "the white race", that is, "the intelligent race," and "the black race", that is, "the loving or affective race." As the "Perpetual President" of the Rio de Janeiro Positivist Society, the abolitionist Miguel Lemos explained,

The African is a venerator by nature, and therefore he submits; it is neither fear, nor interest which holds him in slavery, but the love for the masters whom they regard as their superiors. The submission of the African is similar to the submission of the soldier to the general; we repeat, it is the product of veneration, and not interest.[92]

Given the presence in Brazilian abolitionism of themes such as Africa as a land of vices, the vicious bestial slave, as well as the rationale of race attributing intelligence to white people and stupidity to black people, it is hardly surprising that abolitionists were not prone to praise the slaves' struggle for liberty. Despite some admiring references to African courage in poems by Fagundes Varela, abolitionists could not attribute any honorable meaning to the rebellion of irrational human beings, as they considered the slaves.[93] If there was any meaning, it was that of a mere bloody revenge by the slave, like the one the leading romantic poet Castro Alves lively describes in *The Negro Bandit*.[94]

An abolitionist who differed from most of his peers in applauding the slaves' struggle for liberty was the lawyer Luiz Gama, a former slave himself. Born in 1830 in Salvador, Bahia, of an African free woman and a man of Portuguese descent belonging to one of the state's leading families, he was sold to a slave trader at the age of ten by his indebted father. Subsequently he was shipped to São Paulo, then served as a slave in a household in the city of Santos for about eight years. During this period he induced a young student of Humanities visiting with his master to teach him to read and write. Then Gama ran away, enlisted as a soldier, and finally found means to prove that he had been born a free man. By the end of the 1850's he had already become an outstanding lawyer, who, according to his own estimate, won liberty for more than 500 slaves.[95]

Having experienced slavery himself, Gama went beyond proving the right to freedom for Africans imported to Brazil after the 1831 law, when the slave trade from Africa was first forbidden. He also defended slaves who had caused injuries to or murdered their masters. His arguments were much different from those employed by Nabuco in defending the slave Tomás, whom Nabuco considered a man reduced to irrationality by the violence of slavery. To Gama, the slave who killed his master was always within his rights, for in any circumstance he acted in selfdefense.[96]

Gama was also exceptional in praising in his poems the beauty of being African. Drawing from the memories of the African mother he could never find again—she ran away after supposedly taking part of a Bahia rebellion—he proclaimed himself "an Orpheus of crisp curled hair" who declaims his verses to the sound of an African harp, instead of the conventional lyre, in praising the style of the "adust Libya."[97] Libya was his mother's native country. There she had been queen, and also "the most beautiful black woman," before being captured and shipped as a "poor slave" to Brazil.[98]

Gama's was a voice in the desert among his abolitionist peers. He insisted on building the missing intellectual bridges between the abolitionists' Europeanized world and the African Brazilian world, but died too soon to make his voice heard and assimilated: in 1882, when he died abolitionism in Brazil was just beginning to become a popular campaign. But one wonders how much he could have done, had he lived longer, in extending that bridge. Maybe he would have ended up by discovering that Brazil was just like the beautiful, blond, snow-white woman whom he ardently embraced in one of his poems, only to realize that he had fallen prey to his illusions. The beautiful white woman was no more than an icy statue made of rough marble.[99]

One last point deserves attention in comparing American and Brazilian abolitionists' differing views of the slave. To a researcher previously acquainted with Brazilian abolitionism, it is striking to find numerous slave narratives emerging from American antislavery press. But what is most striking is not the number of narratives, but the fact that the slave of the narratives talks as a person in his or her own right, as an I.

It is interesting to recall here that *The Slave: or Memoirs of Archy Moore*, supposedly the first American abolitionist novel, appeared in 1836 not as a novel, but as a true narrative by a fugitive slave.[100] The author, Richard Hildreth, explained later that it had been necessary to disguise the novel as a slave narrative because of the growing threat of anti-abolitionist mobs.[101] But the fact that

Hildreth chose to write as a slave speaking in the first person singular offers telling evidence of the views of the slave that a white Northerner living detached from slavery could nurture, even after having spent some months as a guest on a Florida plantation.

Although Hildreth, in the voice of Archy Moore, claimed that "men born and bred in slavery, are not men but children", for it is the aim of the masters to keep them in "perpetual imbecility," Archy Moore might have sounded intellectually strong enough to convince his readers of the slave's capacity for reason.[102]

Narratives and, later, the fiction that emerged from the Northern abolitionist movement, all point to American abolitionists' inclination to view the slave as a rational, moral being and therefore, a brother. There is no better picture of the slave as a moral being than Uncle Thomas at the moment of his death. Tortured to force him to disclose the whereabouts of two fugitive slave women, he chooses to die. By facing torture and death, he proves also his moral superiority to his master.[103]

Despite the many references to *Uncle Tom's Cabin* that one may find in the Brazilian abolitionist press, Brazilian abolitionists did not assimilate the novel's view of the slave as a moral being.[104] As young members of the plantation elite, or as people associated with planters by links of kinship, friendship, marriage, and business who themselves relied on the work of urban domestic slaves, Brazilian abolitionists would hardly think of the slaves as people on their own moral level, able to speak in the first person singular.

Since, as this chapter has argued, the view of the slave as evil was the most common view among Brazilian abolitionists, it is not surprising that the slave made his appearance on the Brazilian stage under the name of *The Family Demon*. The play, by José de Alencar, suggests that the only solution for Brazilian society was abolition; not on behalf of the slave and his human rights, but against the slave and his evil acts, which polluted the sanctity of the slaveholder's hearth. To those familiar with the condition to which former slaves were relegated after abolition in Brazil, the words of the offended master to the demoniac slave are prophetic:

> I correct you, by making a man from the automaton; I return
> you to society, but I expel you from the midst of my family and will

close forever the door of my home . . . Take it: it is your liberty letter,
it will be your punishment from now on, because your faults will fall
entirely on you; because morality and law will charge you with a
severe bill for your actions. Free, you will feel the need of honest work,
and will enjoy the noble sentiments which you do not understand
today.[105]

In the opinion of Brazilian abolitionists, the last word should
belong to the slaveholders; backward as they were, their
interests—national interests—were at issue. And the slaves, immoral,
irrational, "the victims-butchers," should not say a word.[106] In
American abolitionism, the slaveholders were not to have the last
word; tyrannts, cruel despots, their interests should not be confused
with the national interests. The slaves, brothers by divine creation
and fellow countrymen by the promise of the Revolution should
have the right to speak out.

IV

REFLECTIONS ON RACISM AND THE
DESTINY OF THE EX-SLAVE

Abolitionists in the United States and Brazil exhibited similar preoccupations about the image and role of their countries in the world at large. They never ceased to call attention to the criticism their countries were drawing from enlightened Europe. As William Lloyd Garrison stressed:

> How abominably hypocritical, how consummately despicable,
> how incorrigibly tyrannical must this whole nation appear in the eyes
> of . . . the people of Europe![1]

By the same token, Ruy Barbosa worried that the Brazilian people might appear unanimously pro-slavery to European eyes. But Europe should be informed, he declared, that in Brazil there were also those who acknowledged the illegitimacy of slavery.[2]

The shame of being the last bastion of slavery was also an ever present sentiment moving abolitionists in each country. As we have already seen in chapter 2, American abolitionists were so sure that slavery in the United States was the worst in the world that they concluded that their country would be the last to abolish it. As David Child foresaw in 1833:

> Our Republic has now in all America only the empire of
> Brazil to keep her in countenance. Even that companion is expected
> soon to leave us, and we will then stand entirely alone. We will then
> take the contempt of the world.[3]

In Brazil, the feeling of shame for being the last bastion of slavery began to take shape among abolitionists only at the time

Brazil did become the last major country to hold slaves on the American continent. In opening the parliamentary debates of 1871 over the possibility of emancipating the new-born children of slaves, the president of the State Council, Viscount of Rio Branco, suggested that while the United States kept slavery, Brazil could rest in peace with its slave institution. But the end of the American Civil War and the defeat of the Southern slaveholders had sealed the destiny of Brazilian slavery.

> The example [of slavery] among an American and democratic people like the one of the United States, was a very strong argument actually giving support to the routine, prejudice, and every concern of individual interest. Well, gentlemen, the idea of emancipation went forward, and the American Union, the last example [of slavery], after a civil war which made rivers of blood, abolished all of a sudden the whole of its slavery!
>
> Spain could not resist this influence pressing it from so close, and the abolition of the servant condition became an almost universal fact.[4]

But the abolitionists' similar preoccupations and sentiments of shame over the continuation of slavery in their countries do not mean similar approaches to the problem of slavery. As we have already seen in the preceding chapters, American and Brazilian abolitionists' different ways of reasoning, their different positions in society, their distinct historical legacies, and their differing links to people of African descent, account for the differences between their views about the slaveholder and the slave. Thus, in contrast to Brazilian abolitionists, who were exclusively concerned with the fact that Brazil was late completing the "universal fact" of abolition, American abolitionists broadened their sentiment of shame over Southern slavery by calling attention to the problem of American racism.

As Aileen S. Kraditor suggests, the central place that abolitionists gave to the religious and moral aspects of their campaign explains why they always struggled toward the double goal of abolishing slavery and abolishing racism.[5] But by intertwining the problem of slavery with the problem of racism, American abolitionists were also trying to show that Northerners themselves were deeply involved in the sin of slavery. For was not racism but a way of invisibly enslaving the so-called free Negro to the lowest levels of society by denying him equal rights with white citizens?[6] Lydia Maria Child made this point clear by stressing that "a whole class" of American citizens were being systematically excluded from opportunities for improvement throughout the nation, "merely on account of complexion."

> Americans mistake if they consider this arrangement as more liberal, or just, than the arbitrary and unchanging distinction of *castes* in benighted Hindostan.[7]

Thus, the fact that abolitionists devoted a considerable part of their writings to the theme of the Southern slaveholder as the most cruel master of the world was not meant to put the Northern conscience at rest. For if American slavery was the worst of the world—as we saw in chapter 2—the racism being increasingly practiced in the North was also the worst ever seen in earth.

To D. Child the United States was unique in its "prejudice against color". In no other country was this prejudice against people of African descent so harsh. The problem was the coexistence of freedom with the oppression of slavery.

> The sting of oppression acquires a new venom in an atmosphere of freedom. The condition of slaves in the United States of America, consists of two component parts, the labor of Sisyphus and the torment of Tantalus. Other countries inflict the ceaseless and fruitless labor of the former, but we add thereto the perpetual exacerbation of the latter. The bitterness of slavery is aggravated by beholding above the sweet and golden fruits of the tree of liberty, which slaves can never touch, and which free colored men find turned to ashes in *their* mouths. There can be no doubt that this circumstance increases very materially the sufferings of colored men in this country, and the guilt of the whites.[8]

The inconsistency of the American Revolution, with its combined legacies of freedom and slavery, explained why the white Americans were exceptional in their cruelty against slaves, as well as in their prejudice against free black people. The implicit conclusion was that in countries which had never experienced such a sharp contrast between freedom and oppression, the relationship between people of European and African descent would be less fraught with conflict. Brazil, where white people did not have any prejudice against the numerous black people, proved that prejudice resulted, not from nature and reason, but from history.

> Brazil contains more Negro slaves than any other nation; and if the prejudice were founded in reason and nature, it ought to be stronger there than elsewhere, because in every nook and corner of the empire, the African hue is associated with servitude and degradation; and yet colored men are eligible to, and do occupy the highest stations; they command armies, plead causes, heal the sick, and minister at the altar. Colored pastors are numerous, and their flocks embrace both white and black.[9]

Thus "prejudice against color" should be considered an irrational element emerging from the peculiar character of American democracy, that is, a democracy paradoxically based on the oppression of part of its population. Child seemed inclined to conclude ironically that people of African descent were better off in countries lacking free political institutions. The case of a Brazilian "colored military officer" who had arrived in Boston a few years before, and had had problems in finding lodgings, illustrated this implicit conclusion.

> Within ten days after his arrival, he was ordered from his lodgings, in Washington Street, ...and was obliged to take shelter in a mean apartment of a sailor boarding-house, because some aspiring young gentlemen of "the most enlightened of nations" declared that if "the niggur" remained, *they* would not. Yet "the niggur" was an exile by reason of his *republican principles*, and of his efforts to establish a free government for his country.[10]

According to Child's reasoning, the origins of racism were not to be sought in oppression alone. Otherwise Brazil, with its despotic institutions combining slavery and monarchy, would also exhibit "prejudice against color." It was the combination of slavery and republicanism that nurtured racism. Had the United States been consistent in its historical democratic foundations, racism would never have been invented. Besides Brazil, the histories of other countries like France, Russia, Turkey, and England pointed to a total lack of prejudice or at least to mild forms of prejudice. England in particular, whose customs and habits most resembled those of America, proved that "prejudice against color" could be considered an invention of the American republic.

> I have seen [in England] colored men at the chess-board, at the card-table, at feasts, at churches, at hotels, and arm-in-arm in the streets, with respectable white men of all ranks. Even in the W.I. Colonies, where cruel and wicked prejudice still survives, white men can sit by the side of black legislators, jurors, and members of the bar.[11]

But the fact that racism was inherent in the paradoxical foundation of the American republic did not mean that it could be contained within the boundaries of America forever. Like slavery, whose expansion was always possible as long as it was allowed to exist, prejudice against people of African descent could also expand throughout the world.

In a lecture delivered in England in 1860, Frederick Douglass made this point clear by calling attention to the rising British racism. No fewer than 40,000 Americans visited Great Britain every year. Since they were accustomed to the American institutions, and were welcome in all areas of British life, they were pouring the "leprous distilment" of their "pro-slavery poison into the ears and hearts" of the British people. Evidence of the evil influence of American visitors was the change of British attitudes toward black people. In reproducing Douglass's lecture, the *British and Foreign Anti-Slavery Reporter* revealed that:

> A change had taken place since he was here—fourteen years ago—in that respect. At that time he traveled over the United Kingdom, ...and he never heard a word, he never saw a look, never a single expression, that indicated the slightest dislike to him on account of the colour with which God had clothed him. (Cheers.)
>
> It was a proud boast, when he went back to America, that he could say to Americans—However you may be disposed, . . . to treat me, on the other side of the Atlantic, among people as refined and as intelligent and as white as yours, I discovered not the slightest ill feeling towards me because of my complexion.
>
> That was a proud boast to make, but he could not make that boast now. American prejudice might be found in the streets of Liverpool and in nearly all our commercial towns.[12]

On the eve of the Civil War, American abolitionists had gotten used to thinking of their country as the chief inventor and exporter of racism. In contrast, Brazilian abolitionists were beginning by the mid-1860's to depict their country as exceptional in tolerance toward people of African descent. As we have already seen, the idea of the American slaveholder as the most cruel one in the world met its counterpart in the idea of the Brazilian slaveholder as a most benign master. By the same token, the counterpart to the American violent "prejudice of color" was Brazil with its colorblindness.

It is interesting here to follow the steps in the rise of the ideology of Brazil as a racial paradise within abolitionism, both at the international and national levels. Like the contrasting ideas of the cruel American slaveholder and the benign Brazilian slaveholder, the belief that the United States and Brazil contrasted as hell to paradise in terms of relations between white and black people also emerged from the numerous comparisons between countries drawn by abolitionists in different moments and places pursuing specific goals of the anti-slavery struggle.

At the international level, foreign travelers to Brazil informed American abolitionists about the mildness of Brazilian slavery, as well as the tolerance of white Brazilians toward free black people.

A frequently quoted source was a book published in 1816 by Henry Koster, who had been born in Lisbon of British parents and had lived in Brazil between 1809 and 1815. He explained that it had not been his intention from the beginning to write a book about Brazil, but that upon returning to Great Britain "I was encouraged."[13] Although he did not reveal who had encouraged him, we know today that Koster became involved with abolitionists, probably after returning to Great Britain. As Manuela Carneiro da Cunha suggests, Koster's article "On the Amelioration of Slavery," published some months after his book on Brazil, "shows the unsuspected links between Koster and British abolitionists, the influence his ideas have derived from theirs and conversely the influence he might have had on their own arguments."[14]

Yet Koster certainly did not travel to Brazil as a spokesman for abolitionism. He seemed, indeed, to be very far from such revolutionary ideas. It was his weak health that first took him to Brazil. He needed to recover in a mild climate, but in the midst of the Napoleonic wars, "the ports of Spain and Portugal were either closed to British subjects, or not in a state to be visited by 'an invalid'." That was his stated reason for arriving in Pernambuco, concerning whose people and climate he had had "favourable reports."[15] But after recovering, he asked himself: why not follow the example of his new Brazilian friends, and try to make ends meet by putting some slaves to work for him? So, at the beginning of April 1812, Koster became a planter. As a renter of a sugar plantation, he received "several slaves, oxen, machinery, and implements," which enabled him to start his business right away. But for him, business as a planter meant the beginning of "a life of quietude". Since "the negroes were already at work for us, and under the direction of ... a manager, ...I had soon very little in which to employ my time, excepting in those things by which I might think proper to amuse myself."[16]

So it was with the eyes of a planter that the abolitionist-to-be Koster first became acquainted with slavery in Brazil. Amid readings in his bedroom and observations of slave life on his own plantation as well as on neighboring plantations where he was received as a guest, Koster concluded that Brazilians were more "indulgent" to their slaves than Europeans, and that slavery in Brazil was mild.[17] Moreover he pointed to the ease with which emancipated slaves were integrated in Brazilian society.

> The degraded state of the people of colour in the British colonies is most lamentable. In Brazil, even the trifling regulations which exist against them remain unattended to. A mulatto enters into holy orders or is appointed a magistrate, his papers stating him to be a white man, but his appearance plainly denoting the contrary. In conversing on one occasion with a man of colour who was in my service, I asked him if a certain *Capitam-mor* was not a mulatto man; he answered, "he was, but is not now." ... I begged him to explain, when he added, "Can a *Capitam-mor* be a mulatto man?[18]

Although Brazilians (in Koster's definition "white persons born in Brazil") seemed especially prone to colorblindness in dealing with "mulattoes" of light complexion holding a good social position, they did not put barriers in the way of the "free Negroes" either. Despite legal barriers to the priesthood and public offices, the "creole negroes of Recife" managed to accumulate "considerable sums of money," as did slave "mechanics of all descriptions."[19]

Koster seems to have been widely read by abolitionists on both sides of the Atlantic. One may find references to his book in the writings of American, Brazilian, and European abolitionists, who seemed equally impressed with his descriptions of mild Brazilian slavery and of harmonious relations between white and black people in Brazil.[20] However abolitionists either were unaware of, or did not sufficiently appreciate, the fact that Koster had observed slavery in Brazil from the position of a planter living within a society of planters. Koster was considered, in every respect, "an Englishman living in Brazil."[21] His subsequent involvement with abolitionism in Great Britain soon won him the *status* of an "accurate" observer of slavery in Brazil.[22]

Since subsequent travelers and writers quoted Koster or simply repeated his observations, by the mid-nineteenth century Brazil had become known as "the very paradise of the negroes."[23] In a paper on Brazil delivered at the Anti-Slavery Conference held in Paris in 1867, the French abolitionist M. Quentin predicted an easy transition from slave to free labor in that huge but tolerant last bastion of slavery on the American continent.

> What will singularly facilitate the transition in Brazil is, that there does not exist any prejudice of race. In the United States, in Cuba, every man of colour, even a freedman, is looked upon as inferior to men of white race. There is nothing like this in Brazil: there all freemen are equal; and this equality is not only of the law, it is also of daily practice. The freedman enters fully into political, civil and social life. I have seen upon the forms at the colleges (I was a professor for six years in Rio de Janeiro) black, mulatto and white pupils follow the same course, assist at the same exercises, and never any sarcasms or jests on the part of the whites against their coloured comrades. At the theatre, in the first tier of boxes, which is called the noble tier, all races are represented; in public stations, even the highest, in the Senate, in the Chamber of Deputies, in the Council of State, the men of colour furnish a very important contingent: it is even rare that there is not a man of colour in the ministry. Equality is, then not only a *right*: it is a *fact*.[24]

The above discourse is impressive for the lecturer's self-confident tone. His words were meant to leave no doubt about the peacefulness of relations between people of European and African descent in Brazil. But what gave the French abolitionist such confidence in picturing that racial paradise on earth was by no means only his six years of teaching in Rio de Janeiro. When he affirmed the absence of racial prejudice in Brazil, he was also relying on an assumption that had been repeated over and over for the last thirty years by American abolitionists stressing the exceptionalism of racism at the United States. Whether in brief references or in long statements, American abolitionists never failed to mention the contrast between Catholic and monarchical, but non-racist, Brazil and the Protestant and republican, but racist United States. As Douglass declared in a long statement during a lecture delivered in New York City in 1858,

> I doubt if there ever were a people more imposed upon, more shamelessly trampled upon, and despitefully used, than are the free colored people of these United States. Even the Catholic country of Brazil—a country which we in our pride stigmatize as semi-barbarous—does not treat the colored people, either free or slave, in the unjust, barbarous and scandalous manner in which we treat them.
> The consequence of this difference is seen in the better condition of the free colored man there than here. The practice in that country is, that when a slave is emancipated, he is at once invested with all the rights of a man—made equal to all other subjects of the Empire. No relic of his past bondage clings to him. He is a freeman. His color and features are lost sight of in the blaze of his Liberty . . . Protestant and democratic America would do well to learn a lesson of justice and Liberty from Catholic and despotic Brazil.[25]

David J. Hellwig suggests that at the beginning of the twentieth century, African Americans and many of their leaders began using "the image of Brazil as an open, colorblind utopia for people of color to instill hope among those who, long after the legal abolition of slavery, lived in social, economic, and politic servitude." Moreover, he argues, the notion of a Brazilian racial paradise served as proof to a skeptical, if not hostile, white audience that racial antipathy was neither inevitable nor innate.[26] In fact, however, Brazil had already achieved an international reputation as a racial paradise by the mid-nineteenth century.

Long before the twentieth century, American abolitionists were talking about the Brazilian racial paradise as a way of emphasizing prejudice and discrimination against people of African descent in the United States. The fact that Brazil was Catholic and governed by a king should add an extra measure of shame to the Protestant American republic, whose white citizens were ever proud of their equalitarian traditions. When the Compromise of 1850, with its toughened Fugitive Slave Law, killed the hopes of many abolitionists for the future of the free black people in their country, abolitionists of African descent like Martin R. Delany began to look toward Brazil as a possible refuge for free African Americans.[27]

Brazilian abolitionists did not miss the lessons coming from their more experienced international comrades. Like American abolitionists, they read the books written by foreign travelers to Brazil. They were also informed about the slavery issue throughout the world by the *Report* of the Paris Anti-Slavery Conference.[28] By reading this *Report* of 1867, they learned that Brazil was exceptional for its benign slavery and smooth relations between white and black people.

Earlier anti-slavery reformers in Brazil had emphasized the danger to a minority of masters of European descent posed by a majority of slaves and impoverished free people of African descent making common cause against them.[29] But from the 1860's onward Brazilian abolitionists began to see Brazil also through the eyes of European and American abolitionists. Yet I would not treat this as simply a case of "importation of ideas"—a thesis advanced by some scholars to explain what they consider the rather artificial history of Brazil.[30] First it is important to bear in mind the international connections of abolitionism, stressed by historians in recent years.[31] Their studies have illustrated the need to analyze the abolitionist movement as a whole, bringing together its national and international dimensions. Second, it is important to remember that Brazilian abolitionists themselves traveled and had the chance to practice comparative skills. Formal segregation, and overt racism did not escape the notice of Brazilian abolitionists visiting the United States.

After a journey through the Northern United States, the engineer André Rebouças, himself of African descent, had much to register, to his horror, in his diary. As a rising professional living in the white world of the Brazilian elite, Rebouças had been accustomed to overcoming prejudice on account of his African descent either by proving his competence as an engineer, or by seeking the protection of sympathetic white people. In hierarchical Brazilian society, a patron's protection seemed almost a natural aspect of the social life of any young man searching for a job, an official position, a marriage, travel for study or a tour abroad, or a simple acknowledgement of his talent. For a young man of African descent rising to the world of the elite, the support of a patron became a crucial matter of survival.[32]

Rebouças's diary testifies to the long hours he had to sit outside someone's office hoping for an opportunity to put his projects of technological improvements in practice. Following the detailed narrative of the many professional problems and barriers Rebouças had to overcome, one suspects that many of them derived from prejudice because of his African descent. How else to explain the long uncomfortable night the young engineer, traveling in an official mission, had to spend in a mill close to the slave quarters, after being denied lodgings by the owner of a plantation at the province of Paraíba?[33] And what about his long months of struggle to prove his right to apply for a teacher's position at the Central School of Rio de Janeiro?[34] Yet Rebouças did not explicitly attribute these hardships to racial discrimination, as did he so attribute those of his brother Antônio, an engineer like himself, living in Chile under an Emperor's commission. The Brazilian diplomats would not introduce him to anyone in Chile, Antônio complained in a letter to his brother.[35]

The fact that André Rebouças did not dwell on the theme of racial discrimination serves to clarify the methods by a young professional of African descent struggling to open his way in the world of the white elites. He had free entrance at the palace of the Emperor Pedro II, whom he considered his highest protector. Yet he declined the minister Zacarias Góis e Vasconcelos's offer to show the Emperor his brother's letter complaining of racial discrimination. He considered "this issue of personal dignity in our condition as mulattoes" too "delicate" to be dealt by the Emperor.[36] As in the episode of the dance with the Emperor's daughter, mentioned in chapter 3, Rebouças preferred to keep private any issue relating to prejudice against his color.[37] He chose, instead, a different method for overcoming racial prejudices: hard work, education, discipline, and a voracious appetite to read everything in as many languages as possible, as many entries in his diary testify.[38] Winning for him should be a matter of competence; and, despite many difficulties, he managed to succeed as an engineer, relying as a matter of course on protection and support from the king and other sympathetic politicians and public officials in high positions.

Rebouças's journey to the United States showed him, however, that competence was not enough in a country where discrimination was explicit and segregation formalized. In the United States, he learned the impossibility of treating the issue of racial prejudice as a private matter. Between the 8th and the 23rd of June, 1873, Rebouças was repeatedly barred from hotels and restaurants in New York, Massachusetts, New Jersey, and Pennsylvania. He complained of hunger after two days during which he was refused service at all the available restaurants. The fact that he was traveling in the company of a white American friend, who insisted upon calling him "doctor" in public, did not stop him from being rejected on account of his color.[39] Possibly never in his life had he heard people say so openly that the problem was his color.

The day after his return to Rio de Janeiro, Rebouças knocked at the door of the royal palace. There the blue-eyed blond, Pedro II, received him with "amiability" and set a special date for another visit a few days later. The Emperor wanted to hear all about his travel to Europe and the United States.[40] For Rebouças, returning from the United States to Brazil may really have been like escaping from hell to paradise.

Differing abolitionist utopias and abolitionists' actual life-experiences in different countries and times intertwined to construct what by the mid-nineteenth century was becoming a self-evident truth: that slavery in the United States and Brazil contrasted as hell to paradise. By the same token, it was generally believed and publicized that former slaves and their descendants in America had the most unjust barriers of color prejudice erected against them, whereas in Brazil the emancipated slaves and their descendants had all the "avenues" of society opened to them. At this point I would like to suggest that these distinct views about slavery, and about relations between people of European and African descent account for differences between the ways abolitionists in each country reflected on the destiny of the ex-slave.

American abolitionists believed that slavery did not cease with emancipation, but rather that color prejudice was a way of subtly perpetuating slavery among the free black people. Their destiny would be forever chained to that of the lowest ranks of society. Therefore the appeal for immediate abolition was two-fold: for the abolition of both slavery and racism. The Declaration of Sentiments adopted at the first convention of the American Anti-Slavery Society in Philadelphia in December 1833, made this point clear by stating both goals in an inextricable manner.

> Therefore we believe and affirm . . . .
>   . . .
> That the slaves ought instantly to be set free, and brought under the protection of law;
>   . . .
> We further believe and affirm—that all persons of color, who possess the qualifications which are demanded of others, ought to be admitted forthwith to the enjoyment of the same privileges, and the exercise of the same prerogatives, as others; and that the paths of preferment, of wealth, and of intelligence, should be opened as widely to them as to persons of a white complexion.[41]

In contrast, the issue of color prejudice never became a central banner for Brazilian abolitionists. For as the Declaration adopted by the Brazilian Anti-Slavery Society at its foundation meeting in Rio de Janeiro in 1880 affirmed: "Slavery has not been able to create the racial hatred [among us] up to now . . . "[42]

Whether Brazilian abolitionists genuinely believed that Brazil was free from the problem of prejudice against black people, or chose instead to keep silent about the issue—as Rebouças did—the fact is that their main focus was the need to abolish slavery in order to overcome backwardness and put the country on the road of progress. As for the destiny of the emancipated slaves and their offspring, abolitionists expected them to easily integrate into Brazilian society. Their presupposition was that the emancipated slaves would not face the barrier of racism as in the United States.

The distinct abolitionist views of the destiny of the slave and the black in general in the two countries can be best visualized if we consider, on the one hand, the debate about colonization of Africa by emancipated American slaves and free black people, and on the other hand, the debate about immigration of Europeans to Brazil to replace the emancipated slaves.

The question "what to do with the emancipated slaves?" was a constant preoccupation of abolitionism in the two countries. In the United States, early abolitionists were inclined to espouse colonizationist plans, that is, plans of sending the emancipated slaves away from the United States or, at least, from land already settled by Americans of European descent. Garrison joined for a time the American Colonization Society, which was founded in 1816 with the intention of sending emancipated slaves to colonize Liberia, in Africa.[43] In 1817 John Kenrick, who like Garrison would become a founder of the New England Anti-Slavery Society in Massachusetts in 1831, defended abolition combined with colonization of the former slaves in Louisiana. The anonymous poem, with which Kenrick concluded his book *Horrors of Slavery*, expresses well his plans to separate white and black people within the same country.

> Ye rulers! Guardians of Columbia's fame!
> Wipe off this shameful odium from her name.
> Redeem from bondage Afric's sons, and "pour
> The wine and oil," their plunder'd rights restore:
> Bind up their broken hearts—their thanks excite,
> By giving something less than what is right.
> In Louisiana's distant, richest oil,
> Afford them lands, with bread, and leave to toil
> Beyond the reach of whips and boist'rous strife,
> With liberty! the sweetest boon of life.
> Instruct, protect, and bless their infant state.
> While young, be friends; and allies when they're great.[44]

In conceding that reserving Louisiana for the emancipated Africa's offspring would be less than they deserved, the author reveals his dissatisfaction with the proposed solution. But his inability to propose anything else in order to "restore" the slaves' proper rights is very revealing of an early period of American abolitionism.

Even abolitionists of African descent, like Prince Saunders, seemed more inclined to espouse colonization plans, which in the long run would reserve the United States for white people only. Saunders believed that the increasing legal restrictions upon free black people living in the Southern slave states would press many of them to flee to the free states for protection. In the New England and middle Atlantic states, many hundreds of free black people were already willing to emigrate in search of a land of their own. In 1818 Saunders suggested that there was no better "Asylum" for the oppressed black people of the United States—slave and free—than "the luxuriant, beautiful and extensive island of Hayti (or St. Domingo)."⁴⁵

However, by the 1820's the people of African descent living in the Northern states had begun to define a better asylum for themselves and their oppressed brethren of the South. If the United States were the asylum for the oppressed people of the world, why should that not also include people of African descent? Should not restoring proper rights to the slaves and their descendants mean acknowledging that the United States belonged to them, who were born there, as much as to the other oppressed people of the world? In 1827 Richard Allen, Bishop of the African Methodist Episcopal Church, put this developing opinion into words in a letter to the editor of the *Freedom's Journal*, the first paper ever published by African Americans.

> Is there not land enough in America, or 'corn enough in Egypt?' Why should they send us into a far country to die? See the thousands of foreigners emigrating to America every year: and if there be ground sufficient for them to cultivate, and bread for them to eat, why would they wish to send the *first tillers* of the land away? Africans have made fortunes for thousands, who are yet unwilling to part with their services; but the free must be sent away, and those who remain must be *slaves*. I have no doubt that there are many good men who do not see as I do, and who are for sending us to Liberia; but they have not duly considered the subject—they are not men of colour.—This land which we have watered with our *tears* and *our blood*, is now our *mother country*, and we are well satisfied to stay where wisdom abounds and the gospel is free.⁴⁶

In 1829 David Walker made Bishop Allen's words his own, declaring that "this country is as much ours as it is the whites," and insisting that slavery as well as color prejudice could and should be destroyed.[47] He suggested three combined paths for achieving these twin goals. The first two paths depended exclusively on the actions of black people. As slaves they should follow the path of violence if they wanted ever to conquer freedom. God would soon give them the leadership of a "Hannibal" and "the whites" who held them as slaves "will curse the day they ever saw us."

> As true as the sun ever shone in its meridian splendor, my colour will root some of them out of the very face of the earth . . . [48]

As free black people they should follow the path of reason. After quoting Thomas Jefferson—"a much greater philosopher the world never afforded"—who considered black people to be inferior to the white, both in the endowments of their bodies and minds, Walker asked his "brethren" to buy a copy of Jefferson's *Notes on Virginia*, and put it in the hands of their sons.[49] For black people should not expect their white friends alone to refute the prejudice against them. The task of proving that black people were children of God and not of "tribes of Monkeys or Orang-Outangs," belonged to black people themselves. Black people should not be content with low employments and low education, which would only make them more subservient to white people. Color prejudice was an invention of white people, but the reproduction of prejudice depended on black people's remaining submissive to white people.[50]

The first two paths proposed by Walker to destroy slavery and racism required black people to break out of their subservience to white people by violence and reason. The third path was to be followed by European Americans if they wished to survive. God expected them to take the path of repentance, for he would soon put a stop to the oppression of black people.

> . . . I speak Americans for your good. We must and shall be free I say, in spite of you . . . God will deliver us from under you. And wo, wo, will be to you if we have to obtain our freedom by fighting. Throw away your fears and prejudices then, and enlighten us and treat us like men, and we will like you more than we do now hate you, and tell us now no more about colonization, for America is as much our country, as it is yours.[51]

The intellectual bridges linking the Northern African American community and the white abolitionists, to which I have already referred in chapter 3, are abundantly evident in the way Garrison assimilated Walker's *Appeal*.[52] Garrison does not mention Walker's influence in explaining his rupture with the American Colonization Society in 1830, but one suspects that his *Thoughts on African Colonization*, published two years after, was meant to be a continuation of the *Appeal*. Like Walker, Garrison strongly attacked the colonization plans by ensuring that:

> The great mass of our colored population were born in this country. This is their native land . . . .; they are descendants of those who were forcibly torn from Africa two centuries ago; their fathers assisted in breaking the yoke of British oppression, and achieving that liberty which we prize above all price; and they cherish the strongest attachment to the land of their birth . . . To see ourselves gravely represented in a British periodical as natives of Great Britain, I doubt not would create great merriment . . .[53]

Besides dwelling on Walker's main theme that the United States was the native land of black people, who had toiled for both its material wealth and its political success, Garrison introduced the issue of the "mulattoes."

> Granting the position assumed by colonizationists, that the *blacks* and the *whites* should occupy different countries, how do they intend to dispose of that numerous and rapidly increasing class who are neither white nor black called mulattoes?[54]

The theme of intermarriage was important for Garrison as a means of challenging the scientific racial theories that were, at that time, opening the way for the rationale that nature had raised up indestructible barriers between the races, barriers requiring that the races should occupy different continents.[55] In refutation, Garrison pointed to amalgamation between white and black people as the very proof that God had "made of one blood all nations of men."[56]

> It is a law of Nature that the lion shall not beget the lamb, or the leopard the bear. Now the planters at the South have clearly demonstrated, that an amalgamation with their slaves is not only possible, but a matter of course, and eminently productive. It neither

ends in abortion, nor produces monsters. In truth, it is often so difficult
in the slave States to distinguish between the fruits of this intercourse
and the children of white parents, that witnesses are summoned at
court to solve the problem![57]

The United States should be acknowledged as the native land
of white and black people alike, Garrison concluded, for both had
behind them many generations who had succeeded not only in
conquering the American land together, but in physically
amalgamating themselves, especially in the Southern part of the
country.

From the 1830's onward, American abolitionism insisted
that the destiny of the emancipated slaves and free black people was
definitively attached to their native land, that is, the United States.
One wonders if this position would have carried the day had it not
been for the militance of African Americans in the North against
slavery and racism. Would Garrison have felt the need to start a
speech by confessing that he never rose to address "a colored
audience," without "feeling ashamed of my own color"?[58] One
should not forget that Garrison included in his *Thoughts on
Colonization* a second part entitled "Sentiments of the People of
Color." By quoting a number of resolutions taken during African
American meetings in different places beginning in 1817, Garrison
emphasized the importance of taking into account the sentiments of
the black people over the issue of colonization.

In all my intercourse with them in various towns and cities, I
have never seen one of their number who was friendly to this
scheme...[59]

During the 1850's, in the aftermath of the Fugitive Slave Law,
the debate over colonization gained new strength with the pro-
colonization pages of Harriet Beecher Stowe's *Uncle Thomas's Cabin*
as well as with the emigrationist proposals of the Reverend Henry
Highland Garnet who had hitherto insisted that "America is my
country."[60] Because the Civil War intervened, we will never know
what the renewed interest in colonization would have meant for
abolitionism. But *Douglass' Monthly* may have captured the sentiment

of thousands of people of African descent—slaves and free—by simply stating that:

> When in slavery, we were liable to perpetual sales, transfers and removals; and now that we are free, we are doomed to be constantly harassed with schemes to get us out of the country. We are quite tired of all this, and wish no more of it.[61]

We have just seen how American abolitionists from the 1830's onward dismissed and attacked colonization plans aimed at expelling blacks from the United States. The introduction of the theme of racism by American abolitionism, and the combining of criticism of slavery with criticism of so-called "color prejudice" from then on, made clear the need to acknowledge the right of the African Americans to work out their destiny in their native land.

Now we will see how Brazilian abolitionists faced the issue of what to do with the emancipated slaves. Living in a slave country where, in contrast to the United States, the majority of the population was of African descent, Brazilian abolitionists had to deal with proposals that aimed not exactly to expel blacks from Brazil, but to replace them with a mass of white immigrants.

Nevertheless, at least one anti-slavery writer judged it necessary to get rid of the black population by adopting a colonization plan similar to the ones already being practiced by Americans and British in Africa. In 1837 Frederico Leopoldo Cezar Burlamaque, a doctor in Mathematics and Natural Sciences, called attention to the evils of the slave trade from Africa, which brought thousands of hostile slaves annually to Brazilian shores. He acknowledged that the slaves were "domestic enemies" because of the slaveholders' cruelty. But for him, there was also a racial issue. As he argued, scientists had not yet proved for sure that Africans had a specific type of brain accounting for their inferior mental capacity. Their stupidity, however, was so visible, that he concluded that Brazil as a nation would have no future if it continued to be inhabited by such a racially heterogenous population, a majority of which was of African descent.[62] Therefore he proposed a plan of gradual abolition, combined with the expulsion of the "emancipated race" from

Brazil. Moreover, the slaves' vacant places were to be occupied by poor Brazilians and foreign workers.[63]

Probably overcome by the difficulties of expelling such a huge mass of people from the country, Burlamaque later reversed the focus of his colonization plan. Instead of sending emancipated slaves to colonize Africa, why not bringing a mass of European urban and rural workers to colonize Brazil? In 1852, Burlamaque became the first secretary of the Society against the Trade of Africans, and Promoter of Colonization, and Civilization of the Indians. The slave trade from Africa had been forbidden by law two years before, but, as the Society's prospectus suggested, there was always the risk of fraud by the slave traders. One way of preventing their clandestine evasion of the law was to constantly enforce the legal measures against them; another was to provide for the gradual abolition of slavery, and simultaneously import free workers from other countries—"with the exception of the sons of Africa"— in substitution for the slaves.[64]

It is worth noting what these early Brazilian abolitionists had in mind when they referred to "free workers". As people living amid slavery, many of them slaveholders themselves, the early Brazilian abolitionists had grown accustomed to associating compulsory work with black people. In contrast, they associated free labor with white people. Their tours through Europe, where they marveled at the progress of nations inhabited mostly by white people, as well as their readings of scientific tracts pointing to the biological and mental inferiority of "the African race," helped to establish in their minds the idea that free labor and the white worker were intrinsically associated.

The program of measures proposed by the anti-African trade Society made clear from the beginning that by free workers they meant European workers. European workers, who had already been employed by a few Brazilian planters, were proving that they were more efficient and more productive than slaves imported from Africa, and even those born in Brazil.[65] As for the destiny of the more of three million slaves who, according to the Society's estimate, inhabited Brazil at that time, the authors of the program were inclined to ignore the subject, apart from one or two brief mentions. They expected that, within thirty years, gradual abolition combined with European colonization would have made the slaves disappear. People born in Brazil who wished to engage as "colonists", and therefore take advantage of the privileges established for foreign workers should apply to the local authorities in charge of the distribution of immigrants among planters and urban entrepreneurs.[66]

From the 1860's onward, more and more intellectuals and politicians took the position that, of the many reforms required to set Brazil on the road to progress, the most important was a radical change of population. They saw European immigration as a means of purifying the Brazilian population; and after the end of the American Civil War, some reformers also proposed the immigration of the defeated Southern slaveholders to Brazil.[67] In criticizing one reformer who opposed the plan of European colonization for Brazil, Antônio Augusto da Costa Aguiar made clear that a thorough rejection of the "African race" lay at the root of the colonizationist position.

> There are men who have a passion for the lugubrious color, the foul smell and the flat nose of the African, . . . we however confess a predilection for the white skin, the blue eyes and blond hair of the European.
>
> . . .
>
> You are willing to reduce [Brazil] to a hybrid-weak-deteriorated-uncertain-unfixed race, tending to Africanism. Oh, then yes, you would have it ready to fall as a submissive, base slave under the feet of the haughty conqueror of the old world. We, on the contrary, are willing to lift it, regenerate it, aiming to prepare it to enter as an equal partner into the congress of the great nations of the world.
>
> . . .
>
> We want a Caucasian Brazil. You want, you want . . . we do not even know how to express it. This is all the difference that separate us.[68]

Brazilian abolitionism, from the 1860's onward, wove into its thought the belief that European colonization would help Brazil to overcome backwardness and achieve progress. However abolitionists should not be considered colonizationists because their main banner was abolition, not European colonization. A parallel could be drawn between the relationship of American abolitionists to free-soilers on one side, and Brazilian abolitionists to colonizationists on the other. For American abolitionists, abolition of slavery as a whole was an essential banner, whereas the free-soil politicians of the 1840's and 1850's fought only to prevent the expansion of slavery to the new territories, sometimes making explicit their goal of preserving a "white man's country."[69] By the same token, Brazilian abolitionists adopted abolition of slavery as a whole as a central banner, whereas the colonizationist reformers of the 1860's onwards focused mainly on plans for European colonization, hoping that slavery, and the slave, would gradually disappear under the pressure of a mass of new inhabitants who would bring progress to Brazil, and make it whiter.

Having as an essential banner the need to abolish slavery as a whole, abolitionists in the two countries had to discuss the destiny of the slave and their descendants. But as we have already seen, Brazilian abolitionists, in contrast to American abolitionists, did not adopt the banner of the struggle against racism. Many reasons account for their failure to recognize the existence of prejudice against people of African descent in Brazil. Abolitionists belonged to a small elite of slaveholders who proudly regarded themselves as people of pure European stock—as the ex-slave Luis Gama sarcastically pointed out in his poems—and despised the surrounding African-Brazilian world.[70] Besides, as we have just seen, the ideology of Brazil as an exceptional racial paradise was taking its first steps at that time.

Last but not least, Brazilian abolitionists lived within an international historical context of increasing secularization of the elite's outlook and the rising prestige of the sciences. By the mid-nineteenth century, when Brazilian abolitionism took its first organizing steps, an international debate was already underway on the future of the so-called hybrid races. In Europe, eminent scientists looked at South America, and especially Brazil, as "the great laboratory of the modern mixed breeds or hybrid nations," and they took their own metaphor literally.[71] Scientists observed South America as a live experiment in the mixing of human races, having in mind one question: what would be the future of the mixed-race countries?

To their astonishment, Brazilians of European descent visiting Europe discovered that, to the eyes of Europeans, Brazil was a black country, something like a new Africa sprouting from the American continent.[72] Therefore, it is by no means surprising that, in confronting the issue of the destiny of the emancipated slaves and their descendants, Brazilian intellectuals followed with great interest the debate between two eminent French scientists about the future of the so-called mixed races. To the Comte of Gobineau, who published the first two volumes of the *Essay on the Inequality of the Human Races* in 1853, the mixed races had no future. With the passage of time, they would degenerate and disappear from the world.[73] He reaffirmed his thesis in 1873, after having spent fourteen months as minister of France at the court of the king of Brazil, that huge, ongoing laboratory of human miscegenation.[74] The only good memories he preserved of Brazil were of his friendship with the blond and enlightened Pedro II.[75] In an article published in France in 1874, he predicted that, despite Brazil's rich and beautiful natural endowments, its population would disappear in less than two hundred years, as would the Haitian people in about fifty years. The problem was that in Brazil, as in Haiti and other countries of mixed races, the different types of "mulattoes" did not reproduce beyond a limited number of generations.[76]

But different conclusions can be drawn from a laboratory experiment. It might have been with relief that the Brazilians of European descent took notice of the writings of another French scientist, Armand de Quatrefages. Professor of Anthropology in the Museum of Natural History of France, and Honorary Fellow of the Anthropological Society of London, Quatrefages, like Gobineau, considered the individual belonging to the "African race" as an intellectual monstrosity."[77] However, he criticized Gobineau's conclusions about the future of the "mixed races." He called attention to the fact that, owing to a history of wars, invasions, and movements of every sort, most Europeans also "retained, to a very high degree, the stamp of mixed races." Should the modern European—"*the hybrid a thousand times crossed from the Allophyllic and the Aryan races*"—be considered inferior to their ancestors? Had Europeans been incapable of constructing a civilization of their own ?[78]

Quatrefages gave to these questions the answer that many Brazilians of European descent wanted to hear. Everything depended on the passing of time as well as "the proportion" of the different "bloods" compounding the human mixture. Differently from the experiments with animals, where "intelligence and artificial selection come in and hasten the final result," "natural selection alone" was at play in the crossing of "human races."[79] However, natural selection of human races was presently under the firm command of "the civilized white man." It was he who everywhere sought out the inferior races, carrying them from one country to another, "mingling his own blood with that of the inferior races, and thereby elevating their position." In sum, Quatrefages predicted that the future human races would be "largely renovated with an infusion of white blood, that is to say, with the ethnological elements which thus far have carried to its highest degree the development of human intelligence."[80]

Brazilian abolitionists assimilated well the teachings of Quatrefages, defending abolition of slavery and simultaneously searching for the right "infusion of white blood" into the population of Brazil. The "right" infusion of white blood had to take into account, first of all, the fact that people of African descent constituted an essential part of the population living among people of European descent throughout the country. As Nabuco explained,

> ... the part of the national population descending from the slaves is at least as considerable as the part exclusively descending from the masters; that is to say that the Negro race gave us a people.[81]

Secondly, Brazil had to pay its respects to the "race" that constructed the country alone, by incessantly putting its work in every conceivable field of social life since the beginning of the colonial era.

> Due to these innumerable sacrifices, due to these sufferings whose horrible concatenation with the slow progress of the country make the history of Brazil one of the saddest events of the colonization of America, the Negro race founded for others a homeland, having with even more reason the right to consider it its own.[82]

In sum, the fact that Brazilians could not consider themselves a truly white people was an important reason for them to endeavor to destroy the "curse of color" of modern slavery, which allowed the enslavement of black people alone.[83]

What Nabuco had in mind was the reconstruction of Brazil on the basis of free labor as well as "the unity of the races in liberty".[84] This unity of the "white race" and the "black race" in liberty would allow the continuation of the amalgamation between races without the oppressive relation between master and slave, and the subsequent conflicts between them.[85] But the success of this amalgamation depended on European colonization to Brazil, which would "incessantly bring to the tropics a current of live, energetic, healthy Caucasian blood." The fact that Nabuco chose to conclude his chief work on the abolitionist mission by warning against planters who were espousing plans of Chinese emigration to Brazil—their goal was "to even more vitiate and corrupt our race"—reveals how profoundly Brazilian abolitionism assimilated the racial ideology of its time.[86]

Since the ideology of race had already become an intrinsic part of the world of the intellectual elites, it is by no means striking to find abolitionists of African descent equally imbued with the racial rationale. In articles for the journal of the Central Society of Immigration, founded in Rio de Janeiro in 1883, Rebouças enthusiastically supported the Society's main goal of constructing a "new Brazil" by colonizing the country with people belonging to the most intelligent and active races of humanity. He hoped that the "present race" inhabiting Brazil would improve under the influence of those superior races from Europe.[87] José do Patrocínio, also of African descent, delivered a lecture at a "meeting of indignation" held at Rio de Janeiro in 1888 under the sponsorship of the same Society. The indignation was against those who insisted on bringing Chinese workers to Brazil. In Patrocínio's view, "the Chim is incompatible with our nationality, not only for ethnic and biological reasons, but because he is an adverse economic factor."[88]

At this point it is interesting to recall Garrison's tone in discussing miscegenation. As we have seen, Garrison introduced the theme of miscegenation to challenge the scientific racial theories which considered "the mulatto" a degenerate being, and which underlay the colonization plan to separate black from white people. Starting from a moral and religious point of departure, Garrison insisted that every human being had been created equal by God and deserved therefore to enjoy equal rights. The fact that black and white people had worked out their destinies in America together, having even physically intermingled, strengthened the abolitionist argument that human beings constituted a single family.

American abolitionists also used the theme of miscegenation to denounce the lust of the slaveholders toward slave women.[89] They saw the question of amalgamation mainly from a moral point of view. Miscegenation happened outside the family of the master in acts of violent and illicit intercourse. By raping their slaves, the master not only destroyed the slave family but brought immorality to his own family. Although always careful not to give the impression that they espoused race mixture, American abolitionists made clear that miscegenation was a matter of reproach primarily because it denied marriage. In commenting on the life of Captain John G. Stedman among the Negroes of Surinam, Lydia Maria Child praised him for having married the "mulatto" slave Joanna. But even though legally married to a "mulatto", the captain committed the sin of inconsistency:

> Yet we find him often apologizing for feelings and conduct, ... and he never calls her his *wife*"[90]

When comparing the approach of abolitionists to miscegenation in the United States and Brazil, one has the sensation of having traveled an inconceivable ideological distance within the framework of international abolitionism. Among the early Brazilian abolitionists, amalgamation was a problem of morality that should be attributed not to the master—as American abolitionists believed—but to the slave woman. She was the one who corrupted his family, by attracting him and his young sons with her lascivious African manners.[91] Later abolitionists, those of the 1870's and 1880's, approached the issue of miscegenation chiefly from a scientific point of view. As we have seen with Nabuco, Rebouças, and Patrocínio, the destiny of the slaves was also the destiny of the Brazilian people. The "new Brazil" of their dreams, a Brazil of liberty, progress, and civilization, depended on the proportion of "bloods" melting in the pot of races. They saw Caucasian blood as essential for the future happiness of the Brazilian people, hitherto too much africanized to advance by their own means toward progress.

It is worth noting that Brazilian abolitionists began to awaken to the problem of prejudice against people of African descent only during the 1880's, with the rise of abolitionism as a popular urban movement. Returning from London in 1884, where he wrote his book about the mission of abolitionism, Nabuco engaged in an electoral campaign for a seat as representative in the Brazilian Parliament. In Recife, the capital of Pernambuco, he met the popular masses in the streets, and suddenly realized that "caucasian blood" might not be essential for their future happiness. In a speech delivered at the Politheama Theater in 1884 he criticized those "sociologists" who opposed abolition with the excuse that the slave needed to be educated first, and at the same time defended foreign colonization. He warned them that:

> . . . the territory of Brazil is not for auction, and belongs to the race that inhabits it. The duty of the good patriots, of those who love their land and their people, is to try to change the present state of things, destroy the motives which keep our population away from work as well as the causes which prevent them from working. For better or for worse Brazil belongs to the Brazilians, and it is theirs, the Brazilians,—that they have incentive and facilities for work and propriety,—this is what the statesman must take care of as a first duty.[92]

The acknowledgment of racism in Brazil was even more explicit in a few articles by abolitionists in São Paulo, a province then known as one of the strongest bastions of slavery in Brazil, along with Rio de Janeiro and Minas Gerais. From August 1887 to May 1888—a period of increasingly massive slave flights from the plantations—the editors of *A Redempção* denounced the unequal and discriminatory treatment of people of African descent by civil and legal institutions. One evidence of the abolitionists' awakening toward the problem of submerged, non-formalized racism was an article denouncing the imprisonment of a former slave by the police for having slapped a white "rascal."

> Why does it matter for the justice that the offended thief is white, has a commercial establishment based on stolen goods, and

that the other is black, in invading the house and imprisoning the one
that is black while the thief remains unpunished to the great danger
of the people's purse?[93]

It is also significant that the first anti-slavery novel to
acknowledge racism in Brazil was published during this same
period. In *O Mulato* [The Mulatto] Aluisio Azevedo called attention
to the invisible mechanisms of social exclusion applied to Brazilians
of African descent. These mechanisms were so subtle that sometimes
even the affected individuals could be unaware of the reasons of
their exclusion. It took some time for Raimundo, Azevedo's main
character, to understand why the upper classes of São Luis, the
capital of the Northern province of Maranhão, were so hostile to
him. As a young, elegant, blue-eyed doctor who had recently
arrived from Portugal for a visit to his native province, Raimundo
suffered under the impression that the whole town looked at him
with suspicion while receiving him as a guest at family parties. The
problem was that he was the only one who did not know that his
mother was an African slave. In trying to conceal this fact from him,
and protect him from the province's color prejudice, his white
father had sent him to Portugal while still a small boy.[94]

Many years before, Luis Gama had dared to denounce this
peculiar Brazilian way of accepting people of African descent at the
level of daily social contacts, and simultaneously excluding them
from more intimate relationships. Having been denied the right to
register for the São Paulo Law School, Gama was invited by a friend
years after, and already as a well-known self-made lawyer, to write
a few words in his album. He did not miss the chance to put in a
poem his feeling of being permanently excluded from the white
world despite living in its midst.

> Sciences and letters
> Are not for you
> A small Black from the Coast
> Is not a human being here.
>
> . . .
>
> Listening to the advice
> Of my reason

I shut up the impulse
Of my heart

. . . Forgive me, my dear friend,
Nothing can I give you;
In the land where the *white* rules,
Prevented are we even from thinking! . . . [95]

By the 1880's white abolitionists were also beginning to realize that Brazil was not free from color prejudice. Yet the issue of racism never became a central banner for Brazilian abolitionism, as it had been for American abolitionism. In contrast to American religious-inspired abolitionists, who insisted on the idea of one human family created by God, the secular Brazilian abolitionists assimilated the rationale of humanity divided by races, which was being preached internationally by scientists.[96] Even the few who did denounce racism were trapped by a rationale that attributed distinct mental inclinations to each race. One good example was the article "The Negro Race" published by *A Redempção* in 1887. The author sought to prove that the "Negro race" was equal to the "white race." But, relying on Auguste Comte's teachings, the author suggested that black people were more capable of withstanding suffering. As for intelligence among black people, he argued, one should remember those intelligent Africans, the Fulas, were not very black for they were descended from Europeans . . .[97]

We have seen that abolitionists in the United States and Brazil similarly concluded that people of African descent—slaves and free—should have the right to the countries they had constructed with their labor and sufferings. More than thirty years before the abolition of slavery, American abolitionists living in the free states, inspired by their peers of African descent, began to suggest that America belonged to the African Americans as much as to the European Americans. In Brazil it took abolitionism considerably more time to conclude that Brazil also belonged to the African Brazilians. Living in the small world of the white elites in a slave country, abolitionists did not have any intellectual empathy for the surrounding African Brazilian world. It was only with the rise of abolitionism as a popular movement in the 1880's, that is, a few years before the abolition of slavery, that Brazilian abolitionists began to appreciate the problem of prejudice and discrimination against people of African descent. However, trapped as they were by the racial rationale of their time, they were not prepared to go very far in their defense of the black people's rights.

It was one thing to acknowledge the right of the slaves and their descendants to work out their destinies in the land to which they had been taken from Africa. It was another, however, to face the question of how to integrate the emancipated slaves into society.

The fact that American abolitionists advocated immediate abolition from the 1830's onwards should not be taken to mean that they were inclined to recognize an instantaneous freedom for the slaves. The New England Anti-Slavery Society's *Annual Report* in 1833 made clear that immediate abolition meant that "all title of property in the slaves shall instantly cease;" but the slaves would remain on the plantations as wage laborers, and under the control of "wholesome regulations." As the *Annual Report* emphasized, "the labor of the blacks is invaluable—the South cannot flourish without them."[98]

American abolitionists seldom discussed in detail what they envisaged for the future of the emancipated slaves. Brief references throughout the 1830's reveal the abolitionists' inclination to imagine the former slave as an eternal worker or tenant under the control of the former slaveholders.[99] Abolitionists also seemed inclined to think of the former slaves as people incapable of exercising political rights. Garrison was very explicit about this topic:

> Immediate abolition does not mean that the slaves shall immediately exercise the right of suffrage, or be eligible to any office, or be emancipated from law, or be free from the benevolent restraints of guardianship.[100]

In Garrison's view, former slaves and their offspring should obtain full citizen's rights only after having been appropriately educated.[101]

During the 1840's and 1850's, as abolitionists concerned themselves more and more with fear about the encroachment of the so-called slave power within the federal government, they had less and less to say about the destiny of the slave. In denouncing the pro-slavery nature of the Constitution and deciding for disunion in 1844, Garrison and his followers were accused of forgetting all about the slave. To the abolitionists of the American Abolition Society—who during the 1850's still hoped that the federal government would be strong enough to challenge the slave power in Congress—abolitionists who espoused the dissolution of the Union were not very different from free-soilers interested only in preventing the spread of slavery to the territories and new states. Both positions left the slaves "without political defenders."[102] Yet the extensive articles of the *Radical Abolitionist*, the journal defending the policy of the American Abolition Society, did not reflect very deeply on the destiny of the former slaves. Douglass summed up the position of the American Abolition Society by reminding readers that the Constitution was anti-slavery and colorblind. Thus, when the Constitution proposed "to provide for the general welfare" of the people, it meant every inhabitant of the United States with no distinctions. But about how the welfare of the emancipated slaves would actually be achieved these abolitionists did not say a word.[103]

With the beginning of the war, the issue of the destiny of the emancipated slave became one of general interest. Douglass did not conceal his irritation in answering a question coming more and more from people who had been always hostile to the Negro.

> My answer to the question, What shall be done with the four million slaves if emancipated? shall be alike short and simple:Do nothing with them, but leave them just as you have left other men, to do with and for themselves.
>
> . . .
>
> Let us alone. Do nothing with us, for us, or by us as a particular class. What you have done with us thus far only worked to our disadvantage. We now simply ask to be allowed to do for ourselves.[104]

Yet, after a few more months of war, Douglass realized that the issue of the destiny of the emancipated slaves deserved a more affirmative treatment. Otherwise they risked becoming "the slaves of the community at large," with no rights at all and subject to a code of black laws which would deny them school privileges, the right of suffrage, the right to sit as jurors, the right to testify in courts of law, the right to keep and bear arms, the right of speech, and the right of petition. [105]

For Douglass there was just one way to secure to the freed men equal rights before the law: to make the whole South a "missionary ground" of abolitionists. Abolitionists' work on behalf of the Negro did not end with the abolition of slavery, but verily began.[106]

Probably the sight of numerous slaves abandoning the plantations in search of the Northern lines as well as the essential role of black troops during the war convinced other abolitionists of the need to struggle for the freedmen's equal rights before law in more positive terms. At the end of the war, Wendell Phillips proposed to banish "the leading men of the South" from the country, and confiscate their properties as well as those belonging to their "subaltern agents," that is, "the subordinate actors in this great conspiracy". The lands were to be distributed among "the loyal white men and black men who are ready to occupy it."[107] But to his view, land was only one element giving effect to the recognition of liberty. The other decisive element was the ballot, the path toward achieving political power. In opposing those who wanted to restrict the vote to the literate, this Harvard graduated abolitionist sarcastically commented:

> I am surprised, and marvel greatly, that so masterly a mind as Stuart Mill should proclaim that a man must read before he votes . . . Does he suppose there was no education in the world before printing was invented? Is education the exclusive prerogative of colleges? Oh, no. The masses of men have their faculties educated by work, not by reading. When God ordained as a condition of our being, that we should earn our living in the sweat of our brows, he gave the guarantee of the development of brain. Whoever works, develops his intellectual faculties . . . I would give the blacks, therefore, and the whites also, suffrage. Then I have got the two elements of State in the hands of the people—Land and the Ballot.[108]

We have seen how American abolitionists evolved from a view of emancipation that foresaw for the freed men "nothing but freedom" to a more affirmative view of emancipation, with freedom defined to include the ensemble of the citizen's rights, like the right to hold property, and the right of suffrage.[109] It is possible to distinguish three moments in this evolution of the abolitionists' views about the freed men and their destiny. During the 1830's, white abolitionists envisioned the Southern freed men as wage laborers or tenants under the control of the planters. No disruption of life on the plantations, or of the planters' interests, would occur, according to this initial view. During the 1840's and the 1850's, abolitionists were more inclined to debate the future of the Union than the future of the slaves. Dissolution of the United States, non-extension of slavery to the new territories, and total abolition decreed by the federal government were the three options available in this debate over the Union's future. As for the slaves, their destiny apparently deserved almost no attention. Thirdly, with the beginning of the Civil War in 1861, the destiny of the freed men became an urgent question. The massive flights of slaves toward the Union's lines made clear that no abolitionist could escape the issue. As Phillips stressed, the so-called "degraded" Negro proved with his valorous action throughout the war that his people deserved to enjoy all the equal rights of American citizenship.[110]

If the Civil War convinced American abolitionists that the emancipated Southern slaves deserved to be integrated into American society as full citizens, the same historical event held different implications for Brazilian abolitionists. The example of the American Civil War convinced Brazilian anti-slavery reformers of the dangers of an unplanned emancipation. The need to carefully plan the integration of the freed men in order not to disrupt the planter's interests, as well as the normal life of the plantations, would be from then on a recurrent theme among abolitionists.

The many references to the American Civil War, that one may find in Brazilian abolitionist writings reveal that Brazilian abolitionists interpreted this historical event as part of their own history. Since the rise of modern slavery had occurred at an international level, the same could be true of its fall, beginning with the countries of the American Continent. As many abolitionists imbued with evolutionist ideologies suggested, the world as a whole evolved toward progress. Yet progress would be achieved only insofar as free institutions replaced despotism. But evolution in history did not mean a linear path toward progress. Without the enlightened intervention of abolitionists, the inevitable fall of slavery in Brazil would only bring war, devastation, and even more backwardness. Francisco Antônio Brandão Jr., a graduate student in Belgium and an enthusiastic follower of Comte, attacked slavery in 1865 by suggesting that Brazil belonged to an international evolutionary chain of countries inevitably marching toward emancipation.

> Despite all the persecution to which they [the slaves] have been exposed . . . the slaves always long for liberty, and the will to rebel to achieve their independence is always present like the echo of some other peoples who have already passed from the same state, . . . inciting them to struggle. Brazil has sometimes experienced some of these bloody scenes . . . —the Republic of Palmares, the rebellion of Cosme at Maranhão, and so many other attempts to conquer their freedom, have been rehearsed by the slaves; and the last act of the drama opened at San Domingo in the beginning of this century, and the second act exhibited in the United States, has been rehearsed at this present hour in Brazil![111]

The debates over a government emancipation bill in the Brazilian Parliament in 1871 opened under the influence of the defeat of the slave South in the American Civil War. Brazil itself had recently emerged from an almost six-year war against neighbouring Paraguay. Besides having had a lively vision of the devastation that war could bring, Brazilian politicans and military realized now that victory did not mean less stress on finances and on the economy in general.[112] In supporting a bill that would begin a gradual process of abolition by attacking slavery in its reproductive principle, that is, by emancipating every newborn slave, the minister of Justice, Sayão Lobato, emphasized that Brazil should not repeat the error of the Southern American slaveholders.

> Gentlemen, when the stone is pulled violently from the top of the mountain and rolls down the precipice, there is no human force that can oppose it.
>
>   . . .
>
> President Lincoln used to say: "I neither want, nor accept the emancipation of slavery in the Southern states, I only require that adequate measures be taken in order to conveniently change it, and obtain in the future its extinction. The slaveholders rejected a fair compromise . . . As a result they suffered complete ruin.
> The same fate will overtake our agriculture if . . . our slaveholders hesitate . . . ; if, nonetheless, they are well guided, if they listen to the advices of prudence, and become persuaded that . . . it is impossible

to perpetuate ... slavery ... they will not only never meet the cruel fate of the slaveowners of the United States, but they will not suffer in their interests which will in this way be protected.[113]

The members of the Conservative Party, which composed the central government at that time, emphasized the need to reject the model of radicalism and violence one could read in the events leading to the American Civil War. If Lincoln had not been heeded by the American Southern slaveholders, Brazilian slaveholders should emulate his moderation and learn the lessons of the subsequent violent American history. Moveover the same United States offered a more convenient model of emancipation—the model of the North—for those who wanted to protect the planters' property from the uncertainties of an unplanned future.

The state of Pennsylvania in 1780 set the example by declaring free the newborn children from the slave womb, with the obligation of serving up to a certain age. In 1784 Connecticut declared free the children born from slave womb, with the obligation of serving until they were 25 years old. Rhode Island proceeded in the same way. New York followed the example in 1799, and New Jersey in 1804. [the slaves] were declared free, or became free with conditions.

. . .

Thus there are many states of the American Union that reached complete emancipation without having suffered any social or politic disturbance by employing the means being advised [now] by the government to the House of Representatives.[114]

Less than a decade after the passing of the Free Womb Law, abolitionists began to show their dissatisfaction with a measure aiming not to end slavery, but only to extinguish the slaves by death.[115] By the end of the 1870's, abolitionists had begun to defend immediate abolition for all slaves. Like the American abolitionists in the 1830's, Brazilian abolitionists did not mean by immediate abolition instantaneous freedom for the slaves. In contrast to American abolitionists, Brazilian abolitionists did not turn gradually to more radical proposals for the social integration of the emancipated slaves.

Despite the abolitionists' criticism of the Free Womb Law, the conservative model of emancipation underlying that law continued to serve as a guide to many leading abolitionists. Control over emancipated slaves' lives, plans for a general abolition of slavery with the obligation for freed men to serve their masters for a certain number of years, plans for forbidding former slaves to move around, and obliging them to settle at the very site of their past enslavement, formed an ensemble of abolitionist proposals up to the eve of the Law of Abolition in 1888.[116] Ironically, these abolitionist proposals for establishing firm control over freed men's lives resembled the provisions of the Black Codes enacted by the Southern American planters before Congress took control of Reconstruction.

But one should not be surprised to find abolitionists in the 1880's concerned most of all with repressing "the liberty of laziness" among freed men, and with instituting a "healthy discipline," seen as necessary to transform the slaves into wage laborers on the plantations.[117] As I have suggested throughout this study, Brazilian abolitionists lived in a slave country, belonged to an elite made up of slaveholders and their connections, interacted daily with slaveholders, depended on the successful conduct of the slaveholders' business, and themselves counted on the labor of domestic slaves, and ultimately on the allowances sent from their parents' plantations for their daily needs.

If in the 1860's and 1870's Brazilian abolitionists were much interested in discussing the Civil War and its outcome, by the 1880's they were trying to take lessons from the experience of the American Reconstruction. No one would be more appropriate to talk about Reconstruction from the point of view of the planters than the new American Minister to Brazil, Henry W. Hilliard. He had been a member of the Whig Party and a representative of Alabama in Congress during the 1840's and 1850's. He served by the side of Henry Clay and Daniel Webster, whom he greatly admired and claimed as an intimate friend.[118] As a member of the defeated Southern planter class, Hilliard had much to tell from the point of view that interested the Brazilian abolitionists most.

From 1877 to 1881, the period of his appointment in Brazil, Hilliard gradually became a frequent object of the abolitionists' attentions. He quickly became a friend to Joaquim Nabuco. By 1880 as a representative from Pernambuco, and the leader of the abolitionists in Parliament, Nabuco requested that he give his views as to the effect of the abolition of slavery in the United States.[119] As

one would expect, Hilliard pictured postbellum relations between
former slaves and former masters in much the same way that David
W. Griffith did, years later, in *The Birth of a Nation*.

> It was supposed, when the war ended, that the freed men of the
> South could not be entrusted to the control of their late masters ... Not
> only were they admitted to equality under the laws, but political
> privileges were immediately conferred upon them. At the same time,
> the leading statesmen of the South were placed under disabilities. The
> anomalous spectacle was presented of colored freedmen suddenly
> elevated to office, while white men, long accustomed to rule, were
> excluded from posts of honor and trust. Not merely were the slaves
> emancipated, but they were permitted to dominate.
>
> Numbers of adventurers from other States found their way to
> the South ... they encouraged distrust and hostility on the part of the
> colored people toward their former masters. Of course, under these
> influences, it was some time before the freedmen adjusted themselves
> to their new conditions. Many wandered from the plantations where
> they had been accustomed to work, and sought employment in the
> cities, leading a migratory and unprofitable life.[120]

Hilliard concluded his remarks on the backward effects of a
"sudden, violent, and universal" abolition by proposing that Brazil
fix a term of seven years before abolishing slavery. It would be well
if abolitionists consulted the experience of other countries, like
England and France, whose emancipation plans included a period
of apprenticeship for the slaves as well as compensation for the
planters. He believed that if slaves could be gradually released from
bondage in Brazil, they would "perform their tasks cheerfully," and
"contribute to the wealth and strength of the country."[121]

Hilliard stated these opinions in a letter to Nabuco in 1880,
which was immediately published by the press. The letter caused
much excitement among abolitionists, as well as among politicians
disturbed at this foreign intervention in national affairs.
Subsequently, abolitionists of the Brazilian Anti-Slavery Society
welcomed the American minister as a true friend of abolitionism,
offering him a special banquet in Rio de Janeiro.[122] Hilliard, a
planter now convinced that the days of slavery were gone forever,
was saying what they wanted Brazilian slaveholders to hear.
Immediate abolition combined with a period of compulsory work
for the freedmen would be the solution for the problem of the

transition to free labor and the social integration of the freedmen. This seemed to many leading abolitionists the only way of achieving peaceful abolition.

On the eve of abolition, abolitionists finally gave up their hope for abolition with apprenticeship. The massive flight of slaves from the plantations robbed those proposals of any meaning. In the years of 1883 and 1884, more radical proposals came from Rebouças and Nabuco, who advocated agrarian reform in order to guarantee the right of property to the landless people. But abolitionism in Brazil ended abruptly with the Law of Abolition on May 13th, 1888.[123] In contrast to those American abolitionists who by the 1860's realized that the integration of the freedmen into American society depended on their achieving civil and political rights, Brazilian abolitionists in the 1880's would not go beyond the banner of nothing but freedom for the emancipated slaves.[124]

EPILOGUE

Abolitionism in the United States and Brazil ended as it began: intent on very distinct tasks. On the eve of abolition, the word best describing American abolitionists' intentions is reconstruction, whereas the word best describing the intentions of Brazilian abolitionists is transition.

We have seen that Frederick Douglass and Wendell Phillips did not believe that abolitionists should regard the defeat of the Confederacy and the subsequent end of slavery as the end of their task. For more than three decades, American abolitionists had stressed a double goal of abolishing both slavery and racism. During the 1840's and 1850's, they split into two different political tendencies. The Garrisonians of the American Anti-Slavery Society regarded the Constitution as a proslavery compromise, which ought to be rejected along with all other compromises with the slave power. In rejecting the Constitution, they also rejected the Union, preferring dissolution to accommodation with the slaveholders. The Radical Abolitionists of the American Abolition Society regarded the Constitution as Anti-Slavery, and therefore capable of legitimizing an act of the federal Government abolishing slavery throughout the country.

The split between the two groups of abolitionists lost much of its meaning with the eruption of the Civil War. From then on, both groups of abolitionists began to imagine what would become of the South after the slave power was defeated and slavery extinguished. Many went beyond imagining and actually traveled to the South, with the aim of transforming the slave states into a "missionary ground," as Douglass put it. They hoped to reconstruct the South by ensuring that the emancipated slaves could live in freedom. But freedom, as Phillips stressed, did not exist in the abstract. In the reconstructed South envisaged by abolitionists, the emancipated slaves would become citizens, that is, individuals who counted on political means—the ballot—and material means—land—to make their rights effective. Moreover, the state should have an active role in defending the new citizens against color prejudice.

In rejecting the version of reconstruction that was taking shape in Louisiana at the beginning of 1865, Phillips made clear his rejection of a period of apprenticeship for the Negro as a model of reconstruction. There should be no distinction among the citizens on account of race or color, he insisted. Therefore, he proposed two amendments to the Constitution, one prohibiting slavery throughout the Union, and another forbidding state laws that discriminated among citizens on account of race or color.[1]

Phillips implied, and Garrison explicitly declared, that the abolitionist model of reconstruction should not be strictly limited to the boundaries of the South. The South was to be an intrinsic part of a new Union. Under the new Union, the national government would be strong enough to make the electoral law uniform in all states and prevent the exclusion from the polls of people of African descent, as had theretofore been the case in some of the Northern and middle states, and in all the western states.[2]

Brazilian abolitionists also dreamed of a new Brazil where, as Joaquim Nabuco stressed, there would be freedom for all and the two "races" would live in peace. Yet in contrast to the American abolitionists, who expected that freedom would be achieved only after slavery and racism were definitively abolished, Brazilian abolitionists visualized freedom for the slave from a much narrower perspective. To be free should mean nothing more for the slaves than to continue on the plantations as docile wage workers or tenants. After abolition, the São Paulo abolitionist paper, *Ça Ira!*, explained in 1882, thousands of freedmen would be searching for jobs in the rural establishments. The increased demand for work would cause a drastic reduction in wages, which would work to the advantage of the planters.[3]

For Brazilian abolitionists, in other words, the main problem was to ensure a smooth transition between slavery and free labor, in order to avoid disrupting the planters' interests. Slaves were to become free workers on the plantations; but what if they did not cooperate with this goal, as their already evident restlessness suggested they might not? José do Patrocínio's paper suggested in

November of 1887, less than six months before the passing of the law of abolition, that the choice was "to save everything," or "to lose everything." By saving everything the abolitionist editor meant "to colonize the freedman", that is, to gradually transform the slave into the free worker through the combined means of "discipline" and payment of wages. Losing everything meant leaving the slaves to find their own way out of slavery by escaping and seizing freedom for themselves.[4]

Having always on their minds the recent historical lessons provided by the American Civil War and the subsequent experience of reconstruction in the South—including Radical Reconst-ruction—Brazilian abolitionists expected that a planned policy of transition would save Brazil from experiencing a sudden rupture of slavery and the subsequent impoverishment of the plantations.

Slavery ended in Brazil all of a sudden on May 13, 1888 with the Emperor's daughter, Princess Isabel, solemnly signing the law of abolition—the Golden Law—at the Parliament building in Rio de Janeiro. But as Ruy Barbosa remarked a few months afterward, there was nothing else to be done. The end of slavery became a fact when the slaves rejected it, with hundreds simply leaving the plantations at the end of 1887 and the beginning of 1888.[5] Transition, by reason of circumstances created by the slaves themselves, ceased to be a key word for abolitionists, and abolitionism passed away amid the many street commemorations, public feasts, and banquets that followed the signature of the law in Parliament.

The fact that hardly any of the former Brazilian abolitionists thought to propose any kind of reparation for the emancipated slaves and their descendants was of some concern to Nabuco. Writing five years after abolition, Nabuco acknowledged that Brazilian abolitionism had ceased to exist on the very day of the so-called Golden law. He sought an explanation for this general lack of concern for the freedmen and their future in a comparison of Brazilian abolitionism to American abolitionism. Although abolitionism in Brazil was a humanitarian and social movement, he suggested, it had nothing of the religiosity of American abolitionism. Therefore, Brazilian abolitionism lacked the moral depth of New England abolitionism. The lack of such a moral depth explained why abolitionists had been able to attack privilege and injustice, while totally failing to envision the future of the country over a new basis, including social measures for the benefit of the freedmen.[6]

A well-traveled man with a keen sense of observation, Nabuco did not miss a basic difference between the two abolitionisms. American abolitionism had a religious underpinning, which partially explains why the struggle against slavery and the struggle for the Negro's citizenship rights were always intertwined. In contrast, Brazilian abolitionism, secular in emphasis, approached the problem of slavery with more expediency and less principle. Brazilian abolitionists were more inclined to stress the need to overcome backwardness and achieve national progress than to promote any kind of reparation for the slaves and their descendants. They thought of progress from the perspective of the class of planters, urban proprietors, and urban professionals. Nevertheless, Nabuco and Rebouças did suggest that the freedmen should also become proprietors. But their proposals soon died along with abolitionism.

And here we come to another of the basic differences between the American and the Brazilian abolitionism. American abolitionists did not live within a slave society; those who once had, like the Reverend George Bourne, the sisters Angelina and Sarah Grimké, and James Birney moved to the North, never to return. By contrasting the free institutions of the North with the slave South, abolitionists were able to forge a demand for change detached from the planters' interests. Brazilian abolitionists, however, lived within a slave society. When they criticized slavery they did so with solicitude for the planters and their interests, which they considered to be intertwined with those of the nation as a whole.

But neither the American abolitionists' religious sentiments, nor the fact that they struggled against slavery from outside slave society lead inevitably to their radical combined assault against slavery and racism. One wonders how radical American abolitionism would have been, but for the intellectual bridges linking abolitionists of European descent and abolitionists of African descent in the Northern states. Although they lived in increasingly segregated communities, abolitionists of diverse origins were able to communicate intellectually by exchanging their views and sentiments over three basic texts: the Bible, the Declaration of Independence, and the

Constitution. And as we have seen, abolitionists of African descent never missed the chance to remind their European American peers that they were brothers by divine creation, and also heirs of the equalitarian promises of the American Revolution.

In contrast, Brazilian abolitionists belonged to the European-oriented world of a small ruling class. They had no connections with the huge surrounding African Brazilian population but those related to daily work relations, business in general, and hierarchical obligations. Brazilian abolitionists had no intellectual empathy for black Catholicism, African religions, or African Brazilian culture at large. As people of the enlightenment, abolitionists recognized the injustice of slavery; but that recognition did not translate into sympathy toward the slaves and their descendants. Moreover abolitionists were constantly informed by foreign travelers and foreign abolitionists that Brazil was exceptional for its tolerance toward the Negro. As they quickly concluded, Brazil would be ready to become a racial paradise once slavery was gone.

These historical differences—in religious orientation, in distance from slave society, and in intellectual contact with people of African descent informed American and Brazilian abolitionists' very different views of the slaveholder and the slave, and their differing reflections on racism and the destiny of the slave. American abolitionists considered the Southern slaveholder the worst of the world, and the slaves their forgotten brothers. Brazilian abolitionists, less emphatic in attacking the slaveholder, considered the slave a victim certainly, but nonetheless a disturbing and evil element within society and within economic life.

American abolitionists extended their criticism to the North, where so-called free institutions were increasingly discriminating against citizens of African descent. In their view, racism had been invented in the United States in order to ensure that the freedmen and their descendants continued enslaved to a life of misery and humiliation. In contrast, racism never became a dominant theme of Brazilian abolitionism. Besides believing that Brazil was an exceptional country for its presupposed tolerance toward blacks, Brazilian abolitionists were themselves imbued with a racial rationale, one of the most fashionable scientific theories of their time.

At the end of the nineteenth century, people in São Paulo, one of the most flourishing provinces of Brazil, began to notice that the black people were gradually "disappearing" from their sight. One common explanation for this fact was that freedmen did not know how to live in liberty. They abused freedom, and died from the vice of drinking. The former abolitionist Antônio Bento labeled this opinion "a lie and a calumny against this unhappy race." Many freedmen were moving to the Northern provinces, from which they had been taken as slaves, in search of relatives and friends. They had no choice. The plan to encourage a massive influx of European immigrants had succeeded by the 1880's and 1890's, especially in the Southern provinces where the wealth of the country was being rapidly concentrated. While European immigrants could count on some privileges and protection from the Brazilian state, as well as from the consulates of their countries of origin, African Brazilians could count on no one but themselves. They suffered persecutions by police and discrimination in looking for jobs. Even religious institutions denied education to black children.[7] Therefore, black people migrated to the North to meet relatives, and try to make ends meet in the most impoverished provinces of Brazil.

At the time African Brazilians were finding out that freedom did not relieve them from poverty and violence, African Americans were being disfranchised in the Southern states. After the failure of Radical Reconstruction during the 1870's, freedmen lost any rights they had briefly enjoyed. Taking the vote away was just one of the first steps of a mounting onslaught against them. As Nate Shaw, a freedman's son, recalled, if the white people could not enslave the black people as they used to do, disfranchising blacks would point in that direction.[8]

As American abolitionists rightly predicted slavery would not cease with abolition. Racism would continue assigning black people to the lowest ranks of society in the United States. But if they had had a chance to take a tour throughout the Brazil of their dreams—the country they imagined for so long as a place free from racism—they might have concluded that, between hell and paradise, there is not such a great distance after all.

NOTES

PREFACE

1. Marc Bloch, "Pour une histoire comparée des sociétés européennes", in *Revue de Synthèse Historique*, nouvelle série, vol. 20 (December 1928): 26; and *Introdução à História* (Lisboa: Publicações Europa-América, 1965), p. 126 [original French edition, *Apologie pour l'histoire ou Métier d'historien*].

INTRODUCTION

1. It is interesting to keep in mind the notion of "genuine slave society" as used by M. I. Finley. The definition of a truly slave society takes into account the role played by slaves in basic production as well as the slaves' central place in a given social structure. From this point of view, both Brazil and the American South can be considered genuine slave societies. M. I. Finley, The Ancient Economy, 2nd. edition (Berkeley: University of California Press, 1985), p. 71-73, 79; and David Brion Davis, *Slavery and Human Progress* (New York: Oxford University Press, 1986), p.28.

2. Florestan Fernandes, *A Integração do Negro na Sociedade de Classes* 2 vols. 3rd ed. (São Paulo: Ática, 1978); and by the same author, *O Negro no Mundo dos Brancos* (São Paulo: Difel, 1971); Octavio Ianni, *As Metamorfoses do Escravo—Apogeu e Crise da Escravatura no Brasil Meridional* (São Paulo: Difel, 1962); Fernando Henrique Cardoso, *Capitalismo e Escravidão no Brasil Meridional* 2nd ed. (Rio de Janeiro: Paz e Terra, 1977); Emília Viotti da Costa, "O Mito da Democracia Racial," in *Da Monarquia à República—Momentos Decisivos* 2nd ed. (São Paulo: Ciências Humanas, 1979).

3. On the destruction of slavery during the American Civil War, see Ira Berlin, Barbara J. Fields, Steven F. Miller, Joseph P. Reidy, and Leslie S. Rowland, "The Destruction of Slavery 1861-1865," in *Slaves No More—Three Essays on Emancipation and the Civil War* (New York: Cambridge University Press, 1993); on the law of abolition in Brazil and the subsequent commemorations, see Robert Conrad, "Abolição," in *Os Últimos Anos da Escravatura da Escravatura no Brasil*, 2nd ed. (Rio de Janeiro: Civilização Brasileira, 1978).

127

4. Gilberto Freyre, *Casa Grande & Senzala—Formação da Família Brasileira sob o Regime da Economia Patriarcal* 20th ed. (Rio Janeiro and Brasília: INL- MEC, 1980), p.53.

5. Ibid., p.335.

6. Ibid., pp.5-8, 189.

7. Ibid., pp.306-307.

8. C. Vann Woodward, *American Counterpoint—Slavery and Racism in the North-South Dialogue* (Oxford: Oxford University Press, 1983), pp.50-56.

9. Frank Tannenbaum, *Slave and Citizen—The Negro in the Americas* (New York: Alfred A. Knopf, 1947), p.42.

10. Ibid., pp.97-98.

11. Ibid., pp.100-104.

12. Ibid., pp.106-107; for a similiar opinion see: Stanley M. Elkins, *Slavery—A Problem in American Institutional Intellectual Life*, 3rd edition (Chicago: The University of Chicago Press, 1976), p.79-80.

13. Ibid., pp.121.

14. Carl N. Degler, *Neither Black Nor White—Slavery and Race Relations in Brazil and the United States* (Madison: The University of Wisconsin Press, 1986), pp.34-35. Degler's book was the winner of the Pulitzer Prize in 1971, and was published in Brazil in 1976.

15. Ibid., pp.43-44.

16. Ibid., pp.44-47.

17. Ibid., pp.224-225.

18. Ibid., p.264. Degler's assumption that in the United States both the slave and the black man were feared, while in Brazil the slave might be feared but not the black man—given the "mulatto escape hatch"—has been dismissed by recent studies of nineteenth-century Brazilian society; ibid., pp.88-89. Manuela Carneiro da Cunha warns against seeing the mestizo race as a rationale underlying nineteenth-century society; she considers this idea an anachronism. See her *Negros, Estrangeiros—Os Escravos Libertos e Sua Volta à África* (São Paulo: Brasiliense, 1985), pp.81-86. I pointed to the elite's preoccupation and fears in having a population basically made up of people of African descent in my *Onda Negra, Medo Branco—O negro no imaginário das elites, século xix* (Rio de Janeiro: Paz e Terra, 1987). Like Degler, Seymour Drescher has recently concluded that "Brazil conceived of itself as intrinsically multiracial" during the nineteenth century. He believes that that self-conception explains why Brazilian slaveholders failed to formulate a proslavery ideology. See his "Brazilian Abolition in Comparative Perspective," in *Hispanic American Historical Review*, vol.68, no.3 (August 1988): 453-454.

19. Barbara J. Fields suggests a most enriching way of considering ideology. In her words: "Ideology is best understood as the descriptive vocabulary of day-to-day existence, through which people make rough sense of the social reality that they live and create from day to day. It is the language of consciousness that suits the particular way in which people deal with their fellows. It is the interpretation in thought of the social relations through which they constantly create and re-create their collective being, in all the varied forms their collective being may assume: family, clan, tribe, nation, class, party, business enterprise, church, army, club, and so on. As such, ideologies are not delusions but real, as real as the social relations for

which they stand."—"Slavery, Race and Ideology in the United States of America,"
in *New Left Review* no.181 (May/June 1990): 110. See also by the same author,
"Ideology and Race in American History," in J. Morgan Kousser and James M.
Macpherson, *Region, Race and Reconstruction* (New York: Oxford University Press,
1982).

20. On the American Revolution, see Edmund Morgan, *The Birth of the
Republic 1763-89*, revised edition (Chicago: The University of Chicago Press, 1977);
Bernard Bailyn, *The Ideological Origins of the American Revolution* (Cambridge: the
Belknap Press of Harvard University Press, 1967). On the process of Independence
in Brazil see Leslie Bethell, "The Independence of Brazil," in *The Independence of Latin
America* (Cambridge: Cambridge University Press, 1989); Caio Prado Jr., *Evolução
Política do Brasil e Outros Estudos* (São Paulo: Brasiliense, 1963); E. V. da Costa,
"Introdução ao Estudo da Emancipação Política do Brasil," in Carlos Guilherme
Mota, ed., *Brasil em Perspectiva* (São Paulo: Difel, 1968). In comparing Brazil to the
U.S. South, Richard Graham points to the very divergent social meanings of the
independence movements in the two countries. As he reminds us, the process of
independence in Brazil signified the unquestioned preeminence of the wealthy in
power whereas students of the American Revolution debate whether or not the
Revolution eased the rise of new social groups to political power. See his, "Economics
or Culture? The Development of the U.S. South and Brazil in the Days of Slavery,"
in Kees Gispen, ed., *What Made the South Different?* (Jackson: University Press of
Mississippi, 1990), p. 122.

21. Paulo Sérgio Pinheiro, ed., *Trabalho Escravo, Economia e Sociedade* (Rio de
Janeiro: Paz e Terra, 1983); E. V. da Costa, *Da Senzala à Colônia* 2nd ed. (São Paulo:
Ciências Humanas, 1982); Robert W. Slenes, *The Demography and Economics of
Brazilian Slavery: 1850-1888* (Ph.D. dissertation, Stanford University, 1976).

22. Eugene Genovese, *The Political Economy of Slavery* (New York: Random
House, 1967); For a comparison of the American slave systems see his *The World the
Slaveholders Made—two essays in interpretation* (Middletown, Connecticut: Wesleyan University Press, 1988). In this book Genovese suggests the need to understand
the nature of power in Brazil and the United States during slavery, investigating
how the ruling classes grew up in relationship to the specific class or classes they
ruled. Only then, he argues, is it possible to understand the disruption of their power
and the implications of that disruption for the dominated classes—p.5.

23. The English revolutionary, Tom Paine, considered America "an asylum
for mankind" for only there did freedom survive after having been expelled from
Europe, Asia and Africa; quoted in Eric Foner, *Tom Paine and Revolutionary America*
(London: Oxford University Press, 1977), p.78. Robert Ernst, "The Asylum of the
Oppressed," in *The South Atlantic Quarterly*, vol.40, no.1 (January 1941); Bernard
Bailyn, *Voyagers to the West—A Passage in the Peopling of America on the Eve of the
Revolution* (New York: Vintage Books/Random House, 1988); *George M. Stephenson,
A History of American Immigration—1820-1924* (New York: Russell & Russell, 1964);
Thomas Archdeacon, *Becoming American—An Ethnic History* (New York: The Free
Press, 1983); John Higham, "Immigration," in C. Vann Woodward, ed., *The Comparati-
ve Approach to American History* (New York: Basic Books, 1968).

24. Michael McDonald Hall, *The Origins of Mass Immigration in Brazil, 1871-
1914* (Ph.D. dissertation, Columbia University, 1969); Thomas Davatz, *Memórias de*

Um Colono no Brasil (Belo Horizonte/São Paulo: Itatiaia/USP, 1980); José de Souza Martins, *A Imigração e Crise do Brasil Agrário* (São Paulo: Pioneira, 1973); Zuleika M.F. Alvim, *Brava Gente! Os Italianos em São Paulo* (São Paulo: Brasiliense, 1986). On the São Paulo representatives' debates on foreign immigration to Brazil in the 1870's and 1880's see my *Onda Negra, Medo Branco.*

25. David Brion Davis, "The Quaker Ethic and the Antislavery International," in *The Problem of Slavery in the Age of Revolution 1770-1823* (Ithaca: Cornell University Press, 1975); Luiz Anselmo da Fonseca, *A Escravidão, o Clero e o Abolicionismo,* facsimile of the 1st ed. of 1887 (Recife: Fundação Joaquim Nabuco, Massangana, 1988); Roger Bastide, *Les Réligions Africaines au Brésil—Vers une sociologie des interpénétrations de civilisations* (Paris: Presses Universitaires de France, 1960).

26. David Brion Davis, *The Problem of Slavery in the Age of Revolution 1770-1823,* pp.41-42.

27. Ibid., pp. 45-48.

28. D. B. Davis, *The Problem of Slavery in Western Culture,* p.227.

29. Evaristo de Moraes, *A Campanha Abolicionista,* pp.231-234; Robert Conrad, *The Destruction of Brazilian Slavery—1850-1888* (Berkeley: University of California Press, 1972), pp.70-89; D.B. Davis, *The Problem of Slavery in the Age of Revolution,* pp.213-254. For the abolitionist societies founded from the beginning of the nineteenth century onward see, Merton Dillon, *The Abolitionists: The Growth of a Dissenting Minority* (New York: W.W. Norton, 1979).

30. D. B. Davis, "The Emergence of Immediatism in British and American Antislavery Thought," in *From Homicide to Slavery: Studies in American Culture* (New York: Oxford University Press, 1986), pp.242-243.

31. M. L. Dillon, *The Abolitionists,* pp.12-13. D. B. Davis, "The Emergence of Immediatism in British and American Antislavery Thought," p.243. E. V. da Costa, *Da Senzala à Colônia,* pp.324-356; C. M. M .de Azevedo, *Onda Negra, Medo Branco,* pp.33-58.

32. D. B. Davis, "The Emergence of Immediatism in British and American Antislavery Thought," p.254; M. L. Dillon, *The Abolitionists,* p.12.

33. D. B. Davis, "The Emergence of Immediatism in British and American Antislavery Thought," pp.255-257; James Brewer Stewart analyzes the differences between the revivals of the eighteenth century and the ones of the 1820's in his *Holy Warriors: The Abolitionists and American Slavery* (New York: Hill and Wang, 1976), pp.35-37. Stewart argues that the revivals of the Revolutionary Era did not generate sustained movements for radical change as the revivals at the 1820's did.

34. Winthrop D. Jordan, *White Over Black: American Attitudes Toward the Negro, 1550-1812* (New York: W.W. Norton, 1977), p.304. Jordan stresses that no one in the South stood up in public to endorse slavery during the Revolutionary Era. On the shift of the focus of the antislavery movement from the South to the North by the 1830's, see M. L. Dillon, *The Abolitionists,* pp.39-40.

35. Gordon E. Finnie, "The Antislavery Movement in the Upper South before 1840," in *The Journal of Southern History,* vol.35, no.3 (August 1969): 320, 336-337, 342.

36. Merton L. Dillon, "*The Abolitionists*: A Decade of Historiography, 1959-1969," in *The Journal of Modern History* vol.35, no.4 (November 1969): 500-502.

37. Ibid., pp.508-512; C. V. Woodward, American Counterpoint, pp.154-157. See also by Woodward, "The Antislavery Myth," in *The American Scholar* (Spring 1962).

38. Ronald G. Walters, "The Boundaries of Abolitionism," in Lewis Perry and Michael Fellman, *Antislavery Reconsidered—New Perspectives on the Abolitionists* (Baton Rouge: Louisiana State University Press, 1979), pp. 14-19.

39. Ibid., p.19. Richard Ellis and Aaron Wildavsky affirm the cultural unity of abolitionism without denying variations within the movement in "A Cultural Analysis of the Role of Abolitionists in the Coming of the Civil War," in *Comparative Studies in Society and History*, vol.32, no.1 (January 1990): 101-102.

40. Evaristo de Moraes, *A Campanha Abolicionista (1879-1888)* (Rio de Janeiro: Livr. Ed. Leite Ribeiro, 1924); *Osório Duque-Estrada, A Abolição (Esboço Histórico) 1831-1888* (Rio de Janeiro: Leite Ribeiro & Maurillo, 1918).

41. Gilberto Freyre, *Novo Mundo nos Trópicos* (São Paulo: Ed. Nacional/ EDUSP, 1971), pp.183-186.

42. Emília Viotti da Costa, *Da Senzala à Colônia*, pp.452-457. Octavio Ianni, *Escravidão e Racismo* (São Paulo: Hucitec, 1978), pp.34-36. Fernando Henrique Cardoso, *Capitalismo e Escravidão no Brasil Meridional:O Negro na Sociedade Escravocrata do Rio Grande do Sul* (Rio de Janeiro: Paz e Terra, 1977), pp. 217-218. I have criticized this historiographical trend in *Onda Negra, Medo Branco*, pp.175-180.

43. Karl Marx, *The 18th Brumaire of Louis Bonaparte* (New York: International Publishers, 1969), p.15. For some recent studies on abolition from a revisionist point of view, see: Célia M. M. de Azevedo, *Onda Negra, Medo Branco;* Sidney Chalhoub, *Visões da Liberdade—Uma história das últimas décadas da escravidão na corte* (São Paulo: Companhia das Letras, 1990); Maria Helena Machado, *O Plano e o Pânico — Os Movimentos Sociais na Década da Abolição* (Rio de Janeiro: UFRJ; São Paulo: EDUSP, 1994). For an index of recent academic literature on slavery, abolition, and race relations in Brazil, see: Luiz Cláudio Barcelos, Olívia Maria Gomes da Cunha and Tereza Cristina Nascimento Araujo, *Escravidão e Relações Raciais no Brasil—Cadastro da Produção Intelectual (1970-1990)* (Rio de Janeiro: Centro de Estudos Afro-Asiáticos, 1991).

CHAPTER I

1. *Daniel O'Connell upon American Slavery with other Irish Testimonies* (New York: The American Anti-Slavery Society, 1860), pp. 14-15.

2. Betty Fladeland, *Men and Brothers: Anglo-American Antislavery Cooperation* (Urbana: University of Illinois Press, 1972), pp. 257-261.

3.. On the eve of the Civil War, slaves in the American South numbered about 4,000,000. On the eve of abolition, Brazil's slaves numbered about 1,500,000, increasingly concentrated in the expanding coffee areas of the Southern provinces. Brazilian planters did not engender an ideology of slavery as the American planters did. But Brazilian planters, especially the Southern coffee planters, made use of political and police channels to resist abolition up to the last minute. They gave up slavery only when slaves began an exodus from the plantations during the 1880's. On the differences between American and Brazilian slaveholding classes and their postures with respect to slavery, see Eugene D. Genovese, *The World the Slaveholders Made: Two Essays in Interpretation* (Middletown, Connecticut: Wesleyan University Press, 1988), p. 81, 96. On the ideology of slavery engendered by the Southern slaveholding class in the United States see Drew Gilpin Faust, *The Ideology of Slavery: Proslavery Thought in the Antebellum South, 1830-1860* (Baton Rouge: Louisiana State University Press, 1981); Eugene D. Genovese, *The Slaveholders' Dilemma: Free-dom and Progress in Southern Conservative Thought, 1820-1960* (Columbia: South Carolina, University of South Carolina Press, 1992).

4. On the history of the pressure from Great Britain against the slave trade from Africa to Brazil, see Leslie Bethell, *The Abolition of the Brazilian Slave Trade: Britain, Brazil and the Slave Trade Question 1807-1869* (Cambridge: Cambridge University Press, 1970).

5. Fladeland, *Men and Brothers*, chapter one.

6. Ibid., p. 30, 187.

7. *Daniel O'Connell upon American Slavery*, pp. 5, 9. In a subsequent speech, O'Connell declared that he would "never pollute" his foot by visiting the United States as long as it was "tarnished by slavery."—"Speech delivered at the Great Anti-Colonization Meeting in London, 1833", ibid., p. 9.

8. David Brion Davis, *The Problem of Slavery in the Age of Revolution 1770-1823* (Ithaca: Cornell University Press, 1975), p.165.

9. Ibid., pp. 41-42.

10. On the economic and social transformations occurring in the United States during the decades preceding independence and during the early years of the American republic see Stephen Innes, ed., *Work and Labor in Early America* (Chapel Hill: University of North Carolina Press, 1988); Bernard Bailyn, *Voyagers to the West: A Passage in the Peopling of America on the Eve of the Revolution* (New York: Vintage Books/Random House, 1988); Richard L. Bushman, *From Puritan to Yankee: Character and the Social Order in Connecticut 1690-1765* (Cambridge: Harvard University Press, 1967); Kenneth A. Lockridge, *A New England Town: The First Hundred Years, Dedham Massachusetts, 1636-1736* (New York: W. W. Norton & Company, 1970); Paulo Boyer and Stephen Nissenbaum, *Salem Possessed: The Social Origins of Witchcraft* (Cambridge: Harvard University Press, 1974); Drew R. McCoy, *The Elusive Republic: Political Economy in Jeffersonian America* (New York: W.W. Norton & Company, 1980). On the sentiment that the American Revolution was failing in its libertarian promises during the first years of the Republic, see Gordon S. Wood, *The Creation of the American Republic, 1776-1787* (New York: W. W. Norton and Company, 1969), pp. 393-396.

11. On the economic and social transformations occurring in Brazil from the mid-nineteenth century onwards see Richard Graham, *Grã-Bretanha e o Início da Modernização no Brasil 1850-1914* (São Paulo: Brasiliense, 1973); Peter L. Eisenberg, *Modernização sem Mudança: A Indústria Açucareira em Pernambuco 1840-1910* (Rio de Janeiro: Paz e Terra; Campinas: Universidade Estadual de Campinas, 1977); Robert Wayne Slenes, "The Demography and Economics of Brazilian Slavery: 1850-1888" (Ph.D. dissertation, Stanford University, November, 1975); Robert Edgar Conrad, *Tumbeiros: O Tráfico Escravista para o Brasil* (São Paulo: Brasiliense, 1985); Emília Viotti da Costa, "Brazil: The Age of Reform, 1870-1889," in *The Cambridge History of Latin America*, vol.5 (Cambridge: Cambridge University Press, 1986).

12. The lives of the brothers Lewis and Arthur Tappan before they became abolitionists may exemplify the revivalist environment in which most abolitionists lived during the 1820's. The revivalist environment nurtured a tendency toward reforms concerned with conversion of the soul and the moral uplift of daily life. On

the brothers Tappan and the revivalist environment of the 1820's, see Bertram Wyatt-Brown, *Lewis Tappan and the Evangelical War Against Slavery* (Cleveland: The Press of Case Western Reserve University, 1969), especially chapter four, "Yankees versus Yorkers." On the rise of voluntary associations inclined to change individuals, and not institutions, during the period of the Second Great Awakening, see Donald G. Mathews, "The Second Great Awakening as an Organizing Process, 1780-1830: An Hypothesis," in *American Quarterly*, vol.21, no.1 (Spring 1969).

13. The life of Joaquim Nabuco before he became an abolitionist may also exemplify the secularized environment in which most abolitionists-to-be lived from the 1850's onwards. The preoccupation with the institutions and the need of reforming them was at the center of the debates and at the root of the literary and political groups created during this period. See Luis Viana Filho, *A Vida de Joaquim Nabuco* 2nd ed. (São Paulo: Livraria Martins Editora/INL/MEC, 1973).

14. "Declaration of Sentiment," in *The Liberator*, vol.5, no.20 (May 16, 1835): 78.

15. "A Nossa Missão," in *O Abolicionista* (November 1, 1880): 1; facsimile edition by Leonardo Dantas Silva (Recife: Fundação Joaquim Nabuco, Editora Massangana, 1988). This quotation refers to the law of November 7th, 1831 which forbade the importation of African slaves to Brazil without ever having enforced it. The African trade to Brazil was abolished only in 1850. Hereafter all the translations from Portuguese, and French, to English are mine.

16. Recent studies of American abolitionism seem inclined to affirm the cultural unity of American abolitionists despite acknowledging internal political variations. See Richard Ellis and Aaron Wildavsky, "A Cultural Analysis of the Role of Abolitionists in the Coming of the Civil War," in *Comparative Studies in Society and History* vol. 32, no.1 (January 1990): 89-116.

17. David Brion Davis, *The Problem of Slavery in Western Culture* (New York: Oxford University Press, 1988), pp. 398-399.

18. João Severiano Maciel da Costa, *Memória sobre a Necessidade de Abolir a Introdução dos Escravos Africanos no Brasil; sobre o Modo e Condições com que esta Abolição se Deve Fazer; e sobre os Meios de Remediar a Falta de Braços que ela Pode Ocasionar* (Coimbra: Imprensa da Universidade, 1821); Frederico Leopoldo Cezar Burlamaque, *Memoria Analytica a Cerca do Commercio d'Escravos e a Cerca dos Males da Escravidão Domestica* (Rio de Janeiro: Comercial Fluminense, 1837). Both epigraphs are in French; the translation to English is mine.

19. Maciel da Costa used the expression "perennial war" in referring to conflicts between masters and slaves; Costa, *Memoria sobre a Necessidade de Abolir a Introdução dos Escravos Africanos no Brasil*, p. 7.

20. On the slave upheavals in Bahia during the 1830's, see João José Reis, *Rebelião Escrava no Brasil: A História do Levante dos Malês (1835)* (São Paulo: Brasiliense, 1986); Clóvis Moura, *Rebeliões da Senzala* 3rd ed. (São Paulo: Ciências Humanas, 1981). On slave rebellions and on abolitionism and its international connections, it is important to keep in mind Fladeland's suggestion: "Too often these insurrections have been viewed separately, but taken together, one can see that their cumulative effect carried much more impact. Because of constant communication, British, West Indians, and Americans reinforced each others' fears."—*Men and Brothers*, pp. 190-191.

21. Davis, *The Problem of Slavery in Western Culture*, p. 405.

22. Peter Gay points to a shift of temper of the Enlightenment from natural law to utilitarianism during this period. He considers Montesquieu as the fountainhead of the enlightened critique of slavery. See Peter Gay, *The Enlightenment: An Interpretation* 2 vols. (New York: W. W. Norton & Company, 1977), vol.2, pp. 416-423.

23. José Bonifácio de Andrada e Silva, *Representação à Assembléa Geral Constituinte e Legislativa do Império do Brasil sobre a Escravatura* (Rio de Janeiro: Typographia de J.E.S. Cabral, 1840), pp. 8-10.

24. During the 1880's, abolitionists like Joaquim Nabuco and André Rebouças criticized the "latifúndio", that is, the large rural property devoted to a single staple, and with a great extension of uncultivated land. Another issue of the 1880's was the subjection of urban-professional interests to the planters' interests. But one senses a line of continuity in the ideology of abolitionism, from the early period to its last years, in the abolitionists' preoccupation with protecting the planters from the threat of a sudden rupture of slavery.

25. Davis, *The Problem of Slavery in Western Culture*, pp. 291-299.

26. On the Quakers' antislavery activities during the eighteenth century see Davis, *The Problem of Slavery in the Age of Revolution*, pp. 213-254.

27. Davis, *The Problem of Slavery in Western Culture*, pp. 334-336.

28. Ibid., pp. 348-351.

29. Ibid., pp. 351-359.

30. "Extracts from an Address, delivered before the N. E. Anti-Slavery Society, by Wm. J. Snelling, Esq.," in *The Abolitionist* vol.1, no.4 (April 1833): 54.

31. "O Espírito de S. Paulo," in Cidade do Rio, no.57 (November 25, 1887): 1.

32. Walter M. Merrill, *Against Wind and Tide: A Biography of Wm. Lloyd Garrison* (Cambridge: Harvard University Press, 1963), p.9. On Garrison's life, see also John L. Thomas, *The Liberator: William Lloyd Garrison a Biography* (Boston: Little, Brown and Company, 1963). In writing about the childhood of Wendell Phillips in Boston, James Brewer Stewart describes a city where people of African descent were segregated in "Nigger Hill," a short distance away from the aristocratic Bostonian neighbourhood where Phillips lived. Stewart, *Wendell Phillips: Liberty's Hero* (Baton Rouge: Louisiana State University Press, 1986), pp. 5-8.

33. Merrill, *Against Wind and Tide*, pp. 18-23.

34. Ibid., p. 23.

35. Ibid., p. 35.

36. Viana Filho, *A Vida de Joaquim Nabuco*, pp. 13-14. On the Praieira Revolution see Izabel Andrade Marson, *O Império do Progresso: A Revolução Praieira* (São Paulo: Brasiliense, 1987).

37. Pedro II ruled from 1840 to 1889, when the monarchy ended and was replaced by the republic. The king was only fifteen years old in 1840. For the liberal upheavals and the politics of "conciliation" from 1853 to 1859 that followed the liberal's defeat, see Heitor Lyra, *História de Dom Pedro II - 1825-1891* 3 vols. (São Paulo: Companhia Editora Nacional, 1938), chapters 4, 8, and 9. Lyra offers a conservative version of the history of the Empire of Pedro II.

38. Joaquim Nabuco, *Minha Formação* (Brasília: Editora Universidade de Brasília, 1963), p. 184. Vianna Filho, *A Vida de Joaquim Nabuco*, p. 16.

39. Viana Filho, *A Vida de Joaquim Nabuco*, pp. 19-40. Viana Filho does not refer to Nabuco's owning slaves during his young adult life. Nabuco's father sold the two slaves Nabuco owned during his childhood on Massangana plantation after Nabuco moved to Rio de Janeiro to live with his parents. Nabuco's political enemies spread rumors, however, that he paid for his travels to Europe by selling his slaves—ibid., pp. 19-40.

40. Joaquim Nabuco, *A Escravidão* (Recife: Fundação Joaquim Nabuco/ Editora Massangana, 1988), p. 32. This book was written in 1870, but it was only published in 1988 by the editor Leonardo Dantas Silva.

41. Davis, *The Problem of Slavery in Western Culture*, p. 363. For a recent debate on this issue, see Thomas Bender, The Antislavery Debate: Capitalism and Abolitionism as a Problem in Historical Interpretation (Berkeley: University of California Press, 1992); and David Eltis, "Europeans and the Rise and Fall of African Slavery in the Americas: An Interpretation," in *The American Historical Review*, vol.98, no.5 (December 1993).

42. David Donald argues that the abolitionist leadership was made up of people who were being displaced by the fast economic and social changes in American society during the 1820's and 1830's. Donald interprets abolitionism as a double crusade: besides seeking freedom for the Negro in the South, the abolitionists were attempting a restoration of the traditional values of their class. See Donald, "Toward a Reconsideration of Abolitionists," in *Lincoln Reconsidered: Essays on the Civil War Era* 2nd ed. (New York: Vintage Book, Random House, 1989), pp. 33-36. Rebeca Baird Bergstresser suggests that Brazilian abolitionists incorporated into their proposals a number of issues related to the needs of the urban masses of Rio de Janeiro. Bergstresser, "The Movement for the Abolition of Slavery in Rio de Janeiro, Brazil, 1880-1889" (Ph.D. dissertation, Stanford University, February 1973).

43. Robin Blackburn, *The Overthrow of Colonial Slavery 1776-1848* (London: Verso, 1990), pp. 27-28.

CHAPTER II

1. On popular indignation at the British navy's violation of Brazilian sovereignty during the 1840's and part of the 1850's see Leslie Bethell, *The Abolition of the Brazilian Slave Trade: Britain, Brazil and the Slave Trade Question 1807-1869* (Cambridge: Cambridge University Press, 1970), pp. 206-208, 335.

2. Francisco Antônio Brandão Jr., *A Escravatura no Brazil Precedida d'um artigo sobre agricultura e colonisação no Maranhão* (Bruxelles, Typographie H. Thiry-Van Buggenhoudt, 1865), p. 52. Written under the influence of Positivism, Brandão Jr.'s book caused a great scandal in Brazil, especially in his native province of Maranhão, where his father was a cotton planter. One of his brothers wrote him that the whole family was sorry that his first published work aimed to make a great number of enemies right at the beginning of his career. The brother reminded him of his parents' enormous sacrifices to pay for his education, which he was paying back by ruining the whole family: "You should not be so ungrateful and selfish for although you can make ends meet with your work, we depend on [the work of] our slaves."

Quoted from Ivan Lins, *História do Positivismo no Brasil* by João Cruz Costa, "O Pensamento Brasileiro sob o Império," in Sérgio Buarque de Holanda, ed., *História Geral da Civilização Brasileira. O Brasil Monárquico* 2nd ed. vol.3 (São Paulo: Difusão Européia do Livro, 1969), pp. 331-332. In 1883, an abolitionist reviewing Brandão Jr.'s book called attention to the influence of the American Civil War on his ideas; *O Abolicionista* (Recife: August 20, 1883), reprinted by Leonardo Dantas Silva, *A Imprensa e a Abolição* (Recife: Fundação Joaquim Nabuco/Editora Massangana, 1988).

    3. Brandão Jr., *A Escravatura no Brazil*, p. 53.

    4. Joaquim Nabuco, *Minha Formação* (Brasília: Editora Universidade de Brasília, 1963), p. 26; Luis Viana Filho, *A Vida de Joaquim Nabuco* 2nd. ed. (São Paulo: Livraria Martins Editora/INL/MEC, 1973), p. 31. It would be interesting to know what Nabuco had in mind in dreaming of his father as a "Brazilian Sumner." In 1869 the American Senator Charles Sumner sent him a letter declaring that his father, Senator Nabuco, was wrong in not demanding immediate abolition of slavery in Brazil. Did Nabuco agree with the advice and might he have pressed his father to become another Sumner in this sense, that is, an immediatist? In any event, Joaquim Nabuco only declared himself in favor of immediate abolition in the 1880's. Letter from Senator Charles Sumner to Joaquim Nabuco quoted by Ana Isabel de Souza Leão Andrade e Carmen Lúcia de Souza Leão Rego, *Catálogo da Correspondência de Joaquim Nabuco 1865-1884* vol.1 (Recife: Ministério da Educação e Cultura/Instituto Joaquim Nabuco de Pesquisas Sociais, 1978), p.9.

    5. "Slavery and the Slave-Trade," in *The Anti-Slavery Reporter* (March 1884): 145-153. The British and Foreign Anti-Slavery Society presented this article as a "short resume of the Anti-Slavery work of the last fifty years." It was to be presented at the Jubilee Meeting at London on August 1st, 1884.

    6. *Special Report of The Anti-Slavery Conference, Held in Paris in the Salle Herz, on the Twenty-Sixth and Twenty-Seventh August, 1867, under the Presidency of Mons. Edouard Laboulaye, Member of the French Institute* (London: The Committee of The British and Foreign Anti-Slavery Society), pp. 115-117.

    7. Ibid., pp. 115-117.

    8. For a list of delegates to the Paris Conference, see "Appendix to Special Report," in *Special Report of The Anti-Slavery Conference*, pp. 55-58.

    9. *The Empire of Brazil at the Paris International Exhibition of 1867* (Rio de Janeiro: E. & Laemmert, 1867), pp. 30-31.

    10. *Special Report of The Anti-Slavery Conference*, p. 14.

    11. Both Quentin and the speaker who followed him, Mons. le Major Taunay, ex French Consul at Rio de Janeiro, emphasized that slavery never constituted an "institution" or a "social system" in Brazil, but only an awkward legacy from the mother-country, that is, Portugal. Taunay minimized the importance of slavery for the economy of the country by stressing the rapid increase in the free part of the population, and the falling number of slaves, ibid., pp. 115-122.

    12. On the Paraguayan War, see Charles J. Kolinski, *Independence or Death! The Story of the Paraguayan War* (Gainesville: University of Florida Press, 1965). In 1865, the abolitionist lawyer and former slave Luis Gama used sarcasm to denounce the violent impressment of people for service in the Paraguayan War. In one of the charges published in his paper, a picture showing a group of chained black men walking behind policemen appears under the words: "Hunting of patriots to be

involuntary volunteers"—*Diabo Coxo* no.7 (September 3, 1865).

13. *Special Report of The Anti-Slavery Conference*, p. 13.

14. The Paris Anti-Slavery Conference decided to send addresses to the Sovereigns and rulers of the following countries: Brazil, Spain, Portugal, Turkey, Egypt, Trans-Vaal Republic, South Africa. The Conference also sent an address to Pope Pius IX; ibid., p. 13, 134-141.

15. Robert Conrad, *Os Últimos Anos da Escravatura no Brasil* 2nd. ed. (São Paulo: Brasiliense, 1978), p. 95. Emília Viotti da Costa, *Da Senzala à Colônia* 2nd. ed. (São Paulo: Livraria Editora Ciências Humanas, 1982), p. 378.

16. I shall return to Luis Gama in chapter three. On the French radical Elisée Reclus, see Marie Fleming, *The Anarchist Way to Socialism: Elisée Reclus and Nineteenth-Century European Anarchism* (Totowa, New Jersey: Croom Helm/Rowman and Littlefield, 1979). Reclus was a member of the International Working Men's Association — the First International—having joined the anarchist Bakunin in the late 1860's; ibid., pp. 61-63, 67.

17. *Special Report of The Anti-Slavery Conference*, p. 118.

18. Only Brazilian slaveholders escaped criticism by speakers at the Paris Anti-Slavery Conference. Cuban and Puerto Rican slaveholders were harshly attacked by Julio L. de Vizcarrondo, Honorary Secretary of the Spanish Abolitionist Society: "The condition of the slave in Cuba is much worse than it is in Porto Rico. This is a consequence of the existence of much more extensive sugar plantations and tobacco estates, demanding a larger number of slaves to work them; and also of the greater toleration by the authorities, of violations of the laws for the protection of the slaves; to wit, in Porto Rico, twelve hours is the extreme of a day's labour, but in Cuba it has reached sixteen in crop time. Under such a system what horrors may not be committed!"; ibid., p. 125.

19. *Special Report of The Anti-Slavery Conference*, p. 13.

20. Marc Bloch, *Introdução à História* (Lisboa: Publicações Europa-América, 1965), p. 31.

21. George Bourne, *Picture of Slavery in the United States of America; Being a Practical Illustration of Voluntarysm and Republicanism* (Middleton, Connecticut: Edwin Hunt, 1834). During the 1830's, Bourne was a member of the New York Anti-Slavery Committee, led by the brothers Arthur and Lewis Tappan, according to Betty Fladeland, *Men and Brothers: Anglo-American Antislavery Cooperation* (Urbana: University of Illinois Press, 1972), p. 208.

22. Bourne, *Picture of Slavery*, p. 10.

23. Ibid., p. 26.

24. Ibid., p. 35.

25. Ibid., p. 12.

26. Ibid., p. 75.

27. Ibid., pp. 77-78.

28. Ibid., pp. 6, 77-103.

29. On the rise of New England nationalism, see Lewis P. Simpson, *Mind and the American Civil War: A Meditation on Lost Causes* (Baton Rouge: Louisiana State University Press, 1989); Barbara Jeanne Fields, "Lost Causes, North and South," in *Reviews in American History* vol.20, no.1 (March 1992): 65-71.

30. Bourne, *Picture of Slavery*, p. 6.

31. Walker's Appeal, in *Four Articles; together with a Preamble, to the Colour-*

ed Citizens of the World, but in particular, and very expressly, to those of The United States of America, written in Boston, State of Massachusetts, September 28, 1829 third and last edition, with additional notes, correction, &c. (Boston: Revised and Published by David Walker, 1830).

32. For Walker's biography, see the account by Henry Highland Garnet, published in 1848 along with a new editon of Walker's Appeal. Garnet's sketch of the life of Walker is in Herbert Aptheker, *"One Continual Cry": David Walker's Appeal to the Colored Citizens of the World 1829-1830. Its Setting & its meaning together with the full text of the third—and last—edition of the Appeal* (New York: Humanities Press, 1965), pp. 40-44.

33. *Walker's Appeal,* p. 2.

34. Ibid., p. 3.

35. Ibid., p. 8.

36. Ibid., p. 2.

37. Ibid., p. 8. The other sources of the "system of cruelty and oppression" against black people in the United States were: ignorance, preachers, and colonization. In Walker's view, color prejudice was born under this system of oppression. I shall return to *Walker's Appeal* and his views about racism in chapter four.

38. Ibid., pp. 11-13.

39. Ibid., pp. 15-16.

40. Ibid., p. 19.

41. For an account of the foundation of the New England Anti-Slavery Society, see Walter M. Merrill, *Against Wind and Tide: A Biography of William Lloyd Garrison* (Cambridge: Harvard University Press, 1963), pp. 57-58. For an account of David Child's life, see the biography of his wife Lydia Maria Child by Helene G. Baer, *The Heart is like Heaven: The Life of Lydia Maria Child* (Philadelphia: University of Pennsylvania Press, 1964), pp. 44-45, 108, 175, 298.

42. David L. Child, *The Despotism of Freedom; or the Tyranny and Cruelty of American Republican Slave-Masters, Shown to Be the Worst in the World; in a Speech, Delivered at the First Anniversary of the New England Anti-Slavery Society, 1833* (Boston: The Boston Young Men's Anti-Slavery Association, for the Diffusion of Truth, 1833), p. iii.

43. Ibid., p. 16.

44. Ibid., p. 20.

45. Ibid., pp. 20-21.

46. Ibid., p. 21, 27, 49.

47. Ibid., pp. 25-26. David Child got this "verbal information" about slavery in Brazil from two Brazilian travelers in the United States—Major Frias e Vasconcellos and S. Marques de Sousa—as he explains in a footnote on p. 26.

48. Ibid, p. 42.

49. Ibid., pp. 28-36, for a detailed travelers' account of such crimes by slaveholders against slaves in the South.

50. Ibid., p. 39.

51. Ibid., pp. 61-62.

52. Ibid., pp. 21-22. Child did not defend disunion at this time, but only the right to debate slavery and change the Constitution by amendment, ibid., p. 25. During the 1840's he became a disunionist along with Garrison, Phillips, and other

members of the American Anti-Slavery Society.

53. "The South Sea Islander," in *The Abolitionist* no. 5 (May 1833): 74.

54. George Bourne, *The Book and Slavery Irreconcilable. with Animadversions upon Dr. Smith's Philosophy* (Philadelphia, J. M Sanderson & Co, 1816), p. 171. Facsimile reprint by John W. Christie and Dwight L. Dumond, *George Bourne and the Book and Slavery Irreconcilable* (Baltimore: The Historical Society of Delaware; Philadelphia: the Presbyterian Historical Society, 1969).

55. I use the expression "neglected period," according to Alice Felt Tyler, *Freedom's Ferment: Phases of American Social History from the Colonial Period to the Outbreak of the Civil War* (New York: Harper & Row, Publishers, 1962), pp.470-472.

56. John Kenrick, *Horrors of Slavery. In Two Parts* (Cambridge: Hilliard and Metcalf, 1817), p.3. Kenrick was the President of the New England Anti-Slavery Society at the time of his death in 1833. For his obituary, see *The Abolitionist*, no.6 (June 1833).

57. Kenrick, *Horrors of Slavery*, pp. 35-37.

58. Child, *The Despotism of Freedom*, p. 30.

59. Lydia Maria Child, ed., *The Oasis* (Boston: Allen and Ticknor, 1834), p. 214.

60. "Continuation of Extracts from the Annual Report," in *The Abolitionist* no.3 (March 1833): 33-35.

61. "Letter to George Washington," in *The Abolitionist* no.1 (January 1833): 12-14. The letter was written in 1796 and "silently returned" to the author, as the editor of the paper explains. Another example of an old letter by an Englishman highlighting the inconsistency of the founding fathers can be found in "Fragment of an Original Letter on the Slavery of the Negroes, written in the Year of 1776," *The Liberator* vol.1, no.16 (April 16, 1831). The author of the letter was Thomas Day, Esq.. The letter was printed in London in 1824. Robert Dale Owen, editor of the New York *Free Inquirer* sent a manuscript to W.L. Garrison as a contribution to the antislavery struggle.

62. Child, *The Despotism of Freedom*, pp. 43-45. Child's source for this account is *Letters* by the Reverend Mr. Rankin who quoted a letter by the Reverend William Dickey, from Bloomingsburg, of October 8, 1824, describing the crime of Jefferson's nephew.

63. Louis Ruchames, ed., *The Abolitionists: A Collection of their Writings* (New York: G.P. Putnam's Sons, 1963), pp. 171-174. The same sentiment of joy and hope could be aroused among abolitionists in relation to the sisters Grimké. Like Birney, Angelina and Sarah Grimké rejected both slavery and their position as mistresses of a South Carolina plantation by moving to the North and engaging in abolitionist activities. On the Grimkés' life, see Gerda Lerner, *The Grimké Sisters from South Carolina Rebels Against Slavery* (Boston: Houghton Mifflin Company, 1967).

64. I use the term imagination as the nearest equivalent to the notion of "imaginaire" used by Cornelius Castoriadis, *A Instituição Imaginária da Sociedade* (Rio de Janeiro: Paz e Terra, 1982). For Castoriadis "imaginaire," does not mean the image of, but the perennial creation of figures, forms, images which allows us to talk about something. That which we define as "reality" and "rationality" are produced by the "imaginaire," p. 13, 410. For the English translation, see *The Imaginary Institution of Society* (Cambridge: MIT Press, 1987).

65. *American Slavery as It Is: Testimony of a Thousand Witnesses* (New York: The American Anti-Slavery Society, 1839), p.9. Facsimile reprint by William Loren Katz, ed., (New York: Arno Press and The New York Times, 1968). This book was published anonymously to protect the authors against possible attack by anti-abolitionist mobs. Theodore Dwight Weld compiled the antislavery testimonies, taken mainly from Southern newspapers of recent date, with the help of his wife, Angelina Grimké, and her sister Sarah. Wendell Phillips referred to Weld's book as "that encyclopaedia of facts and storehouse of arguments," quoted in Ruchames, *The Abolitionists*, p. 164.

66. Richard Hildreth concluded his book *The Slave: Or Memoirs of Archy Moore* (Boston: John H. Eastburn, Printer, 1836) by stressing that the United States was unique in its wickdeness against slaves and free black people. After escaping from slavery and engaging as a sailor in the British navy, Archy Moore says: "I have climbed the lofty crests of the Andes, and wandered among the flowery forests of Brazil. Everywhere I have seen the hateful empire of aristocratic usurpation....But everywhere, or almost every where, I have seen the bondsmen beginning to forget the base lore of traditionary subserviency, and already feeling the impulses and lisping in the language of freedom. I have seen it every where;—every where, except in my native America ... In Catholic Brazil,—in the Spanish islands, where one might expect to find tyranny aggravated by ignorance and superstition, the slave is still regarded as a man, and as entitled to something of human sympathies," ibid., vol.2, pp. 160-163.

67. Child, *The Despotism of Freedom*, p. 47.

68. It is interesting to notice how many of these abolitionist ideas about the American racial hell and the Brazilian racial paradise were incorporated, perhaps unconsciously, by twentieth-century scholars like Gilberto Freyre and Frank Tannenbaum, whose studies I have analyzed in the Introduction.

69. The Rev. Daniel P. Kidder noticed the great demand for French books in Rio de Janeiro in his *Sketches of Residence and Travels in Brazil embracing Historical and Geographical Notices of the Empire and its Several Provinces* 2 vols. (Philadelphia: Sorin & Ball, 1845), pp. 115-116.

70. Joaquim Nabuco, *O Abolicionismo* (Londres: Typographia de Abraham Kingdon & Ca., 1883), p. 133.

71. Ibid., p. 134.

72. Ibid., p. 23.

73. Ibid., p. 23. I shall analyze the American and Brazilian abolitionists' views of racism, as well as the comparisons they drew betweem racism in the two countries, in chapter four.

74. José do Patrocínio, the chief editor and owner of the abolitionist paper *Gazeta da Tarde*, was the son of a Rio de Janeiro planter and priest of European descent and a woman grocer of African descent. He began his career as a journalist in 1877, but he engaged in abolitionist activities from the 1881 onwards. He was a founder of the Abolitionist Confederation on May 12, 1883 at Rio de Janeiro. Evaristo de Moraes, *A Campanha Abolicionista 1879-1888* (Rio de Janeiro: Leite Ribeiro, 1924), pp. 357-377.

75. Cincinnatus, *O Elemento Escravo e as Questões Econômicas do Brazil* (Bahia: Typographia dos Dous Mundos, 1885), p.2.

76. *Folhinha Offerecida pela Redempção aos seus Assignantes—de 1887 a 1888* (January 1888). This special number was published to commemorate the first year of the paper. It put together all the cases denounced in the section, "Chronicle of Years" during 1887.

77. Even the more radical abolitionists of *A Redempção* debated whether a law of abolition should relieve the emancipated slaves of compulsory work at their former masters' plantations for a term of years. Only when the slaves began to leave the São Paulo plantations in large numbers, that is, from October 1887 onwards, did the abolitionists of *A Redempção* decide to demand immediate abolition with no condition of work on the part of the slaves. I have analyzed this shift of positions by the abolitionists of *A Redempção* in *Onda Negra, Medo Branco: O Negro no Imaginário das Elites século xix* (Rio de Janeiro: Paz e Terra, 1987), pp, 227-234. I shall return to the topic of the abolitionists' reflections about the destiny of the slave in chapter four.

78. Luis Anselmo da Fonseca, *A Escravidão, o Clero e o Abolicionismo*, facsimile reprint of 1887 (Recife: Fundação Joaquim Nabuco/Editora Massangana, 1988), p. 576.

79. Nabuco, *O Abolicionismo*, pp. 19-20.

80. Cincinnatus, *O Elemento Escravo e as Questões Econômicas do Brazil*, pp. 7-8.

81. Ibid., pp. 9-10.

82. "Conferência Abolicionista," in *Gazeta da Tarde* no.93 (April 25, 1887).

83. On the assimilation of evolutionist theories by the elite in nineteenth-century Brazil, see Ivan Lins, *História do Positivismo no Brasil* (São Paulo: Nacional, 1964); Richard Graham, "Spencer e o Progresso," in *Grã-Bretanha e o Início da Modernização no Brasil 1850-1914* (São Paulo: Brasiliense, 1973); Thomas E. Skidmore, *Preto no Branco: Raça e Nacionalidade no Pensamento Brasileiro* (Rio de Janeiro: Paz e Terra, 1976). I shall return to this topic in chapter four.

84. *Propaganda Abolicionista. Cartas de Vindex ao Dr. Luiz Alvares dos Santos publicadas no "Diário da Bahia."* (Bahia: Typographia do Diario, 1875), pp. 9-10.

85. "A Revolução de 1817 e a Emancipação," in *O Abolicionista*, no.12 (September 28, 1881): 133, facsimile reprint (Recife: Fundação Joaquim Nabuco/Editora Massangana, 1988); Nabuco, *O Abolicionismo*, pp. 47-49; *Propaganda Abolicionista. Cartas de Vindex*, pp. 3-4.

86. "Ad Perpetuum," in *O Abolicionista* no.2 (December 1, 1880).

87. In 1880 Spain decreed a law of gradual abolition for Cuba establishing a system of apprenticeship for the emancipated slaves. A second law in 1886 decreed total abolition in Cuba. José Martinez Carreras, "Espana y la Abolicion de la Esclavitud Durante el Siglo xix," in Francisco de Solano, ed., *Estudios sobre la Abolición de la Esclavitud* (Madrid: Centro de Estudios Históricos, Departamento de História da America, 1986), pp. 177-179.

CHAPTER III

1. Louis Ruchames, ed., *The Abolitionists—A Collection of their writings.* (New York: G.P. Putnam's Sons, 1963), pp.79-81. The Declaration was written by W. L. Garrison.

2. Ruy Barbosa, "Pelos Escravos às Mães de Família," in *Elogio do Poeta pe-lo Dr. Ruy Barbosa seguido de um escripto do mesmo Autor Pelos Escravos às Mães de Família mandados imprimir pela Commissão do Decennario.* (Bahia: Typographia do "Diário da Bahia," 1881), pp.13-14.

3. *Manifesto da Sociedade Brasileira contra a Escravidão* (Rio de Janeiro: Typ. de G. Leuzinger & Filhos, no date), p.9. This Declaration was written in 1880 by Joaquim Nabuco for the inauguration of the Brazilian Anti-Slavery Society. See J. Nabuco, "Terceira Conferência" [Third Lecture held at Saint Isabel Theather on November 16, 1884], in *Conferências e Discursos Abolicionistas*. Obras Completas. (São Paulo: Instituto Progresso Editorial S.A., 1949), vol. 7, p.310.

4. L. Ruchames, *The Abolitionists*, p. 79.

5. R. Barbosa, "Pelos Escravos às Mães de Família," pp.10-11. On the role of women as seen in Brazilian society by the mid-nineteenth century, see June E. Hahner, *Emancipating The Female Sex: The Struggle for Women's Rights in Brazil, 1850-1940* (Durham and London: Duke University Press, 1990).

6. Among the Northeastern states, Bahia, with 165,403 slaves, or 12.5 percent of the state population, had the greatest number of slaves in 1874. At that time Minas Gerais, more to the South, had 311,304 slaves, representing 15.9 percent of the total population of the state; Rio de Janeiro had 301,352, representing 39.7 percent of the total population; and São Paulo had 174,622 slaves, representing 20.4 percent of the total population. See Robert Conrad, *Os Últimos Anos da Escravatura no Brasil*, 2nd edition, (Rio de Janeiro: Civilização Brasileira, 1978), table 2, p. 345.

7. Lydia Maria Child, ed., *The Oasis* (Boston: Allen and Ticknor, 1834), pp. 19-20.

8. John W. Christie and Dwight L. Dumond, *George Bourne and the Book and Slavery Irreconcilable* (Baltimore, Maryland: The Historical Society of Delaware, Wilmington, Delaware; Philadelphia, Penn.: The Presbyterian Historical Society, 1969), pp.169-170. *The Book and Slavery Irreconcilable with Animadversions upon Dr. Smith's Philosophy* was published in Philadelphia in 1816.

9. Elizabeth Heyrick ("A Member of the Society of Friends"), *Immediate, not Gradual Abolition* (Philadelphia: Philadelphia A. S. Society, 1837), p. 4, pp.11-12. Historians have called attention to the impact of this pamphlet in the Northern United States. See, among others, Betty L. Fladeland, *Men and Brothers: Anglo-American Anti-Slavery Cooperation* (Urbana: University of Illinois Press, 1972). Heyrick first published her pamphlet in England in 1824. The 1837 Philadelphia editors explained on the back of the front cover that this pamphlet changed the "gradualist" views of Wilberforce and other leading British abolitionists: "they now attacked slavery as a sin to be forsaken *immediately*, and the result is known." A limited edition was also published in 1824 in Philadelphia. The 1837 edition was the third to be published in the United States.

10. J. Nabuco, *O Abolicionismo* (Londres: Typographia de Abraham Kingdon E. Ca., 1883), pp.6-7.

11. See Emília Viotti da Costa, *Da Senzala à Colônia*. 2nd ed. (São Paulo: Livraria Editora Ciências Humanas, 1982), p.425; and Richard Graham, "Causes for the Abolition of Negro Slavery in Brazil: an Interpretive Essay," in *The Hispanic American Historical Review*, vol.46, no.2 (May 1966). Rebecca Baird Bergstresser suggests that the abolitionist movement was related to specific needs and problems

of certain professional groups in Rio de Janeiro in the 1880's: for example, the military, the engineers, and urban businessmen. One of these problems was economic policies geared to export agriculture, which constituted a burden for citizens of Rio de Janeiro. See her *The Movement for the Abolition of Slavery in Rio de Janeiro, Brazil, 1880-1889* (Ph.D. dissertation, Stanford University, February 1973), pp. 96-97. But the planters also belonged to urban life, as Cleveland Donald, Jr. shows for Campos, located in the state of Rio de Janeiro. He suggests that "Campos city functioned as the center of planter culture and sociability," in his *Slavery and Abolition in Campos, Bra-zil, 1830-1888* (Ph.D. dissertation, Cornell University, August, 1973), pp.108-111.

12. The main leaders of the abolitionist movement in Brazil in the 1880's, like Joaquim Nabuco, José do Patrocínio, André Rebouças, Raul Pompéia, Carlos Lacerda, had familial or business relations with plantations. The fact that they spent most of their lives living in the cities does not mean that their links with the planters' interest were less strong. I shall return to this topic next chapter in showing the Brazilian abolitionists' views concerning the destiny of the slaves and people of African descent in general.

13. *Propaganda Abolicionista. Cartas de Vindex ao Dr. Luiz Alvares dos Santos publicadas no "Diário da Bahia."* (Bahia: Typographia do Diario, 1875), p. 28.

14. J. Nabuco, *O Abolicionismo*, pp. 6-7.

15. On the perception of slave power by American abolitionists see Larry Gara, "Slavery and the Slave Power: A Crucial Distinction," in *Civil War History*, vol.15, no.1 (March 1969): 5-18. Eric Foner points to the origens of the term "slave power", and the different ways abolitionists made use of this notion during the 1830's, 1840's, and 1850's in *Free Soil, Free Labor, Free Men: The Ideology of the Republican Party before the Civil War* (London: Oxford University Press, 1970), pp. 73-102.

16. For the theme of increasing slave criminality during the 1870's, see my *Onda Negra, Medo Branco. O negro no imaginário das elites, século xix* (Rio de Janeiro: Paz e Terra, 1987), chapter 3. The cited case is on p.186. See also Maria Helena P. T. Machado, *Crime e Escravidão: trabalho, luta e resistências nas lavouras paulistas, 1830-1888* (São Paulo: Brasiliense, 1987); for slave rebellions and criminality during the last century of slavery in Brazil see among others: Lana Lage da Gama Lima, *Rebeldia Negra e Abolicionismo* (Rio de Janeiro: Achiame, 1981); Clóvis Moura, *Rebeliões da Senzala*, 3rd ed. (São Paulo: Ciências Humanas, 1981); Suely R. Reis de Queirós, *Escravidão Negra em São Paulo (Um Estudo das Tensões Provocadas pelo Escravismo no Século XIX)* Rio de Janeiro: José Olympio, 1977); João José Reis, *Rebelião Escrava no Brasil—A História do Levante dos Males (1835)* (São Paulo: Brasiliense, 1986). Leila Mezan Algranti, *O Feitor Ausente—Estudos sobre a Escravidão Urbana no Rio de Janeiro, 1808-1821* (Petrópolis: Vozes, 1988); Maria Helena Machado, *O Plano e o Pânico: Os Movimentos Sociais na Década da Abolição* (Rio de Janeiro: Editora UFRJ; São Paulo: EDUSP, 1994).

17. Padre M. Ribeiro Rocha, *Ethiope Resgatado, Empenhado, Sustentado, Corrigido, Instruido e Libertado* (Lisboa: O. P. Francisco Luiz Ameno, 1758), pp.211-212. David Brion Davis would not consider Rocha a pioneer of abolitionism since he did not challenge the legality of slavery as an institution. See his *The Problem of Slavery in Western Culture* (New York: Oxford University Press, 1988), p.196. Ronaldo Vainfas, *Ideologia & Escravidão—Os Letrados e a Sociedade Escravista no Brasil Colonial* (Petrópolis: Vozes, 1986) , p. 147, and Silvia Hunold Lara, *Campos da*

Violência—escravos e senhores na capitania do Rio de Janeiro 1750-1808 (Rio de Janeiro: Paz e Terra, 1988), p. 47, 54, are of the same opinion. The fact is that Padre Rocha suggested to emancipate children born of slave mothers 22 years before a very similar bill was voted in Pennsylvania in 1780, the first Abolition Law of slavery in the Americas. The difference between Rocha's proposal and the Pennsylvania Emancipation Bill was that the first wanted the children to serve their mother's masters until 14 or 15 years old, whereas the second decreed that Negroes emancipated by the bill were to serve until they were 28 years old. P.Rocha, *Ethiope Resgatado, Empenhado, Sustentado, Instruido e Libertado*, p.75, 81. For the Pennsylvania Emancipation Bill, see Arthur Zilversmit, *The First Emancipation — The Abolition of Slavery in the North* (Chicago: The University of Chicago Press, 1967), pp.126-131. Padre Rocha was acknowledged as a true pioneer of abolitionism during the nineteenth century. In visiting Brazil in 1828 and 1829, the British clergyman R. Walsh searched for Padre Rocha's book at Rio de Janeiro libraries. He had some difficulty finding it, and suspected that copies of it had "disappeared," for the issue of the total abolition of the slave trade was then "of general concern in Brazil." After reading it, he judged it necessary to make "some extracts, as specimens of the notions entertained by the enlightened Portuguese, seventy years ago, on the subject" of slavery. See his *Notices of Brazil in 1828 and 1829*, 2 volumes (London: Frederick Westley and A. H. Davis, 1830), 2nd vol., pp.315-319. For a recent edition of Padre Ribeiro Rocha's book, see Paulo Suess, ed., Manoel Ribeiro Rocha: *Ethiope Resgatado, Empenhado, Sustentado, Instruido e Libertado* (Petrópolis: Vozes, 1992).

18. P. Rocha, *Ethiophe Resgatado, Empenhado, Sustentado, Corrigido, Instruido e Libertado*, pp.276-277.

19. José Bonifácio de Andrada e Silva, *Representação à Assembléa Geral Constituinte e Legislativa do Império do Brasil sobre a Escravatura. Deputado à dita Asembléa pela Provincia de S. Paulo* (Rio de Janeiro: Typographia de J.E.S. Cabral, 1840), p.2.

20. Ibid., p.v.

21. This letter was to be read by Nabuco at the banquet in Paris, which Nabuco held for journalists in commemorating the abolition of slavery at Ceará in 1884. Ceará, in the Northeastern region of Brazil, was the first state to decree the end of slavery. See Osório Duque-Estrada, *A Abolição (Esboço Histórico) 1831-1888*, with a preface by Ruy Barbosa (Rio de Janeiro: Livraria Editora Leite Ribeiro & Maurillo, 1918), p.122. On the Enlightenement and the idea of race, see Leon Poliakov, "A Antropologia das Luzes," in *O Mito Ariano—Ensaio sobre as fontes do racismo e dos nacionalismos* (São Paulo: Editora Perspectiva; EDUSP, 1974), pp.131-159 (chapter 7).

22. Luís Nicolau Fagundes Varela, *Poesias Completas*, 2 volumes (São Paulo: Companhia Editora Nacional, 1957). Miécio Tati and E. Carrera Guerra are the editors. Fagundes Varela's biography is in Guerra's introduction, "Estudo Crítico", pp.19-117, vol.1.

23. L.N. Fagundes Varela, "O Escravo," in *Poesias Completas*, vol.2, pp.117-120.

24. L.N. Fagundes Varela, "Mauro, O Escravo," in *Poesias Completas*, vol.1, pp.191-214. Fagundes Varela wrote this poem during a trip to the hinterland of São Paulo province at a time when coffee plantations were expanding to the West. It was published in 1864 as the opening poem of his *Vozes d'America*. See introduction by Guerra, ibid, p.49, and his footnote to the above poem, p.212.

25. J. Nabuco, *A Escravidão* (edited from the original manuscript by José Antônio Gonçalves de Mello) (Recife: Fundação Joaquim Nabuco; Editora Massangana, 1988), pp. 58-60. This book was written in 1870 when Nabuco was a Law student at Recife, capital of Pernambuco in the Northeastern region of Brazil.

26. J. Nabuco, *O Abolicionismo*, p.25.

27. To David T. Haberly the character of the abolitionist campaign was "uniquely and peculiarly Brazilian," for it made use of "racial stereotypes that were simultaneously anti-slavery and anti-slave." Haberly suggests that Brazilian abolitionists considered slavery bad because it forced white people into close contact with evil and violent Negroes. See his "Abolitionism in Brazil: Anti-Slavery and Anti-Slave," in *Luso-Brazilian Review* vol.9, n.2 (December 1972): 30, 33. Haberly concludes by suggesting that if Brazil is ever to achieve racial justice, "a basic first step is clearly the abolition of Abolitionism." p.46.

28. Michèle Duchet suggests that the theme of the slave rebellion was essential for the formation of antislavery opinion among French philosophers. See her "La Ideologia Colonial: La Critica del Sistema Esclavista," in *Antropologia e História en El Siglo de las Luces* (Siglo XXI, 1984), chapter 3, pp.127-141.

29. J. Nabuco, *O Abolicionismo*, p. 17.

30. Wm. Lloyd Garrison, *Thoughts on African Colonization or An Impartial Exhibition of the Doctrines, Principles and Purposes of the American Colonization Society. Together with the Resolutions, Addresses, and Remonstrances of the Free People of Color* (Boston: Garrison and Knapp, 1832), pp.33-34.

31. According to John W. Blassingame, 68 narratives of fugitive slaves were published before the Civil War. Thirty-three were written by former slaves themselves, or "edited by trustworthy whites, and/or can be corroborated by independent sources." See his *Slave Testimony—Two Centuries of Letters, Speeches, Interviews and Autobiographies* (Baton Rouge: Louisiana State University Press, 1977), p.xli. My point here is not to inquire about the real authorship of the narratives, but to suggest that they were part of an abolitionist effort to create the idea of the brother slave. I will return to this topic later in this chapter. For some of the most important narratives by fugitive slaves see Henry Louis Gates, Jr., ed., *The Classic Slave Narratives: The Life of Olaudah Equiano, the History of Mary Prince, Narrative of the Life of Frederick Douglass, Incidents in the Life of a Slave Girl* (Ontario, Canada: New American Library, 1987).

32. See among others: Leon F. Litwack, "Abolitionism: White and Black," in *North of Slavery—The Negro in the Free States 1790-1860* (Chicago: The University of Chicago Press, 1961), chapter 7; James Brewer Stewart, *Holy Warriors —The Abolitionists and American Slavery* (New York: Hill and Wang, 1976); Jane H. Pease and William H. Pease, *They who would be free—Blacks' Search for Freedom, 1830-1861* (Urbana: University of Illinois Press, 1990); R.J. M. Blackett, *Building an Antislavery Wall— Black Americans in the Atlantic Abolitionist Movement 1830-1860* (Baton Rouge: Louisiana State University Press, 1983).

33. Carol Buchalter Stapp, "Afro-Americans in Antebellum Boston: An Analysis of Probate Records," 2 volumes (Ph.D. dissertation, The George Washington University, 1990), p.259, 26. On the "politics of repression," an expression of L.F. Litwack, see his *North of Slavery*, pp.64-112.

34. J.H. Pease and W.H. Pease, *They who would be free*, pp.3-16.

35. Ira Berlin, "Time, Space, and the Evolution of Afro-American Society on

British Mainland North America," in *American Historical Review* vol.85, n.1 (February, 1980): 45-48, 53.

36. L.F. Litwack, *North of Slavery*, pp.10-12. Black and white Americans were "heirs of the same promise"of liberty and equality, according to Benjamin Quarles. See his *The Negro in the American Revolution* (New York: Norton & Company, 1973), pp.182-200, chapter 10. On "the impact of the American Revolution on the Black Population" see Willie Lee Rose, *Slavery and Freedom* (New York: Oxford University Press, 1982), chapter 1, pp. 3-17.

37. L.F. Litwack, *North of Slavery*, pp.191-196. See also, J.H. Pease and W.H. Pease, *They who would be free*, pp.17-28. On "the humanized, liberating Christology" of black priests see Carol V.R. George, "Widening the Circle—The Black Church and the Abolitionist Crusade, 1830-1860," in Lewis Perry and Michael Fellman, editors, *Antislavery Reconsidered—New Perspectives on the Abolitionists* (Baton Rouge: Louisiana State University Press, 1979), pp.88-91.

38. L.F. Litwack, *North of Slavery*, p.214.

39. J. Nabuco, *O Abolicionismo*, p.17, 25.

40. "Mulatos e negros escravocratas," in *A Redempção*, no.74 (September 25, 1887): p. 3.

41. Agostinho Marques Perdigão Malheiro, *A Escravidão no Brasil—Ensaio Histórico-Jurídico-Social* (Rio de Janeiro: Typographia Nacional, 1867), pp.13-14.

42. Robert Conrad, *Os Últimos Anos da Escravatura no Brasil* 2nd edition (Rio de Janeiro: Civilização Brasileira, 1978), p.345, table 2. According to Herbert S. Klein, the free black population was increasing in Brazil by the mid-nineteenth century. See his "Os Homens Livres de Cor na Sociedade Escravista," in *Dados* no.17 (1978): 3-27.

43. Domingos José Nogueira Jaguaribe, *Algumas Palavras sobre a Emigração—Meios Práticos de Colonisar Colônias do Barão de Porto-Feliz e Estatística do Brasil* (São Paulo: "Diário," 1877), pp.41-42. For the rise of the current of political opinion favoring immigration from Europe, and also from the defeated American South, see my *Onda Negra, Medo Branco*, chapters 1 and 2.

44. See the decade-by-decade estimates from 1781 to 1855 by Herbert S. Klein, "Tráfico de Escravos," in *Estatísticas Históricas do Brasil—Séries Econômicas, Demográficas e Sociais de 1550 a 1985* (Rio de Janeiro: IBGE, 1987), p.58, table 2.2.

45. J. Nabuco, *Minha Formação* (Brasília: Editora Universidade de Brasília, 1963), p.40. Visiting Brazil in 1845, an American minister, the Reverend Daniel P. Kidder, was astonished at "the vast amount of infidel literature in circulation", like the works of Voltaire, Volney, and Rousseau. He also noticed that "the French language has usurped the place of Latin in Brazil." See his *Sketches of Residence and Travels in Brazil, embracing historical and geographical notices of the Empire and its several provinces* 2 volumes (Philadelphia: Sorin & Ball, 1845), vol.1, pp. 115-116.

46. Robert W. Slenes suggests that European travelers discovered Africa in part by visiting Brazil, whereas Africa remained hidden from the Brazilian elite who despised, ignored and feared everything related to African cultures. See his "'Malungu, ngoma vem!': África coberta e descoberta no Brasil," in *Revista USP* no.12 (December/ January/ February, 1991-1992): 49, 67. Slenes suggests that by that time there were "two antagonistic Brazils, two peoples, or ideas of people, in conflict," p.67. Writing during the 1880's, Sylvio Romero noticed that Brazilian scholars did not give any attention to the study of African languages and religions,

whereas British scholars would spend years in the African hinterland researching African culture. "It is a shame for the science of Brazil ... we that have the material at home, that have Africa in our kitchens, as America in our jungles, and Europe in our living-rooms, we have produced nothing about this! It is a disgrace." Quoted in Nina Rodrigues, *Os Africanos no Brasil* 2nd ed. (São Paulo: Cia. Editora Nacional, 1935), pp.10-11.

47. Roger Bastide, *Les Réligions Africaines au Bresil—vers une sociologie des interpénétrations de civilisations* (Paris: Presses Universitaires de France, 1960), p.174.

48. Ibid, pp.165-172, 197.

49. Ibid, pp.152-154.

50. Ibid, pp.186-193. Followers of Black Catholicism might also have been followers of African religions. See Maria Inês Cortes de Oliveira, *O Liberto: o seu Mundo e os Outros* Salvador, 1790/1890 (São Paulo: Corrupio; Brasília, D.F.: CNPq, 1988), pp. 48-51, 77, 82.

51. According to the Rev. Mr. Kidder, "Portugal had never published the Bible, or countenanced its circulation, save in connection with notes and comments that had been approved by inquisitorial censorship." During the 1840's ignorance of the Bible seemed to remain the same as during the Colonial era. Kidder was struck by the fact that he could not find a single copy of the Bible at the library of a deceased bishop of São Paulo. See his *Sketches of Residence and Travels in Brazil*, p. 137, 255-256.

52. See Eugene D. Genovese, "The Rock and the Church", in *Roll Jordan, Roll —The World the Slaves Made* (New York: Vintage Books, 1976), Book 2, pp. 161-284. On Nat Turner and the importance of his knowledge of the Bible for his rise as a slaves' leader see, Herbert Aptheker, *Nat Turner's Slave Rebellion* (New York: Grove Press, Inc., 1966), pp. 35-37.

53. Gilberto Freyre, "Ascensão do Bacharel e do Mulato," in *Sobrados e Mucambos — Decadência do Patriarcado Rural e Desenvolvimento do Urbano* 3 volumes (Rio de Janeiro: José Olympio Editora, 1951), vol.3, chapter 11, pp.949-1038.

54. Ibid, pp. 951-954.

55. Ibid, p. 954.

56. Ibid, pp. 957-959.

57. Ibid, pp. 973-975.

58. Ibid, pp. 976-985. Freyre himself noticed the same phenomenon of passage during a visit to the United States; see, *Sobrados e Mucambos*, pp.974-975. He suggests that in the United States, as in Brazil, the "pink mulattoes," that is, those who were blond and even had blue eyes, were the most successful in passing to the white world, especially in places where their origins were unknown; pp. 984-985.

59. José do Patrocínio, *Motta Coqueiro ou a pena de morte* (Rio de Janeiro: Francisco Alves Editora, 1977), p.36. This book was published in 1877 when Patrocínio was not yet an abolitionist leader. He was born in Rio de Janeiro of a woman of African descent and a priest-planter of Portuguese descent. For another of his hideous black characters, see the description of the woman slave and witch, Balbina, p.67.

60. W. E. B. Du Bois, *The Souls of Black Folk* (New York: New American Library, 1982), p.45.

61. The expression "twoness" is from Du Bois, *The Souls of Black Folk*, p.45.

62. André Rebouças, *Diário e Notas Autobiográficas*, edited by Ana Flora e Inácio José Veríssimo (Rio de Janeiro: José Olympio Ed., 1938), pp.161-162. On Rebouças and the issue of racism, see Leo Spitzer, *Lives in Between—assimilation and marginality in Austria, Brazil, West Africa 1780-1945* (Cambridge: Cambridge University Press, 1989). Thomas Flory suggests that the issue of racism in Brazil had been kept under wraps in Brazil since the mid-1830's owing, among other reasons, to the fear of the possibility of society disintegrating along racial lines. See his "Race and Social Control in Independent Brazil," in *Latin American Studies*, vol.9, no.2, p. 217.

63. On the abolitionist search for empathy with the slave, see Aileen S. Kraditor, *Means and Ends in American Abolitionism—Garrison and his critics on strategy and tactics, 1834-1850* (New York: Pantheon Books, 1969), pp. 237-238.

64. *Walker's Appeal, in Four Articles; together with a preamble, to the Coloured Citizens of the World, but in particular, and very expressly, to those of the United States of America, written in Boston, State of Massachusetts, September 28, 1829*, (Third and Last Edition, with additional notes, corrections, &c.; Boston: Revised and Published by David Walker, 1830), p.22.

65. Wm. Lloyd Garrison, *Thoughts on African Colonization*, p.25, 35. Garrison was so enthusiastic about the civilizing mission of the evangelists in Africa that he expected that even the African climate would "grow sweet and salubrious as her forests disappear, and the purifying influences of Christianity penetrate into the interior," p.37

66. *Walker's Appeal*, p. 22.

67. Ibid, p. 22.

68. Ibid, p. 10, 22.

69. Henry Highland Garnet, *The Past and Present Condition, and the Destiny, of the Colored Race: A Discourse delivered at the fifteenth anniversary of the Female Benevolent Society of Troy, N.Y., Feb. 14, 1848* (Miami, Florida: Mnemosyne Publishing Inc., 1969), pp.5-8.

70. Ibid, p.12. For the thesis that the Africans were the first Egyptians see also Frederick Douglass, "The Claims of the Negro Ethnologically Considered: An Address delivered in Hudson, Ohio, on 12 July 1854," in John W. Blassingame, ed., *The Frederick Douglass Papers*, series one: Speeches, Debates, and Interviews, 3 volumes (New Haven: Yale University Press, 1979) vol.2, pp.497-525.

71. L. M. Child, "Ruins of Egyptian Thebes," in *The Oasis*, pp.212-213.

72. "Danger of Insurrection," in *The Liberator*, vol.8, no.28 (July 13, 1838).

73. "The Insurrection," in *The Liberator*, vol.1, no.36 (September 3, 1831).

74. Ibid.

75. Ibid.

76. "Slavery Happy Consequences of Slavery!! Interesting from Bahia," in *The Liberator*, vol.5, no.19 (May 9, 1835). This rather long article was published on the cover page, second column from the left; this location can be read as an implicit statement of the importance attributed to the event.

77. David L. Child, *The Despotism of Freedom; or the Tyranny and Cruelty of American Repúblican Slave-Masters, shown to be the worst in the world; in a Speech, delivered at the First Anniversary of the New England Anti-Slavery Society, 1833* (Boston: The Boston Young Men's Anti-Slavery Association, for the Diffusion of Truth, 1833), p.68.

78. "Extracts from an Address, delivered before the N.E. Anti-Slavery

Society, by Wm. J. Snelling, Esq.," in *The Abolitionist*, vol.1, no.5 (May 1833): 70. Snelling refers to Hugh Clapperton and Major Denham, the authors of *Narrative of Travels and Discoveries in Northern and Central Africa, in the years of 1822, 1823, and 1824, by Major Denhan, Captain Clapperton, and the late Doctor Oudney, extending across the Great Desert to the tenth degree of Northern Latitude, and from Kouka in Bornou, to Sackatoo, the capital of the Fellath Empire* (London: J. Murray, 1826).

79. E. Heyrick, *Immediate, not Gradual Abolition*, p.9.

80. Prince Saunders, *A Memoir Presented to the American Convention for Promoting the Abolition of Slavery, and Improving the Condition of the African Race, December 11th, 1818; containing some remarks upon the civil Dissentions of the hitherto afflicted People of Hayti, as the Inhabitants of that Island may be connected with Plans for the Emigration of such Free Persons of Colour as may be disposed to remove to it, in case its Reunion, Pacification and Independence should be established. Together with Some Account of the Origin and Progress of the Efforts for effecting the Abolition of Slavery in Pennsylvania and its neighbourhood, and throughout the World* (Philadelphia: Dennis Heartt, 1818), pp.11-12.

81. "History of Hayti—Lessons of Instruction," in *Radical Abolitionist*, vol.1-4, 1855-1858 (New York: Negro Universities Press, 1969). This article is in vol.3, no.4 (November 1857): 29-30. Holley's lecture was published by the Afric-American Printing Co. in 1857.

82. *Walker's Appeal*, p.14.

83. W. L. Garrison, *Thoughts on African Colonization*, p.120.

84. J. Nabuco, *O Abolicionismo*, pp.136-137, 140.

85. Ibid, p.140, 144-145.

86. J. Nabuco, *A Escravidão*, pp.35-36.

87. Domingos José Nogueira Jaguaribe Filho, *Reflexões sobre a Colonisação no Brasil (approvado com distinção pela Academia de Medicina da Corte)* [approved with distinction by the Academy of Medicine of the Court] (São Paulo and Paris: A.L. Garraux e Cia., Livreiros—Editores, 1878), pp.293-294.

88. João Severiano Maciel da Costa (Do Conselho de Sua Magestade), *Memoria sobre a Necessidade de abolir a introdução dos escravos africanos no Brasil; sobre o modo e condiçõis com que esta abolição se deve fazer; e sobre os meios de remediar a falta de braços que ela pode ocasionar* (Coimbra: Imprensa da Universidade, 1821), p.12.

89. For this brief account of Social Darwinism I am relying on Richard Hofstadter, *Social Darwinism in American Thought* revised edition (Boston: Beacon Press, 1955), p.5, 38-44. On Social Darwinism in Brazil see, Richard Graham, *Grã-Bretanha e o Início da Modernização no Brasil—1850-1914* (São Paulo: Brasiliense, 1973).

90. On Spencer's "evolutionary optimism," see R. Hofstadter, *Social Darwinism in American Thought*, pp.39-40.

91. J. Nabuco, *O Abolicionismo*, pp.144-145, 252-253.

92. Miguel Lemos, *O Pozitivismo e a Escravidão Moderna Trechos estraidos das obras de Augusto Comte, seguidos de documentos pozitivistas relativos à questão dA Escravatura no Brazil e precedidos de uma introdução por Miguel Lemos Prezidente Perpetuo da Sociedade Pozitivista do Rio de Janeiro* (Rio de Janeiro: Sede da Sociedade Pozitivista, 1884), p.21, 60.

93. L.N. Fagundes Varela, "O Escravo," in *Poesias Completas*, vol.2, pp.118.

94. Castro Alves, "Bandido Negro," in *Os Escravos* (São Paulo: Livraria Martins Editora, no date), pp.83-91.

95. Sud Mennucci, *O Precursor do Abolicionismo no Brazil (Luiz Gama)* (São Paulo: Companhia Editora Nacional, 1938), pp.20-26, 54-55. See also, Zelbert L. Moore, "Luis Gama, Abolition and Republicanism in São Paulo, Brazil, 1870-1888" (Ph.D. dissertation, Temple University, January 1978).

96. Ibid, pp.149-153.

97. Luiz Gonzaga Pinto da Gama, "Lá Vai Verso," in *Primeiras Trovas Burlescas* 2nd ed. (Rio de Janeiro: Typ. Pinheiro & C.a, 1861), p.14.

98. Luiz G.P.Gama, "Minha Mãe," in *Primeiras Trovas Burlescas*, pp.183-186.

99. Luiz G.P. Gama, "Junto à Estatua," in *Primeiras Trovas Burlescas*, pp.16-19.

100. *The Slave: or Memoirs of Archy Moore* 2 volumes (Boston: John H. Eastburn, 1836). The name of the real author, Richard Hildreth, did not appear on the first edition, which was presented as the work of Archy Moore, a fugitive slave. The "Advertisement" informed that: "It is unnecessary to detain the reader with a narrative of the somewhat singular manner in which the MS. of the following Memoirs came into my possession. It is sufficient for me to say, that I received it, with an injunction to make it public—an injuction which I have not felt myself at liberty to disobey ... As to the conduct of the author, as he has himself described it, there are several occasions on which it is impossible to approve it. But he has written Memoirs, not an apology nor a vindication. No man who writes his own life, will gain much credit, by painting himself as faultless; and few have better claims to indulgence than Archy Moore—The Editor." On the role of the narratives cementing an emphatic sentiment for the slave, Larry Gara quotes an abolitionist's explanation: "Argument provokes argument, reason is met by sophistry; but narratives of slaves go right to the hearts of men." See L. Gara, *The Liberty Line—The Legend of the Underground Railroad* (Lexington: University of Kentucky Press, 1961), p.124.

101. On Richard Hildreth see, Donald E. Emerson, *Richard Hildreth*, series 64, no.2 (Baltimore: The Johns Hopkins Press, 1946), pp.72-78; and Barbara Ritchie, "Introduction," in *Memoirs of a Fugitive—America's First Antislavery Novel* (New York: Thomas Y. Crowell Company, 1971) pp.v-vii. Both Emerson and Ritchie call attention to the fact that Hildreth's book was the first abolitionist novel; but they do not stress the fact that the first editon was read as a true slave narrative.

102. *The Slave: or Memoirs of Archy Moore*, vol.1, p.139.

103. Harriet Beecher Stowe, *Uncle Tom's Cabin* (New York: Washington Square Press, 1971), chapter 40, pp.418-424. According to Russel B. Nye in his "Introduction" to this edition, *Uncle Tom's Cabin* was first published in installments in *The National Era* running from June 5, 1851 to April 1, 1852. The book appeared in two volumes in 1852, ibid., p.x.

104. Translations of *Uncle Tom's Cabin* to Portuguese were published in Paris and Lisbon under the name of *A Cabana do Pai Tomás* in 1853 and 1856. Information according to David Brookshaw, *Raça e Cor na Literatura Brasileira* (Porto Alegre: Mercado Aberto, 1983), footnote n.11, p.29. *A Cabana do Pai Tomás* was also partially published in installments by *A Redempção*, an abolitionist newspaper published in São Paulo. The installments ran from October 13, 1887 to the last number of the newspaper in May 1888. *The Slave: or Memoirs of Archy Moore* was also translated to

Portuguese in its extended version under the name of *O Escravo Branco Companhei-ro do Tio Thomaz ou A Vida de um Fugitivo na Virginia. Romance de Hildreth. Traducção Livre de L. M. do Couto de Albuquerque* (Lisboa: Typographia de Luiz Correia da Cunha, 1854). It is interesting to notice that the title in Portuguese included a reference to *Uncle Tom's Cabin*, published in Lisbon one year earlier; in English it reads: The white slave a companion to Uncle Tom.

105. José de Alencar, "O Demônio Familiar," in *Teatro Completo* 2 volumes (Rio de Janeiro: Serviço Nacional de Teatro, 1977), vol.2 pp. 97-98. The play was presented for the first time at the Teatro do Ginasio, Rio de Janeiro, on September 5, 1857. On the slave and the Negro in the nineteenth-century Brazilian plays see Flo-ra Sussekind, *O Negro como Arlequim: Teatro & Discriminação* (Rio de Janeiro: Achia-mé, 1982).

106. The expression "the victims-butchers" is taken from the title of what is generally supposed to be the first abolitionist Brazilian novel, *As Victimas - Algozes Quadros da Escravidão Romances* 2 volumes, by Joaquim Manoel de Macedo (Rio de Janeiro: Typ. Americana, 1869). According to David Brookshaw there were rumors that the Emperor D. Pedro II himself asked Macedo to write an antislavery novel to prepare the public for the coming Parliamentary debates on a bill emancipating the newborn children of slave women. See his *Raça e Cor na Literatura Brasileira*, p.33. The main thesis of the book was the one already defended by Alencar in his play: that the masters should purify their homes by expelling the slaves, the butchers of their family life. See also Flora Sussekind, "As Vítimas-Algozes e o Imaginário do Medo"; in this preface to the most recent edition of *As Vítimas-Algozes* (Rio de Janeiro: Fundação Casa de Rui Barbosa; Ed. Scipione,1991), Sussekind calls attention to the theme of the increasing Negro danger that underlay Macedo's central thesis of the need for gradual emancipation, without loss to the slaveowners; p.xxiv. For a more sympathetic view of the slave, see Bernardo Guimaraes, *A Escrava Isaura* (Belo Horizonte: Ed. Itatiaia, no date). This novel was first published in 1875. Isaura, a young girl of light complexion, was an exceptional woman slave and therefore deserved to be emancipated; she was exceptional because she had been educated by her owners, and therefore did not have anything to do with the other barbarian slave characters also appearing in the novel.

CHAPTER IV

1. Wm. Lloyd Garrison, *Thoughts on African Colonization or An Impartial Exhibition of the Doctrines, Principles and Purposes of the American Colonization Society. Together with the Resolutions, Addresses, and Remonstrances of the Free People of Color* (Boston: Garrison and Knapp, 1832), pp. 141-142.

2. "O Sr. Ruy Barbosa e os Abolicionistas," in *O Abolicionista*, vol. 2, no. 12 (September 28, 1881), facsimile edition organized by Leonardo Dantas Silva (Recife: CNPq/Fundação Joaquim Nabuco/Ed. Massangana, 1988), p.133.

3. David L. Child, *The Despotism of Freedom; or the Tyranny and Cruelty of American Repúblican Slave-Masters, shown to be the worst in the world; in a Speech, delivered at the First Anniversary of the New England Anti-Slavery Society, 1833* (Boston:

The Boston Young Men's Anti-Slavery Association, for the Diffusion of Truth, 1833), p.66.

4. *Discussão da Reforma do Estado Servil na Câmara dos Deputados e no Senado 1871. Parte 1, de maio a 31 de julho* (Rio de Janeiro: Typographia Nacional, 1871), pp.167-168. Viscount of Rio Branco delivered this speech on July 14, 1871. The representatives were then discussing the first item of the bill, that is, the emancipation of the slaves' newborn children. The newborn children, called "ingenuos," were to serve their mothers' masters until they were 21 years old.

5. Aileen S. Kraditor, *Means and Ends in American Abolitionism—Garrison and His Critics on Strategy and Tactics, 1834-1850* (New York: Pantheon Books, 1969), p.22.

6. On Northern Afro-Americans' "enslavement by racism," see James Brewer Stewart, *Holy Warriors—The Abolitionists and American Society* (New York: Hill and Wang, 1976), p.125.

7. L. M. Child, ed., *The Oasis* (Boston: Allen and Ticknor, 1834), p.ix.

8. D. Child, *The Despotism of Freedom*, pp.11-13. It is important to remember here that the word racism seems to be of very recent origin, and that it was not used by abolitionists. Usually abolitionists referred to "color prejudice" against black Americans. According to Robert Miles there is no reference to the word racism in the *Oxford English Dictionary* of 1910, but only entries for race and racial. See his *Racism* (London: Routledge, 1989), p.42. By the same token, Christian Delacampagne calls attention to the fact that the word racism began to be used in France only during the 1930's. See his, *L'Invention du Racisme—Antiquité et Moyen-Age* (Paris: Fayard, 1983), p.14. I mean by racism an ideology that began to become systematic by the turn of the eighteenth century, and whose key concept is race. On the ideology of race and its historical formation in the United States see Barbara J. Fields, "Ideology and Race in American History," in J. Morgan Kousser and James M. Macpherson, *Region, Race and Reconstruction* (New York: Oxford University Press, 1982); and "Slavery, Race and Ideology in the United States of America," in New Left Review, no. 181 (May/June 1990).

9. D. Child, *The Despotism of Freedom*, pp. 8-9.

10. Ibid, pp. 8-9.

11. Ibid, p. 9.

12. Frederick Douglass, "British Racial Attitudes and Slavery: An Address Delivered in NewCastle-Upon-Tyne, England, on 23 February 1860," in John W. Blassingame, ed., *The Frederick Douglass Papers Series One: Speeches, Debates, and Interviews* vol.3: 1855-63 (New Haven and London: Yale University Press, 1985), pp.334-336.

13. Henry Koster, *Travels in Brazil* (London: Longman, Hurst, Rees, Orme, and Brown, 1816), p.v, 184-186.

14. Manuela Carneiro da Cunha, "Notes and Documents 'On the Amelioration of Slavery' by Henry Koster," in *Slavery and Abolition—A Journal of Comparative Studies*, vol.2, no.3 (December 1990), p. 369. Carneiro da Cunha also reproduces Koster's article, ibid, pp. 377-398. Koster's article was originally published in *Pamphleteer*, no.16, a journal founded in 1813 with the intention of preserving essays circulating as mere pamphlets, according to Carneiro da Cunha, p.370. Carneiro da Cunha calls attention to this article as giving rise to the "the paradox of seeing Bra-

zil, which would be the last American country to abolish slavery, years later, elected to the status of an example to the British abolitionists," p.369.

15. H. Koster, *Travels in Brazil*, p.1.

16. Ibid., pp. 211-215, 281-282.

17. Ibid., p. 390, 402-403.

18. Ibid., p. 391.

19. Ibid., pp. 386-387, 397.

20. Since French was the second language of Brazilian intellectuals throughout the nineteenth century, they might have read Koster's book translated into French two years after the publication of its first edition in London. The title in French is: *Voyages dans la Partie Septentrionale du Bresil: depuis 1809 jusqu'en 1815, comprenant les provinces de Pernambuco (Fernambouc), Seara, Paraiba, Maragnam, etc. 2 t.* (Paris: Delaunay, 1818). The Brazilian abolitionist Elzeário Pinto relies on Koster for his picture of slaveholders in Brazil: "Fortunately in Brazil the *slaveholders* are not as barbarous as the ones in other countries were, as Mr. Koster acknowledges in his writings." See E. Pinto, *Reformas. Emancipação dos Escravos . . . As Sociedades Maçônicas e Abolicionistas do Império* (Bahia: Typ. Constitucional, 1870), p. 21.

21. "Immediate Emancipation," in *The Abolitionists*, vol. 1, no. 3 (March 1833): 37-38. This article quotes Koster's article "On the Amelioration of Slavery."

22. The expression "accurate" in referring to Koster comes from Richard Burton, according to Carneiro da Cunha, "Notes and Documents ʻOn the Amelioration of Slavery' by Henry Koster," p.368. Carneiro da Cunha suggests that many subsequent travelers repeated his observations without quoting him, thus giving the impression of corroborating his information.

23. This is the way a Southern lady — the wife of the United States Consul at Rio de Janeiro—pictured Brazil to Rev. D. P. Kidder, and Rev. J. C. Fletcher. See D. P. Kidder and Rev. J. C. Fletcher, *Brazil and the Brazilians portrayed in Historical and Descriptive Sketches* (Philadelphia: Childs & Peterson; New York: Sheldon Blakeman & CO., 1857), p.133 n. According to Kidder and Fletcher, "In Brazil every thing is in favor of freedom; and such are the facilities for the slave to emancipate himself, and, when emancipated, if he possess the proper qualifications, to ascend to higher eminences than those of a mere free black, that *fuit* will be written against slavery in this Empire before another half-century rolls around . . . Thus, if a man have freedom, money, and merit, no matter how black may be his skin, no place in society is refused him," ibid., p. 133. Kidder suggests that there had been a sympathetic attitude toward the Negro in Brazil since the Colonial era. He identifies philanthropy and the need to Christianize Africans as strong motives leading the Portuguese to trade African slaves to Brazil. See his, *Sketches of Residence and Travels in Brazil embrancing Historical and Geographical Notices of the Empire and its Several Provinces* 2 volumes (Philadelphia: Sorin & Ball, 1845), vol. 2, pp. 44-45. Another traveler to Brazil to whom American abolitionists commonly referred was Rev. R. Walsh. He called attention to the existence of soldiers, respectable citizens, and priests of African descent in Brazil, in his *Notices of Brazil in 1828 and 1829* 2 volumes (London: Frederick Westley and A.H. Davis, 1830), vol.1, pp. 140-141, 366. The article, "Immediate Emancipation, n. iii," in *The Abolitionist*, vol. 1, no. 3 (March 1833) relies both on Walsh and Koster to show that the emancipated slaves were easily integrated in Brazil, among other countries. "Dr. Walsh states that in Brazil there are 600,000

enfranchised persons either Africans or of African descent who were either slaves themselves or are the descendants of slaves. He says they are, generally speaking, `well conducted and industrious persons, who compose indiscriminately different orders of the community. There are among them merchants, farmers, doctors, lawyers, priests and offices of different ranks . . . 'The benefits arising from them, he adds, have disposed the whites to think of making free the whole negro population. . . . Mr. Koster, an Englishman living in Brazil, confirms Mr. Walsh's statement," p.38.

24. "Paper by M. Quintin on the Present Aspect and Future Prospects of the Slavery Question in Brazil," in *Special Report of The Anti-Slavery Conference, Held in Paris in the Salle Herz, on the Twenty-Sixth and Twenty-Seventh August, 1867, under the Presidency of Mons. Edouard Laboulaye, member of the French Institute* (London: The Committee of the British and Foreign Anti-Slavery Society, no date), p.118.

25. F. Douglass, "Citizenship and the Spirit of Caste: an Address Delivered in New York, New York, on 11 May 1858," in J. W. Blassingame, ed., *The Frederick Douglass Papers Series One: Speeches, Debates, and Interviews*, vol. 2: 1847-54 (New Haven and London: Yale University Press, 1979), pp. 211-212. The editor suggests that Douglass's sources were D.P.Kidder and J. C. Fletcher, *Brazil and the Brazilians* (1857), and also Thomas Ewbank, *Life in Brazil* (1856), ibid., pp.211-212, n.3.

26. David J. Hellwig, ed., *African-American Reflections on Brazil's Racial Paradise* (Philadelphia: Temple University Press, 1992), pp. xi-xii. See also on Afro-Americans and the idea of the Brazilian racial paradise in the first decades of the twentieth century, D. J. Hellwig, "A New Frontier in a Racial Paradise: Robert S. Abbott's Brazilian Dream," and Teresa Meade and Gregory Alonso Pirio, "In Search of the Afro-American "Eldorado": Attempts by North American Blacks to Enter Brazil in the 1920s", in *Luso-Brazilian Review*, vol.25, no.1 (Summer 1988).

27. Martin Robison Delany, *The Condition, Elevation, Emigration, and the Destiny of the Colored People of the United States* (New York: Arno Press and The New York Times, 1968), pp.179-180 n., 189. This book was first published in 1852.

28. On the repercussion of the Paris Anti-Slavery Conference in Brazil, see *Propaganda Abolicionista. Cartas de Vindex ao Dr. Luiz Álvares dos Santos publicadas no "Diário da Bahia"* (Bahia: Typ. do Diário, 1875), p.27. Vindex—a possible pseudonym for Augusto Álvares Guimarães—suggests that the Emperor decided to open the debates looking toward an emancipation bill in order to give some satisfaction to the abolitionists of the Conference held in Paris in 1867.

29. For early abolitionists' writings on the dangers of having a country sharply divided between heterogeneous peoples or "races," see my *Onda Negra Medo Branco—O Negro no Imaginário das Elites Século xix* (Rio Janeiro: Paz e Terra, 1987), chapter 1. On the Brazilian elite's perceptions of the Negro as dangerous aliens, see also Manuela Carneiro da Cunha, *Negros, Estrangeiros—Os Escravos Libertos e sua Volta à África* (São Paulo: Brasiliense, 1985), pp. 62-100.

30. For the issue of the importation of ideas in the history of Brazil see: Francisco José de Oliveira Viana, *Populações Meridionais do Brasil* (Rio de Janeiro: Paz e Terra, 1973), p. 21; Roberto Schwarz, "As Idéias Fora do Lugar," in *Revista Estudos Cebrap*, no. 3; Maria Sylvia de Carvalho Franco, "As Idéias Estão No Lugar," in Cadernos de Debate—História do Brasil, no. 1 (São Paulo: Brasiliense, 1976).

31. For historians who work with the international connections of abolitionism see among others: Betty Fladeland, *Men and Brothers—Anglo-American Antislave-*

ry Cooperation (Urbana: University of Illinois Press, 1972); David Brion Davis, *Slavery and Human Progress* (New York: Oxford University Press, 1984); Christine Bolt, *The Anti-Slavery Movement and Reconstruction. A Study in Anglo-American Cooperation 1833-77* (London: Oxford University Press, 1969); Eric Foner, *Nothing But Freedom Emancipation and its legacy* (Baton Rouge and London: Louisiana State University Press, 1983); R. J. M. Blackett, *Building an Antislavery Wall, Black American in the Atlantic Abolitionist Movement 1830-1860* (Baton Rouge and London: Louisiana State University Press, 1983); Lawrence C. Jennings, *French Reaction to British Slave Emancipation* (Baton Rouge and London: Louisiana State University Press, 1988).

32. On the system of patronage in Brazil, see Fernando Uricoechea, *The Patrimonial Foundations of the Brazilian Bureaucratic State* (Berkeley: University of California Press, 1980), pp. 19-22, 58-59; Emília Viotti da Costa, "Brazil: the Age of Reform, 1870-1889," in Leslie Bethell, ed., *The Cambridge History of Latin America*, vol.5, c.1870 to 1930 (Cambridge: Cambridge University Press, 1986), pp.743-744; For a lively description of the importance of patronage in the life of Joaquim Nabuco, see Luis Viana Filho, *A Vida de Joaquim Nabuco*, 2nd ed. (São Paulo: Martins Ed./ INL/MEC, 1973), p. 19, 34, 42, 70-71.

33. André Rebouças, *Diário e Notas Autobiográficas*, ed. by Ana Flora and Inácio José Verissimo (Rio de Janeiro: José Olympio, 1938), p. 55.

34. Ibid., pp. 126-130, 164-166.

35. Ibid., pp. 148, 160.

36. Ibid., p. 160.

37. Ibid., pp. 161-162.

38. For instance, Rebouças was preoccupied with the education of his young brother, whom he daily taught various disciplines like Latin, French, English, and translation of ancient Greek and Roman philosophers, ibid., pp.164-165, 168-169, 175.

39. Ibid., pp. 245, 249, 252-253.

40. Ibid., p. 259.

41. "Declaration of Sentiments of the American Anti-Slavery Society," in Louis Ruchames, ed., *The Abolitionists—A Collection of their Writings* (New York: G. P. Putman's Sons, 1963), pp.80-81.

42. *Manifesto da Sociedade Brasileira contra a Escravidão* (Rio de Janeiro: Typ. de G. Leuzinger & Filhos, no date), pp.12-13. Probably published in 1880, the year of the foundation of the Brazilian Anti-Slavery Society.

43. On the American Colonization Society, see, among others, Merton Dillon, *The Abolitionists—The Growth of a Dissenting Minority* (New York: W. W. Norton & Company, 1979), pp.19-20. On Garrison and his membership to the American Colonization Society see his *Thoughts on Colonization*. He wrote in this respect: "My approval [of the A.C.S.] was the offspring of credulity and ignorance," pp.3-4.

44. John Kenrick, *Horrors of Slavery. In Two Parts* (Cambridge: Hilliard and Metcalf, 1817), p.57.

45. Prince Saunders, *A Memoir Presented to the American Convention for Promoting the Abolition of Slavery, and Improving the Condition of the African Race, December 11th, 1818; containing Some Remarks upon the Civil Dissentions of the hitherto afflicted People of Hayti, as the Inhabitants of that Island may be connected with Plans for the Emigration of such Free Persons of Colour as may be disposed to remove to it, in case its*

Reunion, Pacification and Independence should be established (Philadelphia: Dennis Heartt, 1818), p. 8, 13.

46. Quoted from *Walker's Appeal, in Four Articles; together with a preamble, to the Coloured Citizens of the World, but in particular, and very expressly, to those of The United States of America, written in Boston, State of Massachusetts, September 28, 1829,* third and last edition, with additional notes, corrections, &c. (Boston: revised and published by David Walker, 1830), pp. 64-65. Bishop Allen's letter was published in *Freedom's Journal,* vol. 1, no. 2 (1827).

47. *Walker's Appeal,* p. 62. Herbert Aptheker emphasizes that Walker's Appeal "is the first sustained written assault upon slavery and racism to come from a black man in the United States." See Aptheker, *"One Continual Cry": David Walker's Appeal to the Colored Citizens of the World (1829-1830) Its Setting & Its Meaning together with the full text of the third—and last—edition of the Appeal* (New York: Humanities Press, 1965), p.54.

48. *Walker's Appeal,* p. 23.

49. Ibid., pp. 12, 17-18, 31.

50. Ibid., p. 12, 17-18.

51. Ibid., pp. 79, 49.

52. H. Aptheker shows that Garrison had great respect for *Walker's Appeal.* See his *"One Continual Cry": David Walker's Appeal,* pp. 49-52.

53. W. L. Garrison, *Thoughts on Colonization,* pp. 117-118. I suggest that Garrison can be read as a continuation of Walker's Appeal; but it is important to bear in mind that Garrison did not assimilate the third path proposed by Walker, that is, the insurrection of slaves. Garrison showed his preference for the path of white people's repentance by quoting Walker in his appeal for white Americans to treat black people well before it was too late, p. 134.

54. Ibid., pp. 119.

55. To the physician Edward Long, the "mulatto" personified these natural barriers between races because they were as sterile as the mules. He states his opinions about the "mulatto" in his *History of Jamaica,* published in 1774, according to Leon Poliakov, *O Mito Ariano—Ensaio sobre as Fontes do Racismo e dos Nacionalismos* (São Paulo: Perspectiva/EDUSP, 1974), p.155.

56. W. L. Garrison, *Thoughts on Colonization,* p. 118.

57. Ibid., p. 145.

58. W. L. Garrison, *An Address Delivered Before the Free People of Color, in Philadelphia, New York, and other cities, during the month of June, 1831. by Wm. Lloyd Garrison. Published by request. Third Edition* (Boston: Stephen Foster, 1831), p. 3.

59. W. L. Garrison, *Thoughts on Colonization,* part 2, p. 5.

60. Harriet Beecher Stowe, "Results," in *Uncle Tom's Cabin* (New York: Washington Square Press, 1971), pp.442-443. Henry Highland Garnet, *The Past and the Present Condition, and the Destiny of the Colored Race: a Discourse delivered at the fifteenth anniversary of the Female Benevolent Society of Troy, N.Y., Feb. 14, 1848* (Miami: Mnemosyne Publishing Inc., 1969), p. 29.

61. "African Civilization Society," in *Douglass' Monthly* (vol.1-3 (1859-1861),facsimile ed., Negro Periodicals in the United States, 1840-1960 (New York: Negro Universities Press, 1969), p.19. This article was a critique of Garnet's colonization plan; it was published on February 1859, vol. 1, no. 9.

62. Frederico Leopoldo Cezar Burlamaque, *Memória Analytica a Cerca do*

Commercio d'Escravos e a Cerca dos Males da Escravidão Doméstica (Rio de Janeiro: Comercial Fluminense, 1837), pp. viii, 85.

63. Ibid., pp. 94-97.

64. *Systhema de Medidas Adoptaveis para a Progressiva e Total Extincção do Tráfico, e da Escravatura no Brasil Confeccionado e Approvado pela Sociedade contra o Tráfico de Africanos, e Promotora da Colonisação, e da Civilisação dos Indigenas* (Rio de Janeiro: Typ. do Philanthropo, 1852), pp.4-5, 19.

65. Ibid., p. 12.

66. Ibid., p. 5, 14, 24 (article 30), 21 (article 14).

67. On the rise of colonization plans (or immigrationist, the term more often used by historians in Brazil) and their racist approach, see my *Onda Negra Medo Branco*, chapters 1 and 2.

68. Antônio Augusto da Costa Aguiar,*O Brasil e os Brazileiros* (Santos: Typ. Commercial, 1862), pp.22-23.

69. On the fear that the extension of slavery into the newly acquired territories would exclude free Northern white settlers, and increase the so-called African race, see Eric Foner, "Racial Attitudes of the New York Free Soilers," in *Politics and Ideology in the Age of the Civil War* (Oxford: Oxford Universities Press, 1981), pp.78, 81-85.

70. Luis Gama, "Sortimento de Gorras para *A Gente do Grande Tom,*" and "Pacotilha," in *Primeiras Trovas Burlescas,* 2nd ed. (Rio de Janeiro: Typ. de Pinheiro & C.a, 1861), pp.20-26, 90-96.

71. The expression "the great laboratory . . . " was quoted from M. Perier by Armand de Quatrefages, "The Formation of the Mixed Human Races," in *The Anthropological Review,* vol.7 (London, 1869): 22.

72. Costa Aguiar tells of certain French ladies who, after examining a picture of Pedro II, showed their surprise that the Brazilian king was white—"Mais, Monsieur, est il blanc?" See his *O Brasil e os Brazileiros,* p.22.

73. On Comte of Gobineau, see L. Poliakov, *O Mito Ariano,* pp.217-221.

74. Georges Raeders, *O Inimigo Cordial do Brasil—O Conde de Gobienau no Brasil* (Rio de Janeiro: Paz e Terra, 1988), p.15.

75. Ibid., pp. 45-51, 89-94.

76. Ibid., pp. 215-252.

77. On A. Quatrefages, see L. Poliakov, *O Mito Ariano,* p. 204.

78. A. Quatrefages, "The Formation of the Mixed Human Races," pp. 34-35.

79. Ibid., pp. 36-37.

80. Ibid., pp. 38-39.

81. J. Nabuco, *O Abolicionismo* (Londres: Typ. Abraham Kindon E Ca., 1883), pp.19-20. The abolitionist D.J.N. Jaguaribe, Filho relied on Quatrefage's thesis to defend European colonization to Brazil. He believed that if the Brazilian "mulattoes" "crossed" with Europeans for five generations they would become white. See his *Reflexões sobre a Colonisação no Brasil* (São Paulo/Paris: Garraux, 1878), p.206, 294.

82. J. Nabuco, *O Abolicionismo,* p. 21.

83. Ibid., p. 22.

84. Ibid., p. 19.

85. Ibid., pp. 19-20, 174-176.

86. Ibid., pp. 252-253.

87. A. Rebouças, "Nativismo e Patriotismo," in *A Immigração*, vol.2, no.10 (April 1885): 2-3.

88. *A Immigração*, vol. 5, no. 50 (November 1888): 1.

89. The theme of the lust of the American slaveholders is recurrent in the abolitionist press. See Rev. Theodore Dwight Weld, *American Slavery as it is: Testimony of a Thousand Witnesses*, facsimile of the first anonymous edition of 1839 (New York: Arno Press and The New York Times, 1968), p.24, 51, 97. George Bourne, *Picture of Slavery in the United States of America; being a Practical Illustration of Voluntaryism and Republicanism* (Middleton, Connecticut: Edwin Hunt, 1834), pp.12-26. Richard Hildreth, *The Slave: or Memoirs of Archy Moore* (Boston: John H. Eastburn, 1836), vol.1, pp.52-53; vol.2, p.9. Jules Zanger suggests that the recurrent "tragic octoroon" situation in abolitionist literature reveals propagandistic intentions. "The very existence of the octoroon convicted the slaveholder of prostituting his slaves and of selling his own children for profit". See "The `Tragic Octoroon' in Pre-Civil War Fiction," in *American Quarterly*, vol.18, no.1 (Spring 1966): 65-66.

90. L. M. Child, "Joanna," in *The Oasis*, p.104. The book by Captain John G. Stedman is: *Narrative of a Five Years' Expedition against the Revolted Negroes of Surinam*.

91. See the female slave characters of Joaquim Manuel de Macedo, *As Victimas-Algozes Quadros da Escravidão Romances* 2 volumes (Rio de Janeiro: Typ. Americana, 1869).

92. J. Nabuco, "Conferência no Teatro Politheama," in *Conferências e Discursos Abolicionistas Obras Completas*, vol.7 (São Paulo: Instituto Progresso Editorial S.A., 1949), pp. 238-239.

93. "O Sr. Chefe de Polícia e o Capitão Paulino, Tenente-Coronel dos Indios," in *A Redempção*, March 18, 1888.

94. Aluisio Azevedo, *O Mulato* (Ed. Ouro, no date), pp. 36-38, 102-103, 111-113. This novel was first published in 1881. It is significant that Azevedo wrote three different endings for this novel. In one of them, Raimundo's [the Mulatto] white cousin, expecting a baby of his, tragically dies after she sees two black men carrying his murdered body. But Azevedo chose the end that pictures his cousin years after, already as the happy wife of one of Raimundo's murderers; she had completely forgotten her love for the "mulatto". With this end Azevedo reinforced his message that there was no place for people of African descent among the prejudiced elites of his native province of Maranhão. See on these different versions Josué Montello, *Aluisio Azevedo e a Polêmica d'O Mulato* (Rio de Janeiro: J. Olympio; Brasília: INL, 1975), pp. 51-55.

95. Luis Gama, "No Album do meu amigo J.A.da Silva Sobral," in *Primeiras Trovas Burlescas*, pp.34-39. On Gama's unsuccessful attempt to register for the Law School of São Paulo see Sud Mennucci, *O Precursor do Abolicionismo no Brasil* (Luiz Gama) (São Paulo: Companhia Ed. Nacional, 1938), p. 140.

96. It is convenient to notice here that I am not denying the presence of racism among white American abolitionists. Racism, among them, was evident for example in the patronization to which Frederick Douglass was subjected by Garrison and other white confrères, and in resistance to Douglass's establishing his own paper. See, on this issue, Jane H. Pease and William H. Pease, *They Who Would Be Free— Black's Search for Freedom, 1830-1861* (Urbana and Chicago: University of Illinois Press, 1990), pp.82-93. But I am, instead, using contrast with Brazil to

illustrate importance of formal and explicit disavowal of racism by American abolitionists. On the rationale of humanity divided by races, spread by scientists during the nineteenth century, Hannah Arendt argues that "we owe it to these "scientific" preachers rather than to any scientific findings that today no single science is left into whose categorical system race-thinking has not deeply penetrated." See *The Origins of Totalitarianism*, new edition with added prefaces (San Diego: Harvest/HBJ, 1973), pp. 159-160.

97. "A Raça Negra," in *A Redempção*, July 14, 1887.

98. "Extracts from the Annual Report," in *The Abolitionist*, vol. 1, no. 2 (February 1833): 20-22.

99. For some instances in which abolitionists envisioned the emancipated slaves as wage laborers or tenants on Southern plantations see: "Extracts from an Address, delivered before the N.E. Anti-Slavery Society, by Wm. J. Snelling, Esq.," in *The Abolitionist*, vol.1, no.5 (May 1833); "By abolition, I do no mean that any planter should give up his house and plantation to his slaves. The negroes are laborers now, and if freed would be laborers still. The relations between the two parties would not be much changed," p.73. L.M. Child wrote: " . . . the colored population may be effectually *restrained* by the strong arm of the law, while they are, at the same time, fully *protected* by it . . . If this were done in good faith, the greater proportion of the slaves would remain with their masters, as hired laborers, or free tenants." See *The Oasis*, pp.xii-xiii. See also her *Anti-Slavery Catechism* (1839), partially reproduced by John L. Thomas, *Slavery Attacked: The Abolitionist Crusade* (New Jersey: Englewood Cliffs, 1965), p. 63.

100. W. L. Garrison, *Thoughts on Colonization*, p. 80.

101. Ibid., p. 80.

102. "Appeal of the Executive Committee of the `American Abolition Society' recently organized" in *Radical Abolitionist* vol.1, no.5 (December 1855), facsimile edition, Negro Periodicals in the United States, 1840-1960, volumes 1-4 (New York: Negro Universities Press, 1969), pp.36-37. The radical abolitionists were, among others: Lewis Tappan, William Goodell, Gerrit Smith, and Frederick Douglass; according to *Radical Abolitionist* vol.1, no.1 (December 1855).

103. "Frederick Douglass's Speech," in *Radical Abolitionist*, vol. 1, no. 12 (July 1856): 100.

104. F. Douglass, "The Black Man's Future in the Southern States: An Address delivered in Boston, Massachusetts, on 5 February 1862," in John W. Blassingame, ed., *The Frederick Douglass Papers*, vol. 3, pp. 498-499.

105. "The work of the future," in *Douglass' Monthly* , vol. 5, no. 5 (November 1862): 737.

106. Ibid. Douglass discontinued his paper on August 16, 1863 because he believed he could better serve his "poor bleeding country-men" by "going South and summoning them to assert their just liberty, than I can do by staying here. I am going South to assist Adjutant General Thomas, in the organization of colored troops, who shall win for the millions in bondage the inestimable blessings of liberty and country."—"Valedictory," signed by Douglass, ibid., vol.5, no.10 (August 1863).

107. "Thirty-Second Anniversary of the American Anti-Slavery Society— Speech of Wendell Phillips, Esq.," in *The Liberator* vol.35, no.20 (May 19, 1865).

108. Ibid.

109. I am borrowing here an expression from Eric Foner, *Nothing But Freedom — Emancipation and its Legacy* (Baton Rouge: Louisiana State University Press, 1983).

110. "Thirty-Second Anniversary of the American Anti-Slavery Society Speech of Wendell Phillips, Esq.," ibid. On the role of slaves and the black troops in the Civil War, see Ira Berlin, Barbara J. Fields, Steven F. Miller, Joseph P. Reidy, and Leslie S. Rowland, *Slaves No More: Three Essays on Emancipation and the Civil War* (New York: Cambridge University Press, 1992).

111. F. A. Brandão Jr.,*A Escravatura no Brazil precedida d'um artigo sobre agricultura e colonisação no Maranhão* (Bruxelles: Typ. H. Thiry-Van Buggenhoudt, 1865), pp. 43-45.

112. On the Paraguayan War see Charles J. Kolinski, *Independence or Death! The Story of the Paraguayan War* (Gainesville: University of Florida Press, 1965).

113. *Discussão da Reforma do Estado Servil na Camara dos Deputados e no Senado 1871*, vol.1, pp. 54-55.

114. Ibid, vol.1, pp.123-124. Quoted from the speech of the Representative for Bahia, Junqueira.

115. Propaganda Abolicionista. Cartas de Vindex, p.18. According to his estimate, there would be slaves serving their masters at least until 1937, pp. 16-17.

116. I have detailed these abolitionist plans for controlling freed men's lives and protecting planters' interests in "Batismo da Liberdade: Os Abolicionistas e o Destino do Negro," in *Questões & Debates — Revista da Associação Paranaense de História*, vol.9, no.16 (June 1988): 38-65.

117. Ruy Barbosa, *Projecto No.48* (Rio de Janeiro: Nacional, 1884), pp.149-151.

118. Henry W. Hilliard, *Politics and Pen Pictures at Home and Abroad* (New York: G. P. Putman's Sons, 1892), pp. 1, 207-211, 425.

119. Ibid., pp. 394-395, 381.

120. Ibid., pp. 417-418. Quoted from the letter by Hilliard to Nabuco, October 25, 1880.

121. Ibid., pp. 422-424.

122. Ibid., pp. 395-399.

123. On Nabuco's proposal for agrarian reform, see: "Quarta Conferência, Teatro Santa Isabel, November 30, 1884," in *Conferências e Discursos Abolicionistas*, pp.377-8. For Rebouças's plan to establish a "rural democracy," see: *Agricultura Nacional. Estudos Econômicos* (Rio de Janeiro: Lamoureux, 1883), pp. 118-121.

124. A large part of the Brazilian population had already been disfranchised under the Electoral Reform Law of 1879. Beginning with this law, the illiterate were denied the ballot. The electoral population fell drastically after the passing of this law. In 1874, 1,114 066 people could vote; in 1879, the number was reduced to 145,296. people. In 1881, the total population of Brazil was around 9,941,471. Data according to Sérgio Buarque de Holanda, *História Geral da Civilização Brasileira—O Brasil Monárquico, Do Império à República*, vol.2/5, 4th ed. (São Paulo: Difel, 1985), pp.223-224. The politicians who defended this law were very worried about the danger of the so-called "conscience-less masses" taking part in politics, p.209.

Epilogue

1. "The Annual Meeting," in *The Liberator*, vol.35, No.5 (February 3, 1865).
2. Ibid.
3. *Ça Ira!*, no. 2 (September 23, 1882). The article was signed by the young Law student Raul Pompéia, who a few years later became a well-known writer with his *O Ateneu*.
4. "O espírito de S. Paulo," in *Cidade do Rio*, no. 57 (November 25, 1887): 1. This long article supports the proposal of conservative politicians of São Paulo that slaves be emancipated on condition that they work for their masters for three years. They would receive their wages at the end of the third year, at which time they would finally be free of any obligation to their former holders.
5. As quoted from Ruy Barbosa, *A Queda do Império*, by Evaristo de Moraes, *A Campanha Abolicionista (1879-1888)* (Rio de Janeiro: Leite Ribeiro, 1924), p. 304, n. 226.
6. Joaquim Nabuco, *Minha Formação* (Brasília: Ed. Universidade de Brasí-lia, 1963), pp.209-210.
7. "Os pretos desaparecem d'este Estado," in *A Redempção* (June 27, 1897): 1-2. And "Os pretos excluidos de tudo," in *A Redempção* (May 13, 1895): 2. The history of the African Brazilians after abolition is yet to be told, but some books on the matter have recently come out. See: Miriam Nicolau Ferrara, *A Imprensa Negra Paulista* (1915-1963) (São Paulo: FFLCH/USP, 1986); Cleber da Silva Maciel, *Discriminações Raciais—negros em Campinas* (1888-1921) (Campinas: Editora da UNICAMP, 1987); George Reid Andréws, *Blacks and Whites in São Paulo Brazil 1888-1988* (Madison: The University of Wisconsin Press, 1991). Old militants of the African Brazilian movement of the first decades of the twentieth century have seldom had the chance to put their memories in books. Finally these memories are beginning to come out. See José Correia Leite and Cuti, ed., *E disse o velho militante José Correia Leite* (São Paulo: Secretaria Municipal de Cultura, 1992).
8. Theodore Rosengarten, *All God's Dangers—The Life of Nate Shaw* (New York: Vintage Books, Random House, 1984), p. 35.

BIBLIOGRAPHY

PRIMARY SOURCES

UNITED STATES:

Books and Pamphlets

A Fresh Catalogue of Southern Outrages upon Northern Citizens (New York: The American Anti-Slavery Society, 1860).

American Slavery As It Is: Testimony of a Thousand Witnesses (New York: The American Anti-Slavery Society, 1839).

An Appeal to the Women of the Nominally Free States, issued by an Anti-Slavery Convention of American Women second edition (Boston: Isaac Knapp, 1838). Facsimile Reprint, Freeport: Books for Library Press, 1971.

Anti-Slavery Tracts. Series 1: Nos. 1-20, 1855-1856 reprint (Westport: Negro University Press, 1970).

Bourne, George, *Picture of Slavery in the United States of America; Being a Practical Illustration of Voluntaryism and Republicanism* (Middleton: Connecticut, Edwin Hunt, 1834).

————, *The Book and Slavery Irreconcilable with Animadversions upon Dr. Smith's Philosophy* (Philadelphia: J. M. Sanderson & Co., 1816). Facsimile reprint, John W. Christie and Dwight L. Dumond, eds., *George Bourne and the Book and Slavery Irreconcilable* (Baltimore and Philadelphia: The Historical Society of Delaware and The Presbyterian Historical Society, 1969).

Child, David L., *The Despotism of Freedom; or the Tyranny and Cruelty of American Republican Slave-Masters, Shown To Be the Worst in the World; in a Speech,*

Delivered at the First Aniversary of the New England Anti-Slavery Society, 1833 (Boston: The Boston Young Men's Anti-Slavery Association, 1833).

Child, Lydia Maria, *Right Way The Safe Way* (New York: Negro University Press, 1969). Originally published in 1862; facsimile reprint.

————, *The Duty of Disobedience to the Fugitive Slave Act: An Appeal to the Legislators of Massachusetts* (Boston: The American Anti-Slavery Society, 1860).

————, *An Appeal in Favor of that Class of Americans Called Africans* (Boston: Allen and Ticknor, 1833).

————, ed., *The Oasis*, (Boston: Allen and Tichnor, 1834).

Correspondence Between Lydia Maria Child and Gov. Wise and Mrs. Mason of Virginia (Boston: The American Anti-Slavery Society, 1860).

Daniel O'Connell upon American Slavery with other Irish Testemonies (New York: The American Anti-Slavery Society, 1860).

Delany, Martin Robinson, *The Condition, Elevation, Emigration, and Destiny of the Colored People of the United States*. Originally Published in 1852; facsimile reprint, New York, 1968.

Douglass, Frederick, *The Frederick Douglass Papers. Series One: Speeches, Debates, and Interviews*, 3 volumes, edited by John W. Blassingame. (New Haven: Yale University Press, 1979-85).

————, *Lectures on American Slavery. Delivered at Corinthian Hall, Rochester, N.Y.* (Buffalo: Geo. Reese & Co's Power Press, 1851).

Garnet, Henry Highland, *The Past and the Present Condition, and the Destiny of the Colored Race: a Discourse Delivered at the Fifteeth Anniversary of the Female Benevolent Society of Troy, N.Y., Feb. 14, 1848* (Miami, Florida: Mnemosyne Publishing INC., 1969).

Garrison, William Lloyd, *An Address Delivered Before The People of Color, Philadelphia, New York, and other cities, during the month of June, 1831* (Boston: Stephen Foster, 1831).

————, *Thoughts on African Colonization: or An Impartial Exhibition of the Doctrines, Principles and Purposes of the American Colonization Society. Together with the Resolutions, Address, and Remonstrances of the Free People of Color* (Boston: Merchants' Hall, 1832).

Goodell, William, *Slavery and Anti-Slavery; a History of the Great Struggle in both hemispheres with a view of the slavery question in the United States* (New York: Negro University Press, 1968).Originally published in 1852.

Heyrick, Elizabeth, *Immediate, not Gradual Abolition* (Philadelphia: The Philadelphia A.S. Society, 1837).

Hildreth, Richard Esq., *The White Slave: Or, Memories of a Fugitive. A Story of Slave Life in Virginia, etc.* (London: Ingram, Cooke, & Co., 1852).

————, *O Escravo Branco Companheiro do Tio Thomaz ou a Vida de um Fugitivo na Virginia* (Lisboa: Typographia de Luiz Correia da Cunha, 1854). Translated to Portuguese by L. M. do Couto.

Kenrich, John, *Horrors of Slavery. In Two Parts* (Cambridge: Hilliard and Metcalf, 1817).

Martineau, Harriet, *The 'Manifest Destiny' of the American Union* (New York: The American Anti-Slavery Society, 1857).

No Slave-Hunting in the Old Bay State: An Appeal to the People and Legislature of Massachusetts (New York: The American Anti-Slavery Society, 1860).

Phillips, Wendell, *The Philosophy of the Abolition Movement* (New York: The American Anti-Slavery Society, 1860).

Probus, *The Texas Revolution. Republished with additions from the Northampton (Massachusetts) Gazette, to which is added A Letter from Washington on the annexation of Texas, and the outrage of California* (Northampton: Northampton Gazette, 1843).

Proceedings of the Clerical Convention on the Subject of Slavery (Worcester: Massachusetts Spy Office, 1838).

Quincy, Edmond, *An Explanation of the Changes of Mr. John Scoble & Mr. Lewis Tappan Against the American Anti-Slavery Society* (Dublin: Webb and Chapman, 1852).

Saunders, Prince, *A Memoir Presented to The American Convention for Promoting the Abolition of Slavery, and Improving the Condition of the African Race, December 11th, 1818; Containing Some Remarks upon the Civil Dissentions of the hitherto Afflicted People of Hayti, as the Inhabitants of that Island may be connected with Plans for the Emigration of such Free Persons of Color as may be disposed to remove to it, in case its Reunion, Pacification and Independence should be established. Together with Some Account of the Origin and Progress of the Efforts for effecting the Abolition of Slavery in Pennsylvania and its Neigbourhood, and throuhout the World.* (Philadelphia: Dennis Hearth, 1818).

Speech of John Hossach, Convicted of a Violation of the Fugitive Slave Law, Before Judge Drummond, of the United States District Court, Chicago, Ill. (New York: The American Anti-Slavery Society, 1860).

Stephen, George, *Anti-Slavery Recollections: in a Series of Letters Addressed to Mrs. Beecher Stowe at her request*, second edition with a new introduction by Howard Temperley (London: Frank Cross and Company Ltd, 1971).

Stowe, Harriet Beecher, *Uncle Tom's Cabin*, introduction by Russel B. Nye (New York: Washington Square Books, 1963).

The Constitution. A Pro-Slavery Compact: or Selections From The Madison Papers, &C., second edition, enlarged (New York: The American Anti-Slavery Society, 1845).

The Slave: or Memories of Archy Moore, two volumes (Boston: John H. Eastburn, 1836).

Tribute of William Ellery Channing to the American Abolitionists for their Vindication of Freedom of Speech (New York: The American Anti-Slavery Society, 1861).

Walker's Appeal, In four Articles; together with a Preamble, to the Colored Cities of the World, but in Particular, and Very Expressly, to those pf The United States of America, Written in Boston, Massachusetts, September 28, 1829. Third and Last Edition, with additional notes, corrections, &c. (Boston: David Walker, 1830).

NEWSPAPERS AND PERIODICALS:

American Jubilee, 1854-1855

Douglass' Monthly, 1859-1861

Radical Abolitionist, 1855-1858

The Liberator, 1831-1865

The Abolitionist, 1833

BRAZIL:

Books and Pamphlets:

Aguiar, Antônio Augusto da Costa, *O Brazil e os Brazileiros* (Santos: Typographia Commercial, 1862).

Alencar, José de, *Teatro Completo*, 2 volumes. (Rio de Janeiro: Serviço Nacional de Teatro, 1977).

Alves, Castro, *Os Escravos* (São Paulo: Livraria Martins Editora, no date).

Azevedo, Aluísio, *O Mulato* (Rio de Janeiro: Edições de Ouro, no date).

Barbosa, Ruy, *O Anno Político de 1887* (Rio de Janeiro: Typographia Gazeta de Noticias, 1888).

——, *Elemento Servil. Discurso proferido em 28 de julho de 1884* (Rio de Janeiro: Typographia Nacional, 1884).

——, *Projecto no. 48 Sessão de 4 de agosto de i884. Parecer no. 48 A formulação em nome das comissões reunidas de Orçamento e Justiça Civil, acerca do projecto de Emancipação dos escravos pelo sr. Ruy Barbosa* (Rio de Janeiro: Typographia Nacional, 1884).

——, *Obras Completas*, vol.1 (Rio de Janeiro: Ministerio de Educação e Saúde, 1951).

Barreto, Domingos Alves Branco Moniz, *Memoria sobre a Abolição do Commercio da Escravatura* (Rio de Janeiro: Typographia Imparcial de F. de Paula Brito, 1817).

Blake, Augusto Victorino Alves Sacramento, *Diccionario Bibliographico Brazileiro* (Rio de Janeiro: Typographia Nacional, 1883).

Brandao Jr., Francisco Antônio, *A Escravatura no Brazil precedida d'um artigo sobre a agricultura e colonisação no Maranhão* (Bruxelles: Typographia H. Thiry-Van Buggenhoudt, 1865).

Brito, Peixoto de, *Considerações Geraes sobre a Emancipação dos Escravos no Império do Brasil e Indicação dos meios próprios para realisal-a* (Lisboa: Typographia Portuguesa, 1870).

Burlamaque, Frederico Leopoldo Cezar, *Memoria Analytica á cerca do Commercio d'Escravos e á cerca dos Males da Escravidão Doméstica* (Rio de Janeiro: Typographia Commercio Fluminense, 1837).

Cincinnatus, *O Elemento Escravo e As Questões Econômicas do Brazil* (Bahia: Typographia dos Dous Mundos, 1885).

Costa, João Severiano Maciel da *Memoria sobre a Necessidade de Abolir a Introdução dos Escravos Africanos no Brazil; sobre o modo e condicoes com que esta abolição se deve fazer; e sobre os meios de remediar a falta de braços que ela pode ocasionar* (Coimbra: Imprensa da Universidade, 1821).

Davatz, Thomas, *Memórias de um Colono no Brasil (1850)* (Belo Horizonte: Itatiaia/ São Paulo: EDUSP, 1980).

Debret, Jean Baptiste, *Viagem Pitoresca e Histórica ao Brasil*, 2 volumes (Belo Horizonte: Itatiaia/São Paulo: EDUSP, 1978).

Discussão da Reforma do Estado Servil na Câmara dos Deputados e no Senado, 1871. Parte I, de maio a 31 de julho (Rio de Janeiro: Typographia Nacional, 1871).

Falas do Trono. Desde o Ano de 1823 ate o ano de 1889. Acompanhados dos respectivos votos de graça da Câmara Temporária (São Paulo: Melhoramentos, 1977).

Fonseca, Luis Anselmo da, *A Escravidão, o Clero e o Abolicionismo* (Recife: Massangana, 1988). Originally published in 1887; facsimile reprint.

Frick, João, *Abolição da Escravatura: Breve Noticia sobre A Primeira Sociedade de Emancipação no Brazil* (Lisboa: Lallemant Freres, 1885).

Gama, Luis, *Primeiras Trovas Burlescas*, 2nd. edition (Rio de Janeiro: Typographia de Pinheiro & Co., 1861).

Guimarães, Bernardo, *A Escrava Isaura* (Belo Horizonte: Editora Itatiaia, no date). First published in 1875.

Hilliard, Henry W., *Politics and Pen Pictures at Home and Abroad* (New York and London: G.P. Putnam's Sons, 1892).

Jaguaribe Filho, Domingos, *Reflexões sobre a Colonisação no Brasil* (São Paulo and Paris: A.L. Garrauxe Cia., 1878).

——, *Algumas Palavras sobre a Emigração: Meios praticos de colonisar Colonias do Barao de Porto-Feliz e Estatistica do Brasil* (São Paulo: Typographia do 'Diario', 1877).

Kidder, Rev. D. P. and Fletcher, Rev. J.C., *Brazil and the Brazilians, portrayed in Historical and Descriptive Sketches* (Philadelphia: Childs & Peterson, 1857).

Kidder, Rev. Daniel P., *Sketches of Residence and Travels in Brazil, embracing Historical and Geographical Notices of the Empire and Its Several Provinces*, 2 volumes (Philadelphia: Sorin & Ball, 1845).

Koster, Henry, *Travels in Brazil* (London: Longan, Hurst, Rees, Orme and Brown, 1816).

————, *Voyages dans la Partie Septentrionale du Bresil: depuis 1809 jusqu'en 1815, comprenant les provinces de Pernambuco (Fernanbouc), Seara, Paraiba, Maragnam, etc.* (Paris: Delaunay, 1818).

Leal, Luiz Francisco da Camara, *Consideracoes e Projeto de Lei para a Emancipação dos Escravos - sem prejuizo de seus senhores, nem grave onus para o Estado* (Rio de Janeiro: Typographia de Pinheiro & Co., 1866).

Leao, Polycarpo Lopes de, *Como pensa sobre o Elemento Servil o Dr. Polycarpo Lopes Leao* (Rio de Janeiro: Typographia Perseveranca, 1870).

Lemos, Miguel and Mendes, Teixeira, *A Liberdade Espiritual e a Organização do Trabalho: Considerações historico-filosoficas sobre o movimento abolicionista* (Rio de Janeiro: Centro Positivista do Brasil, 1888).

Lemos, Miguel, *O Positivismo e a Escravidão Moderna* (Rio de Janeiro: Sociedade Positivista, 1884).

Macedo, Joaquim Manoel de, *As Victimas-Algozes: Quadros da Escravidão: Romances*, 2 volumes. (Rio de Janeiro: Typographia Americana, 1869).

Malheiro, Agostinho Marques Perdigão, *A Escravidão no Brasil: Ensaio Historico-Juridico-Social* (Rio de Janeiro: Typographia Nacional, 1867).

Manifesto da Sociedade Brasileira contra a Escravidão (Rio de Janeiro: Typographia G. Leuzinger & Filhos, 1880).

Mendes, Raimundo Teixeira, *Abolicionismo e Clericalismo: Complemento a carta endereçada a S. Exa. o Sr. Dr. Joaquim Nabuco* (Rio de Janeiro: Apostolado Positivista do Brasil, 1888).

Nabuco, Joaquim, *A Escravidão* (Recife: Massangana, 1988).

————, *Campanhas de Imprensa (1884-1887)* (São Paulo: Instituto Progresso Editorial, 1949).

————, *Cartas aos Abolicionistas Ingleses* (Recife: Massangana, 1985).

————, *Conferências e Discursos Abolicionistas* (São Paulo: Instituto Progresso Editorial, 1949).

————, Discursos Parlamentares (1879-1889) (São Paulo: Instituto Progresso Editorial, 1949).

————, Minha Formação (Brasília: Editora Universidade de Brasília, 1963).

————, O Abolicionismo (London: Abraham Kindon & Co., 1883).

Patrocínio, José do, Motta Coqueiro ou a Pena de Morte (Rio de Janeiro: Livraria
Francisco Alves, 1977).

————, L'Affranchissement des Esclaves de la Province de Ceara au Brésil (Paris and Rio
de Janeiro: Gazeta da Tarde, 1884).

————, Conferência Pública do Jornalista José do Patrocínio feita no Theatro Polytheama
em Sessão da Confederação Abolicionista de 17 de maio de 1885 (Rio de Janeiro:
Typographia Central de Evaristo Rodrigues da Costa, 1885).

Pinto, Elzeário, Reformas. Emancipação dos Escravos especialmente após a promulgação
da Lei n.3270 de 28 de setembro de 1885 (Rio de Janeiro: Imprensa Nacional,
1887).

Propaganda Abolicionista: Cartas de Vindex ao Dr. Luiz Alvares dos Santos Publicadas no
'Diario da Bahia' (Bahia: Typographia do Diario, 1875).

Rebouças, André, Agricultura Nacional. Estudos Econômicos (Rio de Janeiro:
Typographia A. J. Lamoureux, 1883).

————, Diário e Notas Autobiográficas Rio de Janeiro: José Olympio, 1938).

Rocha, Padre Manoel Ribeiro, Ethiope Resgatado, Sustentado, Corregido, Instruido e
Libertado (Lisboa: Officina Patriarcal de São Francisco Luiz Ameno, 1758).

Rugendas, João Mauricio, Viagem Pitoresca Através do Brasil 18th edition (Belo
Horizonte and São Paulo: Itatiaia/USP, 1979).

Sampaio, Antonio Gomes de Azevedo, Abolicionismo Um Paragrapho: Considerações
geraes do movimento anti-escravista e sua historia limitada a Jacarehy, que foi um
centro de acção do norte do Estado de São Paulo (São Paulo: Typographia
Louzada & Irmão, 1890).

São Vicente, Visconde de, Trabalho sobre a A Extincção da Escravatura no Brasil (Rio de
Janeiro: Typographia Nacional, 1868).

Silva, Leonardo Dantas da, A imprensa e a Abolição (Recife: Massangana, 1988).

Silva, José Eloy Pessoa da, Memoria sobre a Escravatura e Projecto de Colonisação dos
Europeus e Pretos da Africa no Imperio do Brasil (Rio de Janeiro: Typographia de
Plancher, 1826).

Silva, José Bonifácio de Andrada e, *Representação à Assembleia Geral Constituinte e Legislativa do Imperio do Brasil sobre a Escravatura* (Rio de Janeiro: Typographia J. E. S. Cabral, 1840).

Systhema de Medidas Adoptivas para a Progressiva e Total Extinção do Trafico, e da Escravatura no Brasil. Convencionado e Approvado pela Sociedade Contra o Trafico de Africanos, e Promotora da Colonisação, e da Civilisação dos Indigenas. (Rio de Janeiro: Typographia do Philanthropo, 1852).

The Empire of Brazil at the Universal Exhibition of 1876 in Philadelphia (Rio de Janeiro: Typographia do Imperial Instituto Artistico, 1876).

The Empire of Brazil at the The Paris International Exhibition of 1867 (Rio de Janeiro: E. & Laemmert, 1867).

Varella, J. N. Fagundes, *Poesias Completas*, 2 volumes (São Paulo: Companhia Editora Nacional, 1957).

Walsh, Rev. R., *Notices of Brazil in 1828 and 1829*, 2 volumes (London: Frederick Wesley and A. H. Davis, 1830).

NEWSPAPERS AND PERIODICALS:

A Immigração, 1883-1888

A Redempção, 1887-1888

Ça Ira!, 1882

Cabrião, 1866-1867

Cidade do Rio, 1887-1888

Correio Paulistano, 1888

Diabo Coxo, 1864-1865

Gazeta da Tarde, 1880-1887

O Polichinello, 1876

OTHER PRIMARY SOURCES:

Anti-Slavery Reporter, 1883-1884.

Quatrefages, M. de, "The Formation of the Mixed Human Races", *The Anthropological Review*, vol.7 (1869): 22-40.

Special Report of the Anti-Slavery Conference, Held in Paris, in the Salle Herz, on the Twenty-Sixth and Twenty-Seventh August, 1867, Under the Presidency of Mons. Edouard Laboulaye (London: The Committee of The British and Foreign Anti-Slavery Society).

SECONDARY LITERATURE:

UNITED STATES

Books:

Angle, Paul M., ed., *Created Equal? The Complete Lincoln-Douglass Debates of 1858* (Chicago: The University of Chicago Press, 1958).

Aptheker, Herbert, ed., *"One Centenial Cry": David Walker's Appeal to the Colored Cities of the World (1829 - 1830). Its Setting and Its Meaning* (New York: Humanities Press, 1965).

————, *Nat Turner's Slave Rebellion* (New York: Grove Press, INC.,1966).

Archdeacon, Thomas, *Becoming American: An Ethnic History* (New York: The Free Press, 1983).

Baer, Helene G., *The Heart is like Heaven: The Life of Lydia Maria Child* (Philadelphia: University of Pennsylvania Press, 1964).

Bailyn, Bernard, *The Ideological Origins of the American Revolution* (Cambridge: Harvard University Press, 1967).

————, *Voyagers to the West: A Passage in the Peopling of America on the Eve of the Revolution* (New York: Vintage Books, 1988).

Barnes, Gilbert Hobbs, *The Antislavery Impulse 1830-1844* (Gloucester, Massachusetts: Peter Smith, 1957).

Bender, Thomas, ed., *The Antislavery Debate: Capitalism and Abolitionism as a Problem in Historical Interpretation* (Berkeley: University of California Press, 1992).

Berlin, Ira [et al.], eds., *Slaves No More: Three Essays on Emancipation and the Civil War* (Cambridge: Cambridge University Press, 1993).

———, *Free at Last: A Documentary History of Slavery, Freedom, and The Civil War* (New York: The New Press, 1992).

Bernstein, Barton J., *Towards a New Past: Dissenting Essays in American History* (New York: Pantheon, Random House, 1968).

Blackett, R. J. M., *Building an Antislavery Wall: Black Americans in the Atlantic Abolitionist Movement, 1830-1860* (Baton Rouge: Louisiana State University Press, 1983).

Blassingame, John W., ed., *Slave Testimony: Two Centuries of Letters, Speeches, Interviews and Autobiographies* (Baton Rouge: Louisiania State University, 1977).

Boyer, Paul and Nissenbaum, Stephen, *Salem Possessed: The Social Origins of Witchcraft* (Cambridge: Harvard University Press, 1974).

Bushman, Richard L., *From Puritan to Yankee: Character and the Social Order in Connecticut 1690-1765* (Cambridge: Harvard University Press, 1967).

Christie, John W. and Dumond, Dwight L., *George Bourne and The Book and Slavery Irreconcilable* (Wilmington and Philadelphia: The Historical Society of Dalaware and The Presbyterian Historical Society, 1969).

Davis, David Brion, *The Slave Power Conspiracy and The Paranoid Style* (Baton Rouge: Louisiana State University Press, 1969).

———, *Revolutions: Reflections on American Equality and Foreign Liberations* (Cambridge: Harvard University Press, 1990).

———, *The Problem of Slavery in Western Culture* (New York: Oxford University Press, 1988).

———, *Slavery and Human Progress* (New York: Oxford University Press, 1986).

———, *The Problem of Slavery in the Age of Revolution 1770-1823* (Ithaca: Cornell University Press, 1975).

————, *From Homicide to Slavery: Studies in American Culture* (New York: Oxford Univerity Press, 1986).

Dillon, Merton L., *The Abolitionists: The Growth of a Dissenting Minority* (New York: W. W. Norton & Company, 1979).

Donald, David, *Lincoln Reconsidered: Essays on the Civil War Era* (New York: Vintage Books, 1989).

Du Bois, W. E. Burghardt, *The Souls of Black Folk* (New York: Nal Penguin INC., 1982).

Duberman, Martin, ed., *The Antislavery Vanguard: New Essays on The Abolitionists* (Princeton: Princeton University Press, 1965).

————, *The Antislavery Vanguard: New Essays on the Abolitionists* (Princeton: Princeton University Press, 1965).

Dumond, Dwight Lowell, *Antislavery Origins of the Civil War in the United States* (Ann Arbor: The University of Michigan Press, 1969).

————, *A Bibliography of Antislavery in America* (Ann Arbor: The University of Michigan Press, 1961).

Elkins, Stanley M., *Slavery: A Problem in American Institutional Life*, 3rd edition, revised (Chicago: The University of Chicago Press, 1976).

Emerson, Donald E., *Richard Hildreth* (Baltimore: The John Hopkins University Press, 1946).

Faust, Drew Gilpin, ed., *The Ideology of Slavery: Proslavery Thought in the Antebellum South, 1830-1860* (Baton Rouge: Louisiana State University Press, 1985).

————, *The Creation of Confederate Nationalism: Ideology and Identity in the Civil War South* (Baton Rouge: Louisiana State University Press, 1988).

Fields, Mamie Garvin and Fields, Karen, *Lemon Swamp and Other Places: A Carolina Memoir* (New York: The Free Press, 1983).

Fields, Barbara Jeanne, *Slavery and Freedom on the Middle Ground: Maryland during the Nineteenth Century* (New Haven: Yale University Press, 1985).

Filler, Louis, *The Crusade Against Slavery 1830-1860* (New York: Harper & Row, 1960).

Fladeland, Betty, *Men and Brothers: Anglo-American Antislavery Cooperation* (Urbana: University of Illinois Press, 1972).

Fogel, Robert William, *Without Consent or Contract: The Rise and Fall of American Slavery* (New York: W. W. Norton, 1989).

——, and Engerman, Stanley L., *Time On The Cross: The Economics of American Negro Slavery*, new edition. (New York: W. W. Norton, 1989).

Foner, Eric, *Politics and Ideology in the Age of the Civil War* (Oxford: Oxford University Press, 1980).

——, *Free Soil, Free Labor, Free Men: The Ideology of the Republican Party before the Civil War* (Oxford: Oxford University Press, 1970).

Reconstruction: America's Unfinished Revolution 1863-1877 (New York: Harper & Row, 1988).

Nothing But Freedom: Emancipation and Its Legacy (Baton Rouge: Louisiana State University Press, 1983).

——, *Tom Paine and Revolutionary America* (Oxford: Oxford University Press, 1977).

Foner, Philip S., *Frederick Douglass* (New York: Citadel Press, 1969).

Fox-Genovese, Elizabeth, *Within the Plantation Household: Black and White Women of the Old South* (Chapel Hill: The University of North Carolina Press, 1988).

——, and Genovese, Eugene, *Fruits of Merchant Capital: Slavery and Bourgeois Property in the Rise and Expansion of Capitalism* (Oxford: Oxford University Press, 1983).

Franklin, John Hope, *Race and History: Selected Essays 1938-1988* (Baton Rouge: Louisiana University Press, 1989).

Fredrickson, George M., *The Black Image in the White Mind: The Debate on Afro-American Character and Destiny, 1817-1914* (New York: Harper & Row, 1972).

Fredrickson, George L., ed., *William Lloyd Garrison* (Englewood Cliffs, New Jersey: Prentice-Hall, INC., 1968).

Friedman, Lawrence J., *Gregarious Saints: Self and Community in American Abolitionism, 1830-1870* (Cambridge: Cambridge University Press, 1982).

Gara, Larry, *The Liberty Line: The Legend of the Underground Railroad* (Lexington: University of Kentucky Press, 1961).

Genovese, Eugene D., *The Slaveholders' Dilemma: Freedom and Progress in The Southern Conservative Thought, 1820-1860* (Columbia, South Carolina: University of South Carolina Press, 1992).

————, *Roll, Jordan, Roll: The World the Slaves Made* (New York: Vintage Books, 1976).

————, *The World the Slaveholders Made: Two Essays in Interpretation*, with a new introduction (Middletown, Connecticut: Wesleyan University Press, 1988).

————, *The Political Economy of Slavery* (New York: Random House, 1967).

Gispen, Kees, ed., *What Made the South Different?* (Jackson: University Press of Mississippi, 1990).

Glickstein, Jonathan A., *Concepts of Free Labor in Antebellum America* (New Haven: Yale University Press, 1991).

Greene, Lorenzo Johnston, *The Negro in Colonial New England 1620-1776* (Port Washington: Kennikat Press, INC.).

Gutman, Herbert G., *The Black Family in Slavery and Freedom 1750-1925* (New York: Vintage Books, 1976).

Harding, Vincent, *There Is a River: The Black struggle for Freedom in America* (New York: Vintage Books, 1983).

Heimert, Alan, *Religion and the American Mind: From the Great Awakening to the Revolution* (Cambridge: Harvard University Press, 1966).

Hellwig, David J., ed., *African-American Reflections on Brazil's Racial Paradise* (Philadelphia: Temple University Press, 1992).

Hildreth, Richard, *Memoirs of a Fugitive: America's First Antislavery Novel* adapted by Barbara Ritchie (New York: Thomas Y. Carvell Company, 1971).

Hunt, Alfred N., *Haiti's Influence on Antebellum America: Slumberibg Volcano in the Caribbean* (Baton Rouge: Louisiana State University, 1988).

Innes, Stephen, ed., *Work and Labor in Early America* (Chapel Hill and London: University of North Carolina Press, 1988).

Jordan, Winthrop D., *White over Black: American Attitudes Toward the Negro. 1550-1812* (New York: W. W. Norton & Company, 1977).

Kousser, J. Morgan and MacPherson, James M., *Region, Race and Reconstruction* (New York: Oxford University Press, 1982).

Kraditor, Aileen S., *Means and Ends in American abolitionism* (New York: Pantheon Books, 1969).

Lerner, Gerda, *The Grimké Sisters from South Carolina: Rebels against Slavery* (Boston: Houghton Mifflin Company, 1967).

Lewis, Perry, *Radical Abolitionist Anarchy and the Government of God in Antislavery Thought* (Ithaca and London: Cornell University Press, 1973).

Litwack, Leon F., *North of Slavery: The Negro in the Free States, 1790-1860* (Chicago: The University of Chicago Press, 1961).

Lockridge, Kenneth A., *A New England Town: The First Hundred Years, Dedham Massachusetts, 1636-1736* (New York: W.W. Norton & Company, INC., 1970).

MacPherson, James M., *The Negro's Civil War: How American Negros felt and acted during the war for the Union* (New York: Vintage Books/ Random House, 1965).

———, *Battle Cry of Freedom: The Civil War Era* (Oxford: Oxford University Press, 1988).

Merrill, Walter M., *Against Wind and Tide: A Biography of Wm. Lloyd Garrison* (Cambridge: Harvard University Press, 1963).

Miller, Perry and Johnson, Thomas H., *The Puritans* (New York: American Book Company, 1938).

Morgan, Edmund S., *American Slavery: American Freedom: The Ordeal of Colonial Virginia* (New York: W. W. Norton & Company, 1975).

Morison, Samuel Eliot, *Sources & Documents illustrating the American Revolution 1764-1788 and the formation of the Federal Constitution*, 2nd edition (London: Oxford University Press, 1965).

Ofari, Earl, *"Let your Motto be Resistance": The Life and Thought of Henry Highland Garnet* (Boston: Beacon Press 1972).

Pease, Jane H. and Pease, William H., *They Who Would Be Free: Blacks' Search for Freedom, 1830-1861* (Urbana: University of Illinois Press, 1990).

Perry, Lewis and Fellman, Michael, ed., *Antislavery Reconsidered: New Perspectives on the Abolitionists* (Baton Rouge: Louisiana State University Press, 1979).

Potter, David M., *The Impending Crisis 1848-1861*, completed and edited by Don E. Fehrenbacher. (New York: Harper & Row, 1976).

Quarles, Benjamin, *The negro in the American Revolution* (New York: W. W. Norton & Company, 1973).

———, *Black Abolitionists* (New York: Oxford University Press, 1969).

Ratner, Lorman, *Powder Keg: Northern Opposition to the Antislavery Movement 1832-1840* (New York: Basic Books, 1968).

Remini, Robert V., *The Jacksonian Era* (Arlington Heights, Illinois: Harlan Davison, INC., 1989).

Richards, Leonard L., *"Gentlemen of Property and Standing": Anti-Abolition Mobs in Jacksonian America* (Oxford: Oxford University Press, 1970).

Robinson, Donald L., *Slavery in the Structure of American Politics 1765-1820* (New York: Harcourt Brace Janovich, INC., 1971).

Rose, Willie Lee, *Slavery and Freedom*, edited by William W. Freehling (Oxford: Oxford University Press, 1982).

Rosengarten, Theodore, *All God's Dangers: The Life of Nate Shaw* (New York: Vintage Books, 1974).

Ruchames, Louis, ed., *The Abolitionists: A Collection of their Writings* (New York: G. P. Putnan's Sons, 1963).

Simpson, Lewis P., *Mind and the American Civil War: A Meditation on Lost Causes* (Baton Rouge: Louisiana University Press, 1989).

Stampp, Kenneth M., *The Peculiar Institution: Slavery in the Ante-Bellum South* (New York: Vintage Books, 1989).

Stephenson, George M., *A History of American Immigration, 1820-1924* (New York: Russell & Russell, 1964).

Stewart, James Brewer, *Wendell Phillips: Liberty's Hero* (Baton Rouge: Louisiana State University Press, 1986).

———, *Holy Warriors: The Abolitionists and American Slavery* (New York: Hill and Wang, 1976).

Thomas, John L., *The Liberator: William Lloyd Garrison: A Biography* (Boston: Little, Brown and Company, 1963).

———, *Slavery Attacked: The Abolitionist Crusade* (Englewwod Cliffs, New Jersey: Prentice-Hall, INC., 1965).

Tyler, Alice Felt, *Freedom's Ferment: Phases of American Social History from the Colonial Period to the Outbreak of the Civil War* (New York: Harper & Row, 1962).

Walters, Ronald G., *The Antislavery Appeal: American Abolitionism After 1830* (New York: W. W. Norton & Company, 1984).

West, Cornel, *Race Matters* (Boston: Beacon Press, 1993).

Williamson, Joel, *New People: Miscegenation and Mulatoes in the United States* (New York: New York University Press, 1984).

Woodward, C. Vann, *American Counterpoint: Slavery and Racism in the North-South Dialogue* (Oxford: Oxford University Press, 1983).

————, ed., *The Comparative Approach to American History* (New York: Basic Books, 1968).

Wyatt-Brown, Bertram, *Yankee Saints and Southern Sinners* (Baton Rouge: Louisiana State University Press, 1985).

————, *Lewis Tappan and the Evangelical War Against Slavery* (Cleveland: The Press of Case Western Reserve University, 1969).

Zilversmith, Arthur, *The First Emancipation: The Abolition of Slavery in the North* (Chicago: The University of Chicago Press, 1967).

Articles and Dissertations:

Abzug, Robert H., "The Influence of Garrisonian Abolitionists' Fears of Slave Violence on the Antislavery Argument, 1829-1840," *Journal of Negro History*, (January 1970): 15-28.

Alexander, Thomas B. [et al.], "AHR Forum: Antebellum North and South in Comparative Perspective: A discussion," *The American Historical Review*, vol.85, no.5 (December 1980): 1150-1166.

Berlin, Ira, "Time, Space, and the Evolution of Afro-American Society on British Mainland North America," *The American Historical Review*, vol.85, no.1 (February 1980): 44-78.

Dain, Bruce, "Haiti and Egypt in Early Black Racial Discourse in the United States," *Slavery and Abolition*, vol.14, no. 3 (December 1993): 139-161.

Dillon, Merton L., "The Abolitionists: A Decade of Historiography, 1959-1969," *The Journal of Southern History*, vol.35, no.4 (November 1969): 500-522.

Ellis, Richard and Wildavsky, Aaron, "A Cultural Analysis of the Role of Abolitionists in the Coming of the Civil War," *Comparative Studies in Society and History*, vol.32, no.1 (January 1990): 89-116.

Eltis, David, "Europeans and the Rise and Fall of African Slavery in the Americas: An Interpretation," *The American Historical Review*, vol.98, no.5 (December 1993).

Ernst, Robert, "The Asylum of the Oppressed," *The South Atlantic Quarterly*, vol.40, no.1 (January 1941).

Fields, Barbara Jeanne, "The Nineteenth-Century American South: History and Theory," *Plantation Society in the Americas*, vol.2, no.1 (April 1983): 7-27.

————, "Lost Causes, North and South," *Reviews in American History*, vol.20, no.1 (March 1992):   65-71.

————, "Slavery, Race and Ideology in the United States of America," *New Left Review*, no.181 (May/June 1990): 95-118.

Finnie, Gordon E., "The Antislavery Movement in the Upper South Before 1840," *The Journal of Southern History*, vol.35, no.3 (August 1969): 319-342.

Foster, Gaines M., "Guilt Over Slavery: A Historiographical Analysis," *The Journal of Southern History*, vol.56, no.4 (November 1990): 665-694.

Gara, Larry, "Slavery and the Slave Power: A Crucial Distinction," *Civil War History*, vol.15, no.1 (March 1969): 5-18.

Genovese, Eugene D., "Rebelliousness and Docility in the Negro Slave: A Critique of the Elkins Thesis," *Civil War History*, vol.13, no.4 (December 1967): 293-314.

Kraditor, Aileen S., "A Note on Elkins and the Abolitionists," *Civil War History*, vol.13, no.4 (December 1967): 330-339.

Lynd, Staughton, "The Compromise of 1787," *Political Science Quarterly*, vol.81, no.2 (June 1966): 225-250.

Macleod, Duncan, "From Gradualism to Immediatism: Another Look," *The Abolition of Slavery*, vol.3, no.2 (September 1982): 140-152.

Mathews, Donald G., "The Second Great Awakening as an Organizing Process, 1780-1830: An Hypothesis," *American Quarterly*, vol.21, no.1 (Spring 1969): 23-43.

Ohline, Howard A., "Republicanism and Slavery: Origins of the Three-Fifties Clause in the United States Constitution," *The Willian and Mary Quarterly*, Third Series, vol.28, no.4 (October 1971): 562-584.

Osofsky, Gilbert, "Abolitionists, Irish Immigrants, and the Dilemmas of Romantic Nationalism," *The American Historical Review*, vol.80, no.4 (October 1985): 889-912.

Pessen, Edward, "How Different from Each Other the Antebellum North and South," *The American Historical Review*, vol.85, no.5 (December 1980): 1119-1149.

Stapp, Carol Buchalter, "Afro-Americans in Antebellum Boston: An Analysis of Probate Records" (Ph.D dissertation, 2 volumes, The George Washington University, 1990).

Woodward, C. Vann, "The Antislavery Myth," *The American Scholar* (Spring 1962): 312-328.

Zanger, Jules, "The 'Tragic Octoroon' In Pre-Civil War Fiction," *American Quarterly*, vol.18, no.1 (Spring 1966): 63-70.

BRAZIL

Books:

Algranti, Leila Mezan, *O Feitor Ausente: Estudos sobre a escravidão urbana no Rio de Janeiro, 1808-1822* (Petrópolis: Vozes, 1988).

Almada, Vilma Paraiso Ferreira de, *Escravismo e Transição - O Espirito Santo (1850-1888)* (Rio de Janeiro: Graal, 1984).

Alves, Henrique L., *O fantasma da Abolição* (São Paulo: Secretaria de Estado da Cultura/ Olmo-Kempp Editores, no date).

————, *Bibliografia Afro-Brasileira* (São Paulo: Editora H, 1976).

Andrade, Ana I. S. L. and Rego, Carmen L. S. L., *Catálogo da Correspondência de Joaquim Nabuco, 1865-1884*, 2 volumes. (Recife: Massangana, 1980).

Andrews, George R., *Blacks and Whites in São Paulo, Brazil 1888-1988* (Madison: The University of Wisconsin Press, 1991).

Azevedo, Célia Maria Marinho de, *Onda Negra, Medo Branco. O Negro no imaginário das elites: século XIX* (Rio de Janeiro: Paz e Terra, 1987).

Bakos, Margareth Marchiori, *RS: Escravismo & Abolição* (Porto Alegre: Mercado Aberto, 1982).

Bastide, Roger, *As Americas Negras* (São Paulo: Difel/ EDUSP, 1974).

―――, *Les Religions Africaines au Brésil―Vers une sociologie des interpénétrations de civilisations* (Paris: Presses Universitaires de France, 1960).

Beiguelman, Paula, *Pequenos Estudos de Ciência Política* (São Paulo: Livraria Pioneira Editora, 1968).

―――, *A Crise do Escravismo e a Grande Imigração* 2nd. edition (São Paulo: Brasiliense, 1981).

―――, *Formação Política do Brasil,* 2nd edition (São Paulo: Pioneira, 1976).

―――, *A Formação do Povo no Complexo Cafeeiro. Aspectos Políticos,* 2nd edition (São Paulo: Pioneira, 1977).

Bethell, Leslie, *The Abolition of the Brazilian Slave Trade: Britain, Brazil and The Slave Trade Question, 1807-1869* (Cambridge: Cambridge University Press, 1970).

Brookshaw, David, *Raça e Cor na Literatura Brasileira* (Porto Alegre: Mercado Aberto, 1983).

Campanhole, Adriano, [et al.] *Todas As Constituições do Brasil* (São Paulo: Atlas, 1971).

Campos, Eduardo, *Imprensa Abolicionista, Igreja, Escravos e Senhores* (Fortaleza: Secretaria de Cultura do Estado do Ceará, 1984).

Cardoso, Ciro F. S., ed., *Escravidão e Abolição no Brasil: novas perspectivas* (Rio de Janeiro: Zahar, 1988).

Cardoso, Fernando Henrique, *Capitalismo e Escravidão no Brasil Meridional ,* 2nd edition (Rio de Janeiro: Paz e Terra, 1977).

Chalhoub, Sidney, *Visões da Liberdade. Uma História das Últimas Décadas da Escravidão na Corte* (São Paulo: Companhia das Letras, 1990).

Conrad, Robert, *Os Últimos Anos da Escravatura no Brasil, 1850-1888,* 2nd edition (Rio de Janeiro: Civilização Brasileira, 1978).

―――, *The Destruction of Brazilian Slavery 1850-1888* (Berkeley: University of California Press, 1972).

————, *Tumbeiros. O Tráfico de Escravos para o Brasil* (São Paulo: Brasiliense, 1985).

————, *World of Sorrow: The African Slave Trade to Brazil* (Baton Rouge: Louisiana State University Press, 1986).

Costa, Emília Viotti da, *Da Senzala à Colônia*, 2nd edition (São Paulo: Ciências Humanas, 1982).

————, *Da Monarquia à República Momentos Decisivos*, 2nd edition (São Paulo: Ciências Humanas, 1979).

Cunha, Manuela Carneiro da, *Negros, Estrangeiros. Os escravos libertos e sua volta à África* (São Paulo: Brasiliense, 1985).

Dean, Warren, *Rio Claro - Um Sistema Brasileiro de Grande Lavoura, 1820-1920* (Rio de Janeiro: Paz e Terra, 1977).

Eisenberg, Peter L., *Modernização Sem Mudança. A Indústria Açucareira em Pernambuco, 1840-1910* (Campinas: Ed. UNICAMP/Rio de Janeiro: Paz e Terra, 1977).

————————, *Homens Esquecidos. Escravos e Trabalhadores Livres no Brasil. Séculos XVIII e XIX* (Campinas: Ed.UNICAMP, 1989).

Estatísticas Históricas do Brasil. Séries Econômicas, Demográficas e Sociais de 1550 a 1985, vol.3 (Rio de Janeiro: IBGE, 1987).

Estrada, Osório Duque, *A Abolição. Esboço Histórico, 1831-1888* (Rio de Janeiro: L. Ribeiro, 1918).

Fernandes, Florestan, *O Negro no Mundo dos Brancos* (São Paulo: Difel, 1971).

————, *A Integração do Negro na Sociedade de Classes*, 2 volumes, 3rd edition (São Paulo: Ática, 1978).

Fontaine, Pierre-Michel, ed., *Race, Class and Power in Brazil* (Los Angeles: Center for Afro-American Studies, University of California, 1991).

Franco, Maria Sylvia de Carvalho, *Homens Livres na Ordem Escravocrata*, 2nd edition (São Paulo: Ática, 1976).

Freitas, Décio, *Palmares. A Guerra dos Escravos*, 2nd edition (Rio de Janeiro: Graal, 1978).

Freyre, Gilberto, *Sobrados e Mocambos. Decadência do Patriarcado Rural e Desenvolvimento Urbano*, 3 volumes, 2nd edition (Rio de Janeiro: José Olympio, 1951).

————, *Novo Mundo nos Trópicos* (São Paulo: Cia. Editora Nacional/USP, 1971).

————, *Casa-Grande e Senzala*, 20th edition (Rio de Janeiro/ Brasília: Instituto Nacional do Livro, 1980).

Galliza, Diana Soares de, *O Declínio da Escravidão na Paraíba, 1850-1888* (João Pessoa: Editora Universitária/UFPa, 1979).

Gebara, Ademir, *O Mercado de Trabalho Livre no Brasil, 1871-1888* (São Paulo: Brasiliense, 1986).

Girão, Raimundo, *A Abolição no Ceará* (Fortaleza: Editora A. Batista Fontenele, 1956).

Gorender, Jacob, *A Escravidão Reabilitada* (São Paulo: Ática, 1990).

Gouvea, Fernando da Cruz, *Abolição: A Liberdade veio do Norte* (Recife: Massangana, 1988).

————, *Joaquim Nabuco. Entre a Monarquia e a República* (Recife: Massangana, 1989).

Graham, Richard, *Grã-Bretanha e o Início da Modernização no Brasil, 1850-1914* (São Paulo: Brasiliense, 1973).

Hahner, June E., *Emancipating the Female Sex: The Struggle for Women's Rights in Brazil, 1850-1940* (Durham: Duke University Press, 1990).

Hasenbalg, Carlos A., *Discriminação e Desigualdades Raciais no Brasil* (Rio de Janeiro: Graal, 1979).

Holanda, Sérgio Buarque de, ed., *História Geral da Civilização Brasileira. O Brasil Monárquico*, 5 volumes (São Paulo: Difel, 1969).

Ianni, Octavio, *As Metamorfoses do Escravo. Apogeu e Crise da Escravatura no Brasil Meridional* (São Paulo: Difel, 1962).

————, *Escravidão e Racismo* (São Paulo: Hucitec, 1978).

————, *Raças e Classes Sociais no Brasil*, 2nd edition (Rio de Janeiro: Civilização Brasileira, 1972).

Keith, Henry and Edwards, S. F., eds., *Conflito e Continuidade na Sociedade Brasileira* (Rio de Janeiro: Civilização Brasileira, 1970).

Kolinski, Charles J., *Independence or Death! The Story of the Paraguayan War* (Gainesville: University of Florida, 1965).

Lapa, José Roberto do Amaral, ed., *Modos de Produção e Realidade Brasileira* (Petrópolis: Vozes, 1980).

Lara, Silvia H., *Campos da Violência: escravos e senhores na capitania do Rio de Janeiro, 1750-1808* (Rio de Janeiro: Paz e Terra, 1988).

Lima, Lana Lage da Gama, *Rebeldia Negra e Abolicionismo* (Rio de Janeiro: Achime, 1981).

Lins, Ivan Monteiro de Barros, *História do Positivismo no Brasil* (São Paulo: Nacional, 1964).

————, *Três Abolicionistas Esquecidos* (Rio de Janeiro: Conferência Pública realizada em 24 de maio de 1938).

Lyra, Heitor, *História de Dom Pedro II, 1825-1891* (São Paulo: Cia. Editora Nacional, 1938).

Machado, Maria Helena P.T., *Crime e Escravidão: trabalho, luta e resistência nas lavouras paulistas, 1830-1888* (São Paulo: Brasiliense, 1987).

————, *O Plano e o Pânico — Os Movimentos Sociais na Década da Abolição* (Rio de Janeiro: UFRJ/São Paulo: EDUSP, 1994).

Maciel, Cleber da Silva, *Discriminações Raciais. Negros em Campinas (1888-1921)* (Campinas: Ed. UNICAMP, 1987).

Marson, Izabel Andrade, *O Império do Progresso. A Revolução Praieira* (São Paulo: Brasiliense, 1987).

Mattoso, Katia M. de Queiroz, *Ser escravo no Brasil* (São Paulo: Brasiliense, 1982).

Mennucci, Sud, *O Precursor do Abolicionismo no Brasil (Luiz Gama)* (São Paulo: Cia. Editora Nacional, 1938).

Montello, Josué, *Aluisio Azevedo e a Polêmica d'Mulato* (Rio de Janeiro: José Olympio/INL, 1975).

Monti, Veronica A. Martini, *O Abolicionismo: sua hora decisiva no Rio Grande do Sul-1884* (Porto Alegre: Martins Livreiro Editor, 1985).

Moraes, Evaristo de, *A Escravidão Africana no Brasil. Das origens à extincção* (São Paulo: Cia. Editora Nacional, 1933).

————, *A Campanha Abolicionista,1879-1888* (Rio de Janeiro: Leite Ribeiro, 1924).

Mott, Maria Lucia de Barros, *Submissão e Resistência. A Mulher na Luta Contra a Escravidão* (São Paulo: Contexto, 1988).

Moura, Clovis, *Rebeliões da Senzala*, 3rd edition (São Paulo: Ciências Humanas, 1981).

————, O Negro, de Bom Escravo a Mau Cidadão? (Rio de Janeiro: Conquista, 1977).

Nabuco, Carolina, A Vida de Joaquim Nabuco, 5th edition (Rio de Janeiro: Jose Olympio/ Brasília: INL, 1979).

Neuhaus, Paulo, ed., Economia Brasileira: Uma Visão Histórica (Rio de Janeiro: Campos, 1980).

Nogueira, Oracy, Tanto Preto Quanto Branco: Estudos de Relações Raciais (São Paulo: T. A. Queiroz, 1985).

Nonato, Raimundo, História Social da Abolição em Mossoró (Mossoró: Mossoroense, 1983).

Novaes, Fernando, Portugal e Brasil na Crise do Antigo Sistema Colonial, 1777-1808 (São Paulo: Hucitec, 1979).

Oliveira, Maria Inês Cortes de, O Liberto. Seu mundo e os outros (São Paulo: Currupio, 1988).

Paiva, Tancredo de Barros, Achegas a um Dicionário de Pseudonimos (Iniciais, Abreviaturas e Obras de Autores Brasileiros e de Estrangeiros, sobre o Brasil ou no mesmo Impressos (Rio de Janeiro: 1929).

Pinheiro, Paulo Sérgio, ed., Trabalho Escravo, Economia e Sociedade (Rio de Janeiro: Paz e Terra, 1984).

Prado Jr., Caio, Formação do Brasil Contemporâneo, 13th edition (São Paulo: Brasiliense, 1973).

Queiroz, Suely Robles Reis de, Escravidão Negra em São Paulo. Um Estudo das Tensões Provocadas pelo Escravismo no Século XIX (Rio de Janeiro: José Olympio, 1977).

Raeders, Georges, O Inimigo Cordial do Brasil. O Conde Gobineau no Brasil (Rio de Janeiro: Paz e Terra, 1988).

Reis, João José, Rebelião Escrava no Brasil. A história do Levante dos Malês (1835) (São Paulo: Brasiliense, 1986).

————, ed., Escravidão & Invenção da Liberdade. Estudos sobre o Negro no Brasil (São Paulo: Brasiliense, 1988).

————, Negociação e conflito: a resistência negra no Brasil escravista (São Paulo: Companhia das Letras, 1989).

Rodrigues, José Honório, A Assembléia Constituinte de 1823 (Petrópolis: Vozes, 1974).

Bibliography   187

Rodrigues, Nina, *Os Africanos no Brasil* , 2nd edition (São Paulo: Cia. Editora Nacional, 1935).

Saes, Décio A. M.,*A Formação do Estado Burguês no Brasil, 1888-1891* (Rio de Janeiro: Paz e Terra, 1985).

Salles, Iraci Galvão, *Trabalho, Progresso e a Sociedade Civilizada* (São Paulo: Hucitec, 1986).

Santos, Jose Maria dos, *Os Republicanos Paulistas e A Abolição* (São Paulo: Martins, 1942).

Santos, Ronaldo Marcos dos, *Resistência e Superação do Escravismo na Província de São Paulo, 1885-1888* (São Paulo: IPE/USP, 1980).

Schmidt, Afonso, *A Marcha. Romance da Abolição* (São Paulo: Brasiliense, 1981).

Schwarcz, Lilia, *Retrato em Branco e Negro. Jornais, escravos e cidadãos em São Paulo no final do século XIX* (São Paulo: Companhia das Letras, 1987).

———, *O Espetáculo das Raças -- Cientistas, Instituições e Questão Racial no Brasil 1870-1930* (São Paulo: Companhia das Letras, 1993).

Skidmore, Thomas E., *Preto no Branco. Raça e Nacionalidade no Pensamento Brasileiro* (Rio de Janeiro: Paz e Terra, 1976).

Sodré, Nelson Werneck, *As Razões da Independência*, 2nd edition (Rio de Janeiro: Civilização Brasileira, 1969).

Sussekind, Flora, *O Negro como Arlequim. Teatro & Discriminação* (Rio de Janeiro: Achiamé, 1982).

Toplin, Robert Brent, *The Abolition of Slavery in Brazil* (New York: Atheneum, 1972).

Uricoechea, Fernando, *The Patrimonial Foundations of the Brazilian Bureaucratic State* (Berkeley: University of California Press, 1980).

Vainfas, Ronaldo, *Ideologia & Escravidão - Os Letrados e a Sociedade Escravista no Brasil Colonial* (Petrópolis: Vozes, 1986).

Veríssimo, Ignácio José, *André Rebouças através de sua Auto-Biografia* (Rio de Janeiro: José Olympio, 1939).

Viana Filho, Luis, *A Vida do Barão do Rio Branco* (Rio de Janeiro: José Olympio, 1959).

———, *A Vida de Joaquim Nabuco*, 2nd edition (São Paulo: Livraria Martins Editora, 1973).

Articles and Dissertations:

Azevedo, Célia Maria Marinho de, "Sinal fechado para os negros na rua da liberdade", *Humanidades*, no.17 (1988): 8-12.

————, "Batismo da Liberdade: os abolicionistas e o destino do negro", *História: Questões & Debates*, vol.9, no.16 (June 1988): 38-65.

————, "Abolicionismo e Memória das Relações Raciais," *Estudos Afro-Asiáticos*, vol.26   (September 1994): 5-19.

Bakos, Margareth Machiori, "Repensando o Processo Abolicionista Sul-Rio-Grandense", *Estudos Ibero-Americanos*, vol.14, no.2 (December 1988):117-138.

Bergstresser, Rebeca Baird, "The Movement for the Abolition of Slavery in Rio de Janeiro, Brazil, 1880-1889" (Ph.D. Dissertation, Stanford University, February 1973).

Costa, Emília Viotti da, "Brazil: The Age of Reform, 1870-1889", in Leslie Bethell, ed., *The Cambridge History of Latin America*, vol.5 (Cambridge: Cambridge University Press, 1986).

Cunha, Manuela Carneiro da, "'On The Amelioration of Slavery' by Henry Koster", *Slavery and Abolition*, vol.2, no.3 (December 1990): 368-398.

Donald, Jr., Cleveland, "Slavery and Abolition in Campos, Brazil, 1830-1888 (Ph.D. dissertation, Cornell University, August 1973).

Drescher, Seymour, "Brazilian Abolition in Comparative Perspective", *Hispanic American Historical Review*, vol.68, no.3 (August 1988): 429-460.

Flory, Thomas, "Race and Social Control in Independent Brazil", *Latin American Studies*, vol.9, no.2: 199-224.

Fontes, Alice Aguiar de Barros, "A Prática Abolicionista em São Paulo: os Caifases (1882-1888)" (M.A. dissertation, University of São Paulo, 1976).

Franco, Maria Sylvia de Carvalho, "As Idéias estão no lugar," *Cadernos de Debates — História do Brasil*, no.1 (São Paulo: Brasiliense, 1976).

Graham, Richard, "Causes for the Abolition of Negro Slavery in Brazil: An Interpretative Essay", *The Hispanic American Historical Review*, vol.46, no.2 (May 1966): 123-137.

Hall, Michael M., "The Origins of Mass Immigration in Brazil, 1871-1914" (Ph.D. dissertation, Columbia University, 1969).

Hellwig, David J., "A New Frontier in a Racial Paradise: Robert S. Abbott's Brazilian Dream", *Luso-Brazilian Review*, vol.25, no.1 (Summer 1988): 59-67.

————, "Racial Paradise or Run-around? Afro-North American Views of Race Relations in Brazil", *American Studies*, vol.31, no.2, (Fall 1990): 43-60.

Kennedy, James H., "Luiz Gama: Pioneer of Abolition in Brazil", *The Journal of Negro History*, vol.59, no.3 (June 1974): 255-267.

Klein, Herbert S., "Os Homens Livres de Cor na Sociedade Escravista Brasileira", *Dados*, no.17, 1978.

Meade, Teresa and Pirio, Gregory Alonso, "In Search of the Afro-American 'Eldorado': Attempts by North American Blacks to Enter Brazil in the 1920s", *Luso-Brazilian Review*, vol.25, no.1 (Summer 1988): 85-110.

Moore, Zelbert L., "Luis Gama, Abolition and Republican in São Paulo, Brazil,1870-1888" (Ph.D. dissertation, Temple University, January 1978).

Mott, Luiz R. B., "A Revolução dos Negros do Haiti e o Brasil", *Questões & Debates*, vol.3, no.4 (June 1982).

Pena, Eduardo Spiller, "Escravos, libertos e imigrantes: fragmentos da transição em Curitiba na segunda metade do século XIX", *História: Questões & Debates*, vol.9, no.16 (June 1988): 83-103.

Reis, Elisa Maria P. & Reis, Eustáquio J., "As elites agrárias e a abolição da escravidão no Brasil", *Cad. EIAP*, no.1 (Rio de Janeiro: Fundação Getulio Vargas, 1979).

Saes, Flavio A. M., "O Término do Escravismo: Uma Nota Sobre a Historiografia", *Estudos Econômicos*, vol.12, no.3 (December 1982): 29-40.

Slenes, Robert W., "Escravos, cartórios e desburocratização: o que Rui Barbosa não queimou será destruído agora?", *Revista Brasileira de História*, vol.5, no.10 (March-August 1985): 166-196.

————, "The Demography and Economics of Brazilian Slavery: 1850-1888" (Ph.D. dissertation, Stanford University, November 1975).

————, "'Malungu, ngoma Vem!': África coberta e descoberta no Brasil", *Revista USP*, no.12 (December 1991/February 1992): 48-67.

GENERAL BIBLIOGRAPHY

Books:

Arendt, Hannah, *The Origins of Totalitarianism* (New York: Harcourt Brace Jovanovich, Publishers, 1979).

Berghe, Pierre L. van den, *Race and Racism: A Comparative Perspective* (New York: John Wiley & Sons, INC., 1967).

Bethell, Leslie, ed., *The Independence of Latin America* (Cambridge: Cambridge University Press, 1987).

Bloch, Marc, *Intodução à História* (Lisboa: Publicações Europa-América, 1965).

Bolt, Christine, *The Anti-Slavery Movement and reconstruction: A Study in Anglo-American Co-operation 1833-77* (Oxford: Oxford University Press, 1969).

———, and Drescher, Seymour, *Anti-Slavery, religion and Reform: Essays in Memory of Roger Anstey* (Hamden, Connecticut: Wm. Dawson & Sons, 1980).

Blackburn, Robin, *The Overthrow of Colonial Slavery 1776-1848* (London: Verso, 1988).

Castoriadis, Cornelius, *A Instituição Imaginária da Sociedade* (Rio de Janeiro: Paz e Terra, 1982).

Degler, Carl N., *Neither Black Nor White: Slavery and Race Relations in Brazil and the United States* (Madison: The University of Wisconsin Press, 1986).

———, *Nem Preto Nem Branco: escravidão e relações raciais no Brasil e nos Estados Unidos* (Rio de Janeiro: Labor, 1976).

Delacampagne, Christian, *L'invention du racisme. Antiquité et Moyen-Age* (Paris: Fayard, 1983).

Drescher, Seymour, *Capitalism and Antislavery: British Mobilization in Comparative Perspective* (Oxford: Oxford University Press, 1987).

Duchet, Michele, *Antropologia y Historia en el Siglo de las Luces* (Madrid: Siglo XXI, 1984).

Edwards, G. Franklin, ed., *E. Franklin Frazier on Race Relations: Selected Writings* (Chicago: The University of Chicago Press, 1969).

Fleming, Marie, *The Anarchist Way to Socialism: Elisée Reclus and Nineteenth-Century European Anarchism* (London: Croom Helm / Rowman and Littlefield, 1979).

Finley, M. I., *The Ancient Economy*, 2nd edition (Berkeley, University of California Press, 1985).

Gay, Peter, *The Enlightenment: An Interpretation*, 2 volumes (New York: W. W. Norton & Company, 1977).

Graham, Richard, ed., *The Idea of Race in Latin America, 1870-1940* (Austin: University of Texas Press, 1990).

Harris, Marvin, *Patterns of Race in the Americas* (Westport, Connecticut: Greenwood Press, 1980).

Hobsbawm, Eric J., *Nations and Nationalism since 1780: Programme, Myth, Reality* (Cambridge: Cambridge University Press, 1990).

————, *The Age of Capital, 1848-1875* (New York: New American Library, 1979).

————, *The Age of Revolution, 1789-1848* (New York: Mentor Books, 1962).

Hoetink, H., *Caribbean Race Relations: A Study of Two Variants* (Oxford: Oxford University Press, 1971).

Hofstadter, Richard, *Social Darwinism in American Thought* (Boston: Beacon Press, 1955).

Holt, Thomas C., *The Problem of Freedom: Race, Labor, and Politics in Jamaica and Britain, 1832-1938* (Baltimore: The John Hopkins University Press, 1992).

James, C. L. R., *The Black Jacobins: Toussaint L'Ouverture and the San Domingo Revolution* (New York: Vintage Books, 1963).

Jennings, Lawrence C., *French Reaction to British Slave Emancipation* (Baton Rouge: Louisiana State University Press, 1988).

Klein, Herbert, *African Slavery in Latin America and The Caribbean* (Oxford: Oxford University Press, 1986).

Miles, Robert, *Racism* (London: Routledge, 1989).

Morse, Richard M., *O Espelho de Próspero: culturas e idéias nas Américas* (São Paulo: Companhia das Letras, 1988).

Patterson, Orlando, *Slavery and Social Death: A Comparative Study* (Cambridge: Harvard University Press, 1982).

Poliakov, Leon, *O Mito Ariano. Ensaio sobre as fontes do racismo e dos nacionalismos* (São Paulo: Perspectiva, 1974).

Solano, Francisco de, ed., *Estudios sobre la Abolición de la Esclavitud* (Madrid: Consejo Superior de Investigaciones Cientificas, 1986).

Spitzer, Leo, *Lives in Between: Assimilation and Marginality in Austria, Brazil, West Africa 1780-1945* (Cambridge: Cambridge University Press, 1989).

Tannenbaum, Frank, *Slave and Citizen: The Negro in the Americas* (New York: Alfred A. Knopf, 1947).

Toplin, Robert Brent, *Freedom and Prejudice: The Legacy of Slavery in the United States and Brazil* (Westport: Greewood Press, 1981).

Weber, Max, *A Ética Protestante e o Espírito do Capitalismo* (São Paulo: Pioneira, 1981).

Williams, Eric, *Capitalismo e Escravidão* (Rio de Janeiro: Cia. Editora Americana, 1975).

Articles:

Andrews, George R., "Racial Inequality in Brazil and the United States: A Statistical Comparison", *Journal of Social History* (Winter 1992): 229-263.

_____ , Review Essay: Comparing the Comparisons: White Supremacy in the United States and South Africa", *Journal of Social History* (Spring 1987): 585-599.

Bloch, Marc, "Pour une histoire comparee des societes europeénnes", *Revue de Synthèse Historique*, nouvelle série, vol.20 (December 1928): 15-50.

Grew, Raymond, "The Case for Comparing Histories", *The American Historical Review*, vol.85, no.4 (October 1980): 763-778.

Hill, Arlette Olin and Hill, Jr., Boyd H., "Marc Bloch and Comparative History", *American Historical Review*, vol.85, no.4 (October 1980): 828-846.

Holt, Thomas C., "Explaining Abolition", *Journal of Social History* (Winter 1990): 371-378.

Scott, Rebecca, "Comparing Emancipations: A Review Essay", *Journal of Social History* (Spring 1987): 565-583.

———, "R"Exploring the Meaning of Freedom: Postemancipation Societies in Comparative Perspective", *Hispanic American Historical Review*, vol.68, no.3 (August 1988): 407-428.

Sio, Arnold A., "Interpretations of Slavery: The Slave Status in the Americas", *Comparative Studies in Society and History*, vol.7, no.3 (April 1965): 289-308.

INDEX

European American culture, 61
Evolutionism, 77

Fagundes Varela, Nicolau, 57,
    79
Family Demon, The, 81
Female Benevolent Society, 69
Fladeland, Betty, 4
Fonseca, Luis Anselmo da, 45
France, 59, 73, 86, 105, 119
free black people, xvii, 62-63,
    74, 92, 95, 97-98
free soilers, 103, 113
Free Womb Law (Brazil, 1871),
    62, 117
Freedom's Journal, 97
French Abolitionists, 23, 90
French Revolution, xx, 38
Freyre, Gilberto, xii-xiii, xvi,
    xxiii, 66-67
Fugitive Slaves, xxi, 60, 109,
    115, 120
Fugitive Slave Law, 92, 100

Gama, Luiz, 25, 79, 80, 104, 110
Garnet, Henry Highland, 69,
    100
Garrison, William Lloyd, 15,
    18, 36, 59, 61-62, 64, 68,
    75, 83, 99-100, 107,
    112-113, 121-122
Garrisonians, xxii, 121
Gazeta da Tarde, 44-45
Genius of Universal
    Emancipation, 16
Gobineau, Comte of, 105
Góis e Vasconcelos, Zacarias, 93
Goodell, William, 36

gradual abolition
    (emancipation), xix,
    101-102
gradualism, xx
Great Britain, 4, 46, 53, 55, 86-
    88, 90, 92, 99, 119
Greece, 33, 68, 70
Griffith, David W., 119
Grimké, Angelina and Sarah,
    124

Haiti, xiv, xx, 72-76, 99, 105
Haitian Revolution, 25-26, 72-
    74
Ham, 69
Hellwig, David. J., 91
Herald, 15
Heyrick, Elizabeth, 53, 55, 73
Hildreth, Richard, 80
Hilliard, Henry W., 118, 121
Holley, James T., 74
Horrors of Slavery, 96
Hugo, Victor, 57
Hume, David, 11

Ignatius, 25
immediate abolition
    (emancipation), 28,
    112, 117, 119
immediatism, xx-xxi, xxiii, 61
immigration (Brazil), xviii, 63-
    64, 96, 103, 107, 109,
    126
immigration (U. S.), xviii
Isabel, Princess, 67, 123
Israel, 31